A
Psychology
of
Hope

"Jonah, V—a sketch" by Nahum Gutman. The reproduction of the etching was provided graciously by Dr. David Gutmann and Joanna Gutmann.

A
PSYCHOLOGY
OF
HOPE

An Antidote to the Suicidal
Pathology of Western Civilization

KALMAN J. KAPLAN
AND
MATTHEW B. SCHWARTZ

Foreword by David Bakan

Westport, Connecticut
London

Library of Congress Cataloging-in-Publication Data

Kaplan, Kalman J.
    A psychology of hope : an antidote to the suicidal pathology of
Western civilization / Kalman J. Kaplan and Matthew B. Schwartz.
        p.   cm.
    Includes bibliographical references (p.   ) and index.
    ISBN 0-275-94379-8 (alk. paper)
    1. Suicide — Psychological aspects.   2. Suicidal behavior.
    3. Suicide in literature.   4. Suicide — Biblical teaching.
    I. Schwartz, Matthew B.   II. Title.
    HV6545.K35   1993
    362.2'8 — dc20   92-36551

British Library Cataloguing in Publication Data is available.

Library of Congress Catalog Card Number: 92-36551
ISBN: 0-275-94379-8

First published in 1993

Praeger Publishers, 88 Post Road West, Westport, CT 06881
An imprint of Greenwood Publishing Group, Inc.

Printed in the United States of America

The paper used in this book complies with the Permanent
Paper Standard issued by the National Information Standards
Organization (Z39.48–1984).

10 9 8 7 6 5 4 3 2 1

To my parents, Lewis C. (Yehuda Leib) Kaplan and Edith (Yehudit) Saposnik Kaplan, and to my uncle, Dr. Joseph (Yehoshua) Saposnik, who raised me with a sense of hope and purpose, and to my son, Daniel Lewis Kaplan, in whom I have attempted to instill this tradition.

KJK

To my dear wife, Nechama.

MS

Contents

     Family: Isaac and Ruth   137

IV.   **The Prevention of Suicide**   **155**

10.   From Tragedy to Therapy: A Psychology of Hope   157

      Bibliography   165
      Index   175

Illustrations

Foreword

In the course of the development of psychoanalytic psychotherapy Freud went through some interesting steps with respect to his dealing with history. First, he focused on the memory of the individual as the major determinant of human experience and conduct, especially its sufferings and the failures of the normal volitionary mechanisms. He allowed that most of the content of memory was unconscious and that the recall of historical events in the life of the individual comprised the essential therapeutic operation.

However, this history began with the birth of the individual. Freud's next step was to conceive of history as something that went back further. In order to truly understand and help the individual one had to look to the history that extended way back, back even before the beginning of civilization and especially the crises of the beginning. Freud thus went from individual to the group, from the short history that began with the birth of the individual to the long history of culture. He went from works such as his contributions in *Studies in Hysteria* and highly temporally local considerations such as those that fill the pages of *The Interpretation of Dreams* to the larger history as expressed in such works as *Totem and Taboo, Civilization and Its Discontents,* and *Moses and Monotheism*.

Durkheim came upon a somewhat different consideration in his *Suicide,* yet, in a certain way, the position of Durkheim bore a similarity to the second position of Freud noted above. A single phenomenon caught the attention of Durkheim—the extraordinary constancy of the suicide rate over time in various groups. The finding led to his notion of the "social fact," the trans-individual characteristic of groups not identifiable in individuals. This notion would become the ground for a science of sociology for him. His reasoning was that if suicide were an individual phenomenon, the suicide rate of any group would change over time, since the suicidal individuals were separated from the group by their act of suicide. However, the suicide rate remained constant. It even remained constant in groups that had major population turnover, such as the army. Thus Durkheim concluded that the suicide rate was an essential reflection of some characteristic of the group as such. That characteristic of the group reflected itself in the determination of the relative numbers of people committing suicide in the group. He took a strong position against the relevance of psychological considerations for the understanding of suicide.

I find this work by Kaplan and Schwartz an intellectually remarkable synthesis of these two lines of thought, combined with direct applicability to psychotherapy with suicidally inclined people. Both the Freudian and the Durkheimian positions strain credibility. The Freudian approach went towards the uncomfortable assumption of some kind of genetic inheritance of history, a kind of Lamarckianism, which even alienated some of Freud's closest supporters. The Durkheimian approach went against the obvious truth that individual psychological factors play a role in suicide. Kaplan and Schwartz have transcended both of these difficulties, and bring what is credible in both positions together.

Kaplan and Schwartz recognize the continuity of cultural history and have placed the individual within it, albeit born into it. They see the facticity of suicide as embedded in our collective culture including its very complexities. They have identified the two great historical cultures of Western Civilization, the Greek and the Hebraic, that have given rise to the culture in which we live. They take full cognizance of the fact that contemporary culture derives from both of them and carries within it both syntheses and abiding conflicts. Most important, they identify social forms and attitudes that bear on suicide in the historical cultures. Every person living in our society draws his being from the culture that combines the two cultures. It is not that the culture is carried genetically, as Freud suggested. It is not a mysterious transcendental social fact with respect to which psychological considerations are irrelevant as Durkheim argued.

And from this arises a moral direction, a practical direction and some research directions, all very valuable.

The moral direction is the implicit recognition that suicide is a casualty of our collective culture, of the culture which each of us is *in*, each of us *is*, and each of us is the *agent* of the future of. The rate of suicide is an index of the health of the society at large. When anyone commits suicide we must look to the nature of the culture which is generating that suicide, and take steps to rectify it. When, for example, the rate of suicide in some sub-group is high, we should move to improve the conditions in that sub-group. And should the rate of suicide rise for the whole group, or for any particular group within it, we should take it as a major signal calling for rectifying action.

The practical direction is the ready emergence of guidelines for psychotherapy with suicidal individuals that are indicated in this work. I have little doubt but that the application of these guidelines can save lives that might have been lost otherwise. Hopefully, this work will encourage more therapists to undertake therapy with suicide-prone individuals.

Of the research paths that seem to open, two are clear. First, there is a great need for more critical study of history as the basis of contemporary psychological conditions, including suicide proneness. History, in this sense, is the patent extension of the psychoanalytic method. The study of history should be the act of the culture in the conduct of its own psychoanalysis towards promoting its perfection. Second, it would be hoped that there be continued work in the assessment of the guidelines indicated and their improvement.

David Bakan

Acknowledgments

We gratefully acknowledge the help of Mr. David Nelson, supervisor of the Word Processing Center of Wayne State University, and especially of his secretary, Ms. Christine Waters, in the preparation of this volume. We also are appreciative of the assistance of the staff of the Wayne State University Library, Ms. Sarah Bell of the Midrasha Library, Southfield, Michigan, and Dr. Ernest Ament, Chairperson of the Classics Department at Wayne State University, and the resources provided by Grant MH26341 of the National Institute of Mental Health under the direction of Dr. Martin Harrow, Chairman of Psychology in the Department of Psychiatry at Humana Hospital-Michael Reese, Chicago. Our work has likewise benefited from the devoted labor of the staff at Praeger, especially Mr. Paul Macirowski, Acquisitions Editor, Ms. Susan Wladaver-Morgan, Copy Editor, and Ms. Diane Spalding, Production Editor.

Introduction

Ask any group of people this question: "Is it more difficult to kill yourself or not to kill yourself?" Invariably, two equally strong opinions emerge. The "kill yourselves" and "not kill yourselves" groups are similar in size, and each camp finds it difficult, if not impossible, to comprehend the other's point of view. This variation tells us a great deal about the lack of unanimity in our culture about the question of suicide. One wonders about the source of these opinions.

This book is about suicide and suicide prevention in both ancient and modern times. The focus is at once historical and psychological, theoretical and practical. The development of a suicide-preventive therapy in modern society can gain much from the ancient sources. After all, the question of suicide is linked to the larger issue of human existence, both at the level of individual psychopathology and in a more general societal milieu.

Sigmund Freud noted the pervasive "death instinct" in the human being. In *The Ego and the Id*, he stated that "the aim of all life is death" or a return to an early inanimate state that existed before the animate one. In this same work, Freud argued that the superego could become "a pure culture of the death instinct" that could turn its strength against the ego. In *Mourning and Melancholia*, Freud suggested that suicide, like depression, results from the turning inward of anger and aggression toward the outside world.

Historians too have pointed to an apparent cycle in human affairs, in which primitive but warlike peoples conquer great civilizations, then become highly civilized but less vigorous, themselves, and at last collapse before new waves of primitive aggressors. The ancient near-Eastern empires, Greece, and Rome all rose and fell. Twentieth-century scholars have seen possible signs of the collapse of Western civilization in the wholesale destruction of the two world wars.

Our work has led us to the conclusion, surprising to us, that these historians have not merely created an artificial theoretic structure. They have correctly sensed a trend of rising and falling that characterizes the history of most nations. They have, however, fallen short of an important finding. This pattern is established neither by universal forces nor by some predetermined cosmic doom. We argue that there is instead a feeling of despair, alienation, and worthlessness that eats at the inner core of a civilization even as it reaches its peak of military and cultural strength.

This response is in large part not a realistic weltanschauung but rather a suicidal pattern that closely parallels that of an individual who moves toward hopelessness and self-destruction. Nations as well as individuals often need a "stopper," a saving intervention to restore them to the road toward healthy self-fulfillment. For the Stoics of Classical Greece and Rome, the right to kill oneself represented the highest degree of human freedom. In contrast, Biblical thought saw freedom as fulfilling the divine command to live. The way in which an individual, or indeed a society, deals with this issue is manifest in every fiber of its being and does much to form its character and progress. If life indeed has little or no meaning, then wisdom will not help.[1] Further, does not ending such a life become a viable and sensible alternative? Some have answered this last question with a clear "yes" and look favorably upon self-destruction. Others give an equally strong "no" and are unalterably opposed to it.

In this book, we unite our skills as a psychologist and a historian to study Graeco-Roman, Biblical, and post-Biblical views on suicide in order to connect the influence of these civilizations to modern thought. In the mental health field, a new specialty has emerged — suicidology. In the last few years, it has grown quickly to deal with both individuals and families. The clergy have been quite prominent in this movement, and many crisis centers and hotlines are affiliated with churches and synagogues. Yet there has been very little systematic use of Biblical materials in this regard. It is as if the clergy put aside their religious backgrounds when they practice suicide prevention, adopting instead the dominant psychological and psychiatric models, many of which are subtly based on a Graeco-Roman view of life. The treatment of the "psyche" and the emphasis on the Oedipus complex are but two examples. This curious self-limitation may be especially relevant when dealing with suicide and suicide prevention. The study of Graeco-Roman and Biblical precedents is fundamental both for an understanding of intellectual history and for practical treatment in individual counseling situations.

Earlier social thinkers who have written on these matters, such as Henry Romilly Fedden and Alfredo Alvarez, have been consistently and quite correctly faulted by historians for their lack of care for historical sources.[2]

Émile Durkheim (1979) has been criticized for viewing religion as "an elaborate reflection of more basic social realities" rather than as an important motivating force in human life (Pope 1976). Thus, Durkheim argues that Protestants have higher suicide rates than do Catholics, because of the lower level of social integration provided by the Protestant church and the potentially suicidal aspects of the highly individualized Protestant desire for knowledge. Jews, because of their persecuted status, have greater social integration and thus show lower suicide rates than either Protestants or Catholics.[3] This may be, but Durkheim showed his unfamiliarity with Biblical and Jewish historical viewpoints on suicide. For example, he incorrectly stated that the Hebrew Bible contains no law forbidding a man to kill himself and that the only Jewish proscription against suicide is mentioned by Flavius Josephus in the *Jewish War* (3.25).

Durkheim's weakness with regard to Biblical materials may well typify a general antireligious bias among social scientists. R. Stark, D. P. Doyle, and J. L. Rushing (1983) have argued this strongly:

Despite Durkheim's reputation as a founding father of the sociology of religion, we found his writing to display amazing innocence of elementary facts about religion in Europe at the time he wrote. Time and again in *Suicide* (1897) his open contempt for religion and his lack of knowledge of it led him to frame obviously wrong arguments. Nor were these directed towards peripheral concerns. Critical parts of his analysis rest on arguments that never should have passed even moderately informed inspection. That these matters were not recognized long ago probably reflects the persistence among social scientists of the same biases and unfamiliarity that led Durkheim himself into error. (Stark, Doyle, and Rushing 1983, 120)

Such an antireligious bias is especially unfortunate given Durkheim's brilliance and his own statement that "a religious nature . . . is very different from the egoistic involvement . . . which leads man to suicide" (Durkheim 1897, 336).

A more serious attempt to explore the relationship between religion and suicide has been made by A. Bayet (1922) in his work *Le Suicide et la Morale.* In this work, Bayet attempted to distinguish two sorts of morality. The first and primitive sort, *morale simple,* is founded on religion and represents the basis for the morality of the common people; the second, *morale nuancée,* is the morality of the educated and intellectual minority and has its roots in reason. Bayet then sought to apply this idea of twin moralities to an understanding of the fluctuation in attitudes toward suicide. As reason increases, he suggested, the penalties for suicide decrease; as religion increases, the penalties for suicide increase. Thus, the Classical and Renaissance tolerance of suicide follows the defeat of the *morale simple* of earlier times and of the Age of Faith. A fuller and more direct comparison of the place of suicide in Biblical and Greek societies could be expected to help explain this issue.[4]

In our examination of these contrasting views of life, death, and suicide, a number of important questions stand out: What is the meaning of life and death? To whom does life belong? Why do people terminate their own lives? What sort of internal or external circumstances may be involved? Is there something that a person may know or may not know that brings him to suicide? Finally, do the Biblical and Classical civilizations provide different wisdoms for the treatment of these problems?

In the Bible, God is man's guide, protector, and indeed partner. No matter how bad things get for man, he need never lose hope. God placed a rainbow in the clouds as a sign of his covenant (*Genesis* 9:12–17). This hope provides a stopper that is simply unavailable to Greek man, on whom Pandora loosed all the ills from the box of Epimetheus; hope alone is locked up inside the box (Hesiod, *Works and Days*, 90–96).

The widespread incidence of suicide and the obsession with self-destruction in Classical literature are astonishing. Clearly, self-destruction was a pervasive motivating theme in Greek and Roman thought. The Greek world seemed consistently undone by a tragic confusion implicit in the heroic impulse and by a commitment to unsatisfactory choices that were always destructively rigid and harsh. In this world, hubris brings nemesis, and families are often pathological, making matters worse. The gods are capricious, narcissistically preoccupied with their own affairs, and incapable of providing any stopper in the individual's rush to self-destruction. Suicide often seems the only way out. These themes appear uncomfortably similar to many varieties of suicidal thought in modern society.

The right-to-die debate has been raging in America. The questions of euthanasia (itself a combination of two Greek words meaning a good death) and assisted suicide have been posed by the Hemlock Society in terms of the philosophical freedom to die. Left untouched in much of this debate, however, is the religious question of why an individual would want to end his life and the therapeutic issue of how to restore hope.

In contrast to the Greek world-view, the ancient Hebraic writings speak little of suicide and approach duty and freedom in vastly different and more realistic terms. God is an involved parent who cares for His children. Heroism in the Greek sense is not needed, nor is the individual compelled to choose between impossible and unlivable alternatives. Biblical families are typically supportive. Even when they are not, there is still hope. God protects His children and allows them to develop, to recover when they err, and to avoid the polarities of egoism and altruism, of hubris and nemesis, even in the absence of supportive families.[5] Many of these ideas may be critical to preventing suicide and the obsession with self-destruction in the modern world.

The book is divided into four sections: The Problem of Suicide, Individual Case Studies, Family Influences, and The Prevention of Suicide. In each of the first three sections, we began by discussing the issue of suicide in a comparative framework (chapters 1, 4, and 7), then the suicide-inducing effects of the Graeco-Roman society (chapters 2, 5, and 8), and finally the suicide-preventing effects of the Hebrew world (chapters 3, 6, and 9). The final section (chapter 10) draws on this material to suggest a psychology of hope that may serve as a suicide-preventive therapy designed to overcome the tragic confusion of Western man.

NOTES

1. This reflects the Classical Greek bias against knowledge that emerges in Sophocles' *Oedipus Rex:* "What good is wisdom if it does not benefit the wise?" See also the myth of Narcissus: "He will live a long life so long as he does not come to know himself."

2. For example, David Ladouceur (1987, 113) has referred to the uncritical approaches of Henry Romilly Fedden and Alfredo Alvarez in their treatment of Roman and Jewish suicides.

3. The single exception to this rule, curiously, was Bavaria, where Jews killed themselves twice as often as Catholics. This anomaly led Durkheim to ask prophetically in 1897, "Is there something exceptional about the position of Judaism in this country [Bavaria] we do not know?" The rise of Adolf Hitler there some thirty years later provided a tragic affirmative answer to Durkheim's speculations.

4. Note also Arthur Droge and James Tabor, *A Noble Death* (1992).

5. What is often required is a regression from this impossible axis and a return to a more harmonious yet possibly less developed position. Anna Freud (1936) referred to this as regression in the service of development.

I

THE PROBLEM OF SUICIDE

Chapter 1

To Be or Not to Be?
The Question of Suicide

To be or not to be, that is the question, whether 'tis nobler in the mind
to suffer the slings and arrows of outrageous fortune, or to take arms
against a sea of troubles, and by opposing end them.

Shakespeare, *Hamlet*

There is but one truly serious philosophical problem, and that is suicide.

Camus, *The Myth of Sisyphus,* 3

"To be or not to be, that is the question," ponders Hamlet in the best-
known soliloquy in Western letters. This musing on suicide grows clearer in
each succeeding line. First a hint: "Whether 'tis nobler in the mind to suffer the slings and arrows of outrageous fortune, or to take arms against a
sea of troubles, and by opposing end them." He then addresses the question
of death head on: "To die: to sleep; no more; and, by a sleep to say we end
the heartache and the thousand natural shocks that flesh is heir to, 'tis a
consummation devoutly to be wished." Finally, the question of suicide is
posed directly: "For who would bear the whips and scorns of time . . .
When he himself might his quietus make with a bare bodkin [dagger]?"
(Shakespeare, *Hamlet*, act 3, sc. 1, lines 55–75).

Seldom has the question of life and death been posed so earnestly. Hamlet is placing life and its attendant suffering in one hand and death and the
supposed cessation of suffering in the other. The centrality of the question
of suicide in the human agenda has been stated very directly by the French
existentialist, Albert Camus, "There is but one truly serious philosophical
problem, and that is suicide. Judging whether life is or is not worth living

amounts to answering the fundamental question of philosophy" (Camus 1955, 3). There has been no agreement on this question in Western society and hence on the permissibility of suicide.

VIEWS OF SUICIDE

Dante's *Divine Comedy* places the "violent against themselves" in the wood of the suicides in the second round of the seventh circle of Hell. The souls of the suicides are encased in thorny trees where the leaves are eaten by harpies, causing their wounds to bleed. Only as long as the blood flows are the souls of the trees able to speak. They are permitted to speak only through that which injures and destroys them (Dante Alighieri, *The Inferno*, canto 13).

In Germany some centuries later, Immanuel Kant (1785) argued strongly against suicide because he felt it to be incompatible with the affirmation of a universal law of self-love. At about the same time, Johann Wolfgang von Goethe (1774) romanticized suicide in his novel *The Sorrows of Young Werther.* Indeed, Goethe's book was associated with a veritable epidemic of romantic suicides throughout Europe.

Many of the greatest names in French philosophy were sympathetic to suicide. Voltaire (1973), for example, argued that at times suicide must be defensible, even though he was himself temperamentally opposed to it. While regarding it as abnormal, he admitted the possibility of its social and moral validity. Paul d'Holbach (1770) strongly favored the permissibility of suicide on two grounds. First, suicide is not contrary to the law of nature; second, suicide is not antisocial. The individual's contract with society is based on mutual benefit. Therefore, if society can give him nothing, the suicide has every right to consider the contract void. Jean-Jacques Rousseau too was sympathetic. The twenty-first letter in the *Nouvelle Héloise* (1761) contains an extensive apology for suicide from a young man disillusioned with life. First, suicide is not against the law of nature; it is up to us to leave life when it no longer seems good. Second, suicide is not akin to deserting one's post (see Plato's argument in Chapter 2) but is like moving to a more hospitable town. Third, suicide does not remove one from the providence of God; it destroys one's body but not one's soul, which actually comes closer to God through death. Fourth, suffering sometimes becomes unendurable. Fifth, the Scriptures have no word to say against suicide.

At the same time, France produced a great voice against suicide. Madame Anne Louise de Stael, in her 1814 essay *Reflections on Suicide,* reversed the support that she had shown in her earlier essay, *On the Influence of Passions* (1796). She offered a threefold argument. First pain serves to regenerate the soul; to escape from pain through suicide is thus a refusal to recognize the possibilities of one's own nature. Second, God never abandons the true believer; there is thus no reason or right to commit suicide. Finally, suicide is not consonant with the moral dignity of man.

The English poet and churchman John Donne (1608) expressed a very different point of view in his classic work on suicide, *Biathanatos* (1648, 29). He argued that, under certain limited conditions, suicide might not be a sin: "for we say . . . , That this may be done only, when the Honor of God may be promoted by that way and no other" (136). Donne did present a general plea for charity toward suicides, however, and a proof that no set of rules can govern all instances (145).

David Hume went even farther in *An Essay On Suicide*. For suicide to be criminal, he argued, it must be a transgression of duty toward God, one's self, or one's neighbors. That it cannot be the first stems from Hume's assertion that all our powers are received from our creator. Therefore, suicide can be no more ungodly than any other form of death. That suicide cannot involve a transgression against one's self seemed obvious to Hume, as no one has ever thrown away his life while it was worth keeping. That suicide does not involve transgression against one's neighbors was also obvious to him. All one's obligations to do good to society, according to Hume, imply something reciprocal. So long as one receives benefit from society, one is obligated to promote its interests, but when one withdraws altogether from society, one is no longer so bound.

A very different point of view was taken by a clergyman named Adams at the beginning of the eighteenth century. In a publication entitled *An Essay Concerning Self-Murder* (1700), Adams stated that human life is God's own property, entrusted to man only for a certain end. Therefore, man has no liberty to destroy it. He extended this viewpoint into the political realm. A man may hazard his life for his country — but he may not destroy himself for it.[1] Another English clergyman, the Reverend Mr. Tuke, attempted to bridge this gap by differentiating between two types of suicide, one permissible and the other not.

> There be two sorts of voluntarie deaths, the one lawful and honest such as the death of Martyrs, the other dishonest and unlawful, when men have neyther lawfull calling, nor honest endes, as of Peregrinus, who burnt himself in a pile of wood, thinking thereby to live forever in men's remembrance.[2] (1613, 21)

Views in contemporary Western society are similarly mixed. The American psychiatrist Thomas Szasz (1971) has attacked the view that suicide is necessarily a manifestation of mental illness. Suicide, he has argued, is a product of choice by an agent, not a symptom of disease. Such a choice must be respected by psychiatrists, police, and others who might attempt to intervene in suicide. To do otherwise involves the infantilization and dehumanization of the suicidal person.

An equally compelling antisuicide position has been taken by Austrian psychiatrist Ewin Ringel, the founder of the International Association for Suicide Prevention. Ringel (1981) has argued that suicide cannot be freely chosen, and he therefore opposes libertarian attitudes toward suicide, including those that would allow planned deaths to the terminally ill. Arguing that every human life is important, his work presents the purpose of suicide prevention as the reinvigoration of human life, through the help of psychiatry and crisis intervention, to all human beings.

Middle-ground positions have been taken by Brandt (1975) and by Lebacqz and Englehardt (1977). Brandt, a past president of the American Philosophical Association, has attempted to distinguish between rational and irrational suicide. His opinion is that a person may, on utilitarian grounds, reach a rational decision to take his life but that the rational decision process is often distorted by emotional disturbances. He has argued that intervention to prevent suicide may be justified if the decision is an irrational one. If the decision is rational, however, such intervention is not justified, and Brandt has even argued for an obligation to assist a person attempting a rational suicide. Lebacqz, a professor of Christian ethics, and Englehardt, a professor of the philosophy of medicine, have taken a slightly different approach. While acknowledging on libertarian grounds that persons might have a *prima facie* right to commit suicide, they have maintained that this right is nevertheless usually overridden by contravening duties that grow out of our covenantal relations with others. Still, there may be a right to suicide in at least three kinds of cases: voluntary euthanasia, covenantal suicide, and symbolic protest, for in these cases suicide would affirm the covenants we have with others.

These views, of course, represent only a sample of those existing in past and present Western society. They reflect, however, confusion and vacillation with regard to many issues involving suicide.[3] Is suicide to be viewed as mental illness, when judgment is, by definition, distorted and irrational, or can the choice be based on a rational decision? What implications would this definition have for mental health professionals, religious leaders, and concerned lay people? Should they respect an individual's "right to die" and even assist him? Or are they morally bound to attempt to preserve life even against the expressed will of the potential suicide? To whom does an individual's life belong—to himself, to the state, or to God?[4] And, finally, how is suicide related to the basic idea of freedom? Suicide must be understood in the context of the larger issues of life and death and the historical antecedents to this problem. To this we now turn.

DEFINITIONS OF SUICIDE

In his book, *Definition of Suicide*, Edwin Shneidman (1985), the father of the suicidology movement in America, has offered what many regard as a state-of-the-art definition of suicide: "Currently in the Western world, suicide is a conscious act of self-induced annihilation, best understood as a multidimensional malaise in a needful individual who defines an issue for which suicide is perceived as the best solution" (Shneidman 1985, 203).

The emphasis on "currently" reflects Shneidman's awareness that the meaning of suicide may vary from one historical period to another. The emphasis on "Western world" implicitly recognizes that the meaning of suicide may be a function of the cultural matrix in which it occurs. The word "conscious" limits suicide to *human* acts, while the word "act" calls for a narrowing of our usage of the term suicide to a particular behavior that leads to death. As such, this passage seems to suggest that the word "suicide" not be so readily used to refer to attempts and/or threats. The word "self-induced" indicates a death by one's own hand, and "annihilation" is meant to imply the end of experiential aspects of life and of the actual cessation of life itself. Suicide thus represents the permanent cessation of individual consciousness.

Nevertheless, Shneidman's definition fails to capture many nuances apparent in the suicides that we explore in this book. First, Jewish law, for example, addresses the question of when a person is compelled to accept death rather than actively to commit suicide. Second, many Greek suicidal themes, especially in the plays of Euripides, take the form of ritual murder in which the victim does not literally take his or her own life. Iphigenia, for example, allows herself, without protest, to be sacrificed by others (Euripides, *Iphigenia in Aulis*). Another example is Macaria who refuses the chance to escape her sacrifice through a lottery (Euripides, *Heracleidae*). Third, Shneidman's definition leaves open the relationship between martyrdom and suicide — where does one end and the other begin? Our examination of Graeco-Roman, Jewish, and especially Christian materials shows how complicated this question may be. Fourth, many of the suicides in ancient narratives may not be fully "conscious." Sophocles' Ajax is a good example of this. He kills himself while in a state of severe depression and agitation (Sophocles, *Ajax*). Finally the question arises as to whether the individual equates suicide with total "self-annihilation." What if he believes in an afterlife?

Still Shneidman and Farberow (1957) have argued that "suicidal logic" presupposes a belief in one's immortality after death. Thus, a potential suicide thinks that he will be able to experience others' reactions to his death. He may think, "You will be sorry after I kill myself." Equally destructive is the belief that the world ends with one's own death. Such a breakdown is evident in Eugene Ionesco's play *"Exit the King"* (1963). Here the dying King Berenger shows no investment in the future. When told by his wife that "the younger generation's expanding the universe," the King replies, "I'm dying." When he is told that they are "conquering new constellations," he again replies, "I'm dying." Finally, when informed that the younger generation is "boldly battering at the gates of Heaven," he responds "they can knock them flat for all I care" (67). Berenger has lost any investment in the world beyond him.

Many of the assumptions underlying Shneidman's definition of suicide are therefore tenuous. More useful for present purposes is Durkheim's definition in his classic study *Le Suicide* (1897/1951) as "all cases of death resulting directly or indirectly from a positive or negative act of the victim himself, which he knows will produce this result" (44). Durkheim's inclusion of the term "indirectly" in his definition of suicide suggests that martyrs may sometimes be classified as suicides.[5] Durkheim's taxonomy of suicide types is also extremely valuable.[6] He suggested three common types of suicide: *egoistic, altruistic,* and *anomic.*[7] *Egoistic* suicides are people insufficiently bonded to the society around them. *Altruistic* suicides lack the autonomy to differentiate themselves from the surrounding milieu. *Anomic* suicides occur when there is confusion or disruption in the relationship of an individual to the society around him. In addition, this work suggests a nonsuicidal category (which Durkheim labeled religious) that unites the individual personality with society (336). Durkheim's thinking seems overly influenced by outmoded utopian idealism, and his reference to religion is vague. Nevertheless, he seemed to be groping toward the possibility of a category where there is unity or congruence between individuation and attachment.

An understanding of the processes of individuation and attachment is essential to the problem of healthy versus pathological human development and specifically to the problems of suicide and suicide preventions. The dimension of individuation-deindividuation refers to the degree to which an individual can stand on his own two feet—that is, can show autonomous or independent thought, feeling, and action. An individuated person is separated or differentiated from those around him but is not necessarily isolated from them. (Figure 1.1 denotes this person as having a strong or articulated self-definition or ego boundary thus— $\bigcirc$). A deindividuated person, in contrast, is not capable of independent thought, feeling, and action and is not separated or differentiated from those around him. (Figure 1.1 denotes this person as having a weak or inarticulated self-definition or ego boundary thus— $\bigcirc$).

The attachment-detachment dimension describes the degree to which an individual can extend his hand to another—that is, can show a capacity for bonding or cooperating with others in thought, feeling, and action. An attached individual is integrated or involved with those around him but is not necessarily enmeshed with them. (This person is represented as having a permeable or flexible defensive structure or wall $\square$). A detached individual, in contrast, is not integrated or involved with those around him. (He is denoted by an impermeable or rigid defensive structure or wall $\blacksquare$).

These two dimensions should be seen as separate and independent of one another. A number of different positions are visible in this drawing and may be placed on one of two axes. The first, labeled the AC axis (Figure 1.2) throughout this book, represents fixation and a pathological incongruence

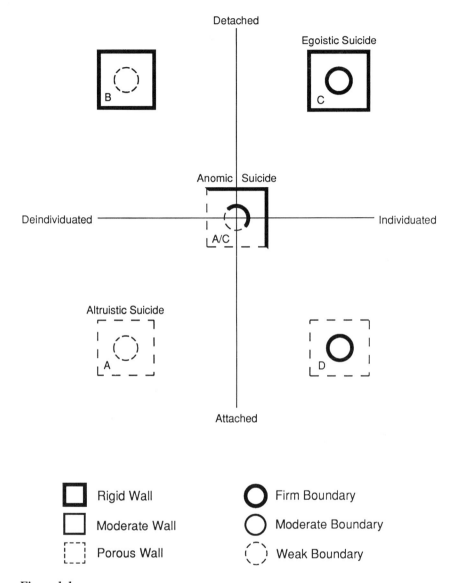

Figure 1.1
A Bidimensional Distancing Representation of Suicide Types

or disintegration between individuation and attachment. The suicide of an individual at position A is, by Durkheim's definition, *altruistic* — a suicide insufficiently differentiated from the environment around him. Position C, in contrast, represents Durkheim's *egoistic* suicide — an individual insuffi-

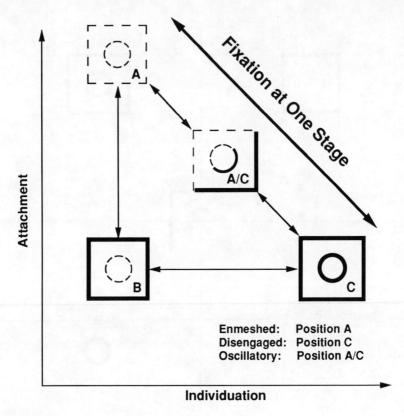

Figure 1.2
The Individual Clinical Axis

ciently integrated with his environment. An *anomic* suicide is represented by position A/C—an afflicted individual torn between enmeshment and disengagement. Someone fixated on this AC clinical axis cannot move ahead in development (Markus-Kaplan and Kaplan 1984; Kaplan 1988; Kaplan and O'Connor in press; Kaplan and Worth in press).

The second axis, labeled BED (see Figure 1.3), represents healthy congruence or integration between individuation and attachment. Positions B, E, and D denote levels of developmental progression along a maturity dimension at a given life stage. Level B represents an individual not sufficiently differentiated from others to integrate with them. This position, if permanent, has aspects of Durkheim's fatalistic suicide (see note 3, Chapter 1). As a temporary position, however, this B level may actually represent a suicide-preventive haven from the AC axis. Such protection allows the individual to mature at his own pace through E (a state of semi-individuation and semi-attachment) to D (a state of full individuation and at-

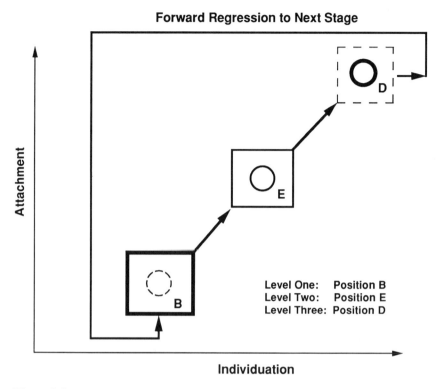

Figure 1.3
The Individual Developmental Axis

tachment). D, of course, represents exactly the nonsuicidal position that Durkheim seems to have been groping for in his previously mentioned attempt to define a religious, nonsuicidal position.[8]

We have come to see the entire BED axis as a suicide-preventive alternative to the suicidal AC axis. Individuation and attachment are congruent and integrated rather than incongruent and disintegrated. This book will attempt to demonstrate that the suicide-preventive BED axis emerges from the Biblical, covenantal perspective. This perspective contrasts with the suicide-promoting AC axis, which, we will argue, emerges from the Classical (Graeco-Roman) narcissistic culture.

NOTES

1. The clergyman Adams is referred to by Henry Romilly Fedden (1938, 216–217).

2. Reverend Mr. Tuke is discussed by Faber (1967, 31, 32).

3. Studies of the attitudes of African and Asian societies toward suicide also indicate variation (Bohannan 1960; Elwin 1943; Hankoff 1969b; Thakur 1963; Yap 1958; Ohara 1961). India practiced *suttee*, the custom in which widows were placed on the funeral pyres of their husbands (Thakur 1963). Japanese history is filled with incidents of suicide, ranging from the traditional story of the *forty-seven ronin*, in which servants killed themselves *en masse* upon their master's death, through the practice of *hara-kiri* or *seppuku* conducted by the Samurai warriors, to the modern Kamikaze pilots who dive-bombed to their death in World War II (Ohara 1965; Tatai and Kato 1974). Suicide in China has never been ritualized to the same extent as in Japan and has therefore attracted less attention. Yet suicide has played an important role throughout Chinese history, and an astounding number of eminent men and women are reported to have taken their own lives. These suicides were often committed as expiation for violations of loyalties, even if they were committed inadvertently (Yap 1958; Lindell 1973; Rin 1975).

4. Ross and Kaplan (1993) have recently developed a questionnaire designed to measure an individual's life-ownership orientation. The Life-Orientation Ownership Questionnaire (LOOQ) assesses whether an individual feels his life belongs to himself, to the state, or to a divine being. Ross and Kaplan have begun to investigate the influence of this orientation on attitudes toward abortion, suicide, and capital punishment.

5. In contrast, van Hooff (1990) has not counted martyrs "as self-killers because they cause their own deaths indirectly" (54).

6. A number of other classification systems of different types and motives for suicide have emerged in the professional literature over the past century (Douglas 1967; Shneidman 1968; Baechler 1979; Hill 1983).

7. Durkheim also suggested a fourth, "rare" type of *fatalistic* suicide, which is likely to occur when there is excessive regulation and rigidity in an individual's relation to the society around him.

8. One final point should be made. An individual who reaches level D at one life stage may *forwardly regress* (retreating in level to advance in stage) at the next.

Chapter 2

Suicide in Graeco-Roman Thought

Those who pursue philosophy aright study nothing but dying and being dead.

Socrates, Phaedo, 64a

For, if pure knowledge is impossible while the body is with us, one of two things must follow, either it cannot be acquired at all or only when we are dead; for then the soul will be by itself apart from the body, but not before.

Socrates, Phaedo, 68d

You see that yawning precipice? It leads to liberty. You see that flood, that river, that well? Liberty houses within them. You see that stunted, parched, and sorry tree? From each branch, liberty hangs. Your neck, your throat, your heart are so many ways of escape from slavery. . . . Do you inquire the road to freedom? You shall find it in every vein of your body.

Seneca, De Ira, 3.15.3–4

The philosopher may choose his own mode of death as he chooses a ship or a house. He leaves life as he would a banquet — when it is time.

Seneca, Epistle, 70.11

Many famous individuals took their own lives in Ancient Greece and Rome. John Donne listed three pages of suicides in his *Biathanatos*. The works of ancient biographers like Plutarch and Diogenes Laertius recount many suicide tales: Pythagoras, Socrates, Zeno, Demosthenes, Marc Antony, the statesman Seneca and his wife Paulina, and many more.

In addition, Graeco-Roman literature provides a number of examples of collective suicide in the ancient world, in which men slaughtered their families and then themselves. Cohen (1982) has discussed sixteen Graeco-Roman accounts of mass suicides. Only one of these cases involved the Greeks themselves, however (the Phocians' nonactualized pact to slay their families and free themselves in order to avoid capture by the Thessalians in the 480s BCE; Pausanias 10.1.6–9), and one other involved the Romans (the inhabitants of the city of Norba set fire to the city and slew themselves after being betrayed to Aemilius Lepidus in 82–81 BCE; Appian, *Civil War*, 1.94). Six cases concerned townspeople in Asia Minor, and eight instances involved "barbarians."[1] Certain ideas and perceptions in Greek and Roman life tended to make suicide a suitable action.[2]

THE HOMERIC PERIOD

The Epic Hero

The epic hero of the Homeric period is consumed by the search for glory. A prime example is Achilles who earns greatness by slaying Trojans, particularly Hector, their great prince. Achilles does this although he knows through a prophecy that slaying Hector will hasten his own death (Homer, *Iliad*, 18.95–96). Ajax, perhaps the second greatest warrior in the Achaean host before Troy, kills himself in a fit of madness after being judged the loser in an athletic contest (see Sophocles, *Ajax*). Generally, the *Iliad*, like most epics, glories in describing how warriors destroy each other in the field of battle, cleaving and hacking each other's flesh and bones, piling corpses all around them.

In Homer's world, the warrior-hero is the highest type of individual. Although always a nobleman and often descended from a god, the hero is fundamentally flawed and can never really win. Ultimately, no amount of heroism is enough, no pinnacle of glory is sufficient to bring him satisfaction or give any value to his life. In the last book of the *Iliad*, Achilles is reduced to tears by the seeming pointlessness of his life (24.505). Other Achaean heroes also later come to unhappy ends. Agamemnon returns home to be brutally murdered by his wife Clytemnestra and her lover Aegisthus. Ajax the Lesser is punished by the gods after he rapes the prophetess Cassandra on the altar of Zeus. Odysseus wanders the seas for ten years, consumed by a terrible homesickness (Homer, *Odyssey*, 1.59) until he finally reaches Ithaca, his homeland. Penelope, his wife, also suffers from the heroic trap of Odysseus. Though Hirzel (1908, 884) makes much of the fact that neither she nor Odysseus commits suicide to end their anguish, it is significant that Penelope begs the gods to give her death to preserve her faithfulness to her husband (*Odyssey*, 26.61). In addition, Hades is portrayed as a place of horror. The *Odyssey* offers the scene of the shades of heroes lapping blood and speaking of their miseries (*Odyssey*, 11).

One can achieve success and recognition in the Homeric world only by means of heroism and competition, but the heroic life typically ends in miserable destruction. A good example of the potentially suicidal aspect of heroism lies in the legend recounted to the first American Olympic team in Athens by its coach in 1896. According to this legend, the already spent runner Pheidippides ran twenty-six miles from the battlefield of Marathon to the city of Athens to give the news of the Athenian victory. After blurting out the story, he fell dead of exhaustion. One must wonder, given the victory, why it was necessary for Pheidippides to run himself to death rather than stop to rest along the way or why, unlike Paul Revere who was faced with a more pressing message, he did not take a horse.[3]

Finley (1959, 128–129) has pointed out that the Greeks extended the idea of competition from physical prowess to the realm of intellect, poetry, and dramatic composition. "The Greeks used to stage contests in everything that offered the bare possibility of a fight" (Huizinga 1955, 73). Slater (1968, 36) has argued that nothing had meaning for the Greeks unless it involved the defeat of an opponent.

A number of factors in Homeric thought contribute to this pattern. The hero is more than a great but tragic warrior. His behavioral pattern also seems to contain a strain of sado-masochism. As powerful and destructive as he is on the field of battle, he is more essentially a passive-aggressive personality. The first episode of *The Iliad* describes how Achilles refuses to go into battle after the general of the Greek forces, Agamemnon, takes a captured slave girl from him. The theme of that epic poem is broached in its very first line: "Sing muse of the wrath of Achilles."

The hero typically brings misery on himself by his own acts. For example, Theseus reacts in haste to a false message and curses his innocent son, Hippolytus. Hippolytus is killed soon after when thrown from his chariot. In another myth, King Aegeus of Athens hastily jumps into the sea and drowns when wrongly convinced that his son, Theseus, has been slain by the Minotaur. Similarly, Erigone hangs herself after discovering the murdered body of her father, Icarius.

Stories of this type are manifold in Greek literature. The great problem, however, is not that Greek heroes make errors. It is rather that there seems to be no recourse, no way out of the so-called heroic pattern. Even worse, the errors often seem to be quite minor and accidental. Nevertheless, they spell a pattern of doom. There is no stopper in Greek society — no way out. If this view is carried to its ultimate, especially for a serious thinker, then the most logical conclusion of human life is suicide.

THE CLASSICAL PERIOD

Suicidologist Henry Romilly Fedden (1938, 70–85) has placed Greek attitudes toward suicide into three camps: Pythagoras, Aristotle, and the Epicureans were opposed to it; Plato and Socrates took a guarded middle position; and the Cynics and Stoics accepted it. Although this view is over-simplified, it provides not a bad beginning for a discussion of these schools of thought.

Pythagoras

Athenaeus (prominent around 200 CE) stated the Pythagorean position as follows:

that the souls of all men were bound in the body, and in the life which is on earth, for the sake of punishment. . . . On which account all men, being afraid of those threatenings of the gods, fear to depart from life by their own act, but only gladly welcome death when it comes in old age. (Athenaeus, *The Deipnosophists*, 2.216)

For the Pythagoreans, suicide is a rebellion against an almost mathematical discipline set by the gods. Death comes when it should and then it can be welcomed. There is a set number of souls, according to Pythagoras, that is available in the world at any one time. Killing oneself creates a gap by upsetting this mathematical equilibrium, and thus it must be rejected. Despite this philosophy, several accounts portrayed Pythagoras as letting himself be killed or actively committing suicide. According to one, Pythagoras allowed pursuers to catch and kill him in preference to trampling on a field of beans (Diogenes Laertius, 8.45).

Socrates and Plato

Three general themes in the teaching of Socrates eased the road to suicide in the classical period. First, he made several references to the nature of the afterworld. For Socrates, Hades (if it existed at all) was not so frightening a place as it was to the Homeric hero. In the closing section of Plato's *Apology* (41a–42a) Socrates asked rhetorically:

If on arrival in the other world, beyond the reach of our so-called justice, one will find there the true judges who are said to preside in those courts, Minos and Rhadamanthes and Aeacus and Triptolemus . . . to meet Orpheus and Musaeus, Hesiod and Homer . . . would that be an unrewarding journey? . . . What would one not give . . . to be able to question the leader of that great host against Troy, or Odysseus, or Sisyphus?

At the conclusion of Plato's *Republic*, Socrates related the myth of Er, which describes the wonderful gifts and rewards awaiting the good man in the life after death (*Republic*, 10.3, 1.614).

Second, the idealized harmony of man evident in the statues of classical

Greece gave way in Plato's thinking to a sense that the relationship between body and soul is conflictual and unfortunate. "The soul is a helpless prisoner chained hand and foot in the body, compelled to view reality not directly but only through its prison bars, and wallowing in utter ignorance" (*Phaedo*, 83a). The evil acts of the body pollute the soul; they prevent the soul from achieving a complete and clean separation and returning to the world of Ideal Forms. Only the soul can perceive Ideal Truth but it cannot do so as long as it must perceive Reality through the use of the five bodily senses. Thus, the real attainment of truth can come only in the higher world when souls can perceive directly without the interference of the body. This position does not necessarily lead to a direct call to suicide, but it does foster a habit of thought in which earthly life is belittled and the philosopher is encouraged to believe that separation from earthly life is the only road to the Ideal human existence.

The third point that may facilitate suicide was Socrates' general view, expressed in different forms upon a number of occasions, that philosophy is "preparation for death." While awaiting execution after his trial, Socrates maintained in an argument to Simmias and Cebes:

Other people are likely not to be aware that those who pursue philosophy aright study nothing but dying and being dead. Now if this is true, it would be absurd to be eager for nothing but this all their lives, and then to be troubled when that came for which they had all along been eagerly practicing. (*Phaedo*, 64a)

In a subsequent passage, Socrates again stated that philosophers desire death, even though people do not understand why: "For they do not know in what way the real philosophers desire death, nor in what way they deserve death" (*Phaedo*, 64b). Later in this dialogue, Socrates explained that death frees the soul!

For, if pure knowledge is impossible while the body is with us, one of two things must follow. Either it cannot be acquired at all or only when we are dead; for then the soul will be by itself apart from the body, but not before. (*Phaedo*, 66e)

True philosophers practice dying and thus fear death less than other men (*Phaedo*, 68a). The argument continues along the line that, unlike the ordinary man, the philosopher understands that death is not a great evil. "You know, do you not, that all other men count death among the great evils" (*Phaedo*, 68d).

Given the concern with death as compared to life, it seems only a short step for Cebes to ask Socrates what the grounds are for saying that suicide is not legitimate (*Phaedo*, 62a). Socrates conceded Cebes' point (*Phaedo*, 62b) and gave the famous guard-post allegory as an argument against suicide. Life is a sorry business, but we must not leave our guard-post unless we are relieved:

We men are put in a sort of guard-post, from which one must not release one's self or run away . . . the gods are our keepers, and we men are one of their possessions. . . . If one of your possessions were to destroy itself without intimation from you that you wanted it to die, wouldn't you be angry with it and punish it, if you had any means of doing so? . . . so if you look at it this way I suppose it is not unreasonable to say that we must not put an end to ourselves until God sends some compulsion like the one which we are facing now. (*Phaedo*, 62b–c)

The *Phaedo* is hardly a ringing endorsement of life. Indeed, it is said to have inspired the suicides of the Spartan King Cleombrotus and of the Roman Cato.

There is no question that Plato expressed different ideas about suicide in different writings. On the one hand, he called for the denial of regular burial for a suicide (*Laws*, 9.12). On the other, at least according to Olympiodorus, Plato seemed to admit that "suicide may be proper to the worthy man, to him of a middle character, and to the multitude and depraved." To the worthy man, as in *The Phaedo* (62b–c); to him of a middle character, as in *The Republic* (3.406d), if he "is afflicted with a long and incurable disease, as being useless to the city"; and to the vulgar character, as in *The Laws* (8.838), if he is "possessed with certain incurable passions, such as being enamored of his mother[4] . . . and who is incapable of governing himself" (Plotinus, *On Suicide*, 1a).

This view generally permeated Socrates' reaction at his trial. In his concluding speech to the jury after his conviction for atheism and for corrupting the minds of the youth of Athens, Socrates described death in a speech reminiscent of Hamlet's soliloquy:

Death is one of two things . . . like a sleep in which the sleeper does not even dream, death would be a wonderful gain. For I think if anyone were to pick out that night in which he slept a dreamless sleep and, comparing with it the other nights and days of his life, were to say, after due consideration, how many days and nights in his life had passed more pleasantly than that night. . . . if death is, as it were, a change of habitation from here to some other place, and if what we are told is true, that all the dead are there, what greater blessing could there be, judges? (Plato, *Apology*, 40c–e)

That this speech was not simply Socrates' denial and rationalization about his own upcoming death is supported by an earlier statement by him before he knew that he would be convicted.

For to fear death, gentlemen, is nothing else than to think one is wise when one is not; for it is thinking one knows when one does not know. For no one knows whether death be not even the greatest of all blessings to man, but they fear it as if they knew that it is the greatest of evils. (Plato, *Apology*, 29a)

Socrates' disciple Xenophon wrote that Socrates was gerophobic and feared the suffering of old age. "I know I must now suffer evils of old age, sight, hearing, learning slow, and forgetfulness. If I am discontent in life, where can I find any pleasure in continuing to live" (Xenophon, *Apology*, 6). The trial seemed a golden opportunity to terminate his life "not only at a proper season but in the easiest manner" (Xenophon, *Apology*, 7).

Xenophon pointed out two curious aspects of Socrates' defense plea. First, Socrates seemed to go out of his way to antagonize the jury by boasting that the oracle at Delphi had termed him the wisest of men (Xenophon, *Apology*, 14). Second, he further angered the jury by proposing as his penalty free meals at the city hall rather than a fine (23, note 1). This served to push the jury to vote for the death penalty. Clearly, Socrates "thought that the proper time was then come for him to die." Seeing his friends weeping after the trial, Socrates said to them, "How is this? Do you now weep? Do you not know that from the moment I was born, death was decreed for me by nature?" (27).

One can hardly find a man possessed of a greater *joie de vivre* than Socrates. Still, he seems to have epitomized Greek thinking in his view of death. All of his life is only to die; all of philosophy is but preparation for death. Indeed, life is permeated and clouded over by the inevitability of death. Xenophon offered his view of the trial of Socrates in his usual direct, matter-of-fact style. He quite agreed with Socrates that at that point "to die was better for him than to live" (Xenophon, *Apology*, 31).[5]

Aristotle

Aristotle seemed less obsessed with the idea of suicide than his mentor Plato, and the subject occupies only a few lines in his many extant writings. He argued that suicide for certain reasons is the act of a coward— suicide as an escape from "poverty or disappointed love or bodily or mental anguish is the deed of a coward. . . . The suicide braves death not for some noble object but to escape ill" (*Ethics*, 3.7). Aristotle added that suicide is an injustice against the state that the state may punish. Unlike Socrates' allegory in *The Phaedo*, Aristotle made no mention of man being the property of the gods, but only as obligated to the state.

But the man who cuts his throat in a fit of temper is voluntarily doing an injury which the law does not allow. It follows that the suicide commits an injustice. But against whom? Is it not the State rather than himself? For he suffers of his own volition, and nobody suffers injustice voluntarily. It is for this reason that the State attaches a penalty, which takes the form of a stigma put on one who has destroyed himself, on the ground that he is guilty of the offense against the State. (*Ethics*, 5.11)

Durkheim (1897/1951, 329–332) argued that Aristotle is the key to understanding the Greek laws on suicide. Suicide is thus illegal when it is not
authorized by the state and legal when it is so authorized.

Greek Law

In Athens, Cyprus, and Thebes, a suicide was denied regular burial
and, perhaps because of some primitive superstition, the hand (seen as
alien to the body) was cut off and buried separately. This rule was even
more severe in Sparta (Aeschines, *Against Ctesiphon*, 244.8; Plato, *Laws*,
9.12; Dio Chrysostom, *Orations*, 4.14). On the other hand, suicide was
tolerated and even assisted when it had received prior state approval. In
Athens, as well as in Massilia and Ceos, such a suicide was actually supplied with hemlock (Valerius Maximus, 2, 6.7–8). According to Libanius
(quoted by Durkheim), the laws in Athens read as follows:

Whosoever no longer wishes to live shall state his reasons to the Senate; and after
having received permission shall abandon life. If your existence is hateful to you,
die; if you are overwhelmed by fate, drink the hemlock. If you are bowed with
grief, abandon life. Let the unhappy man recount his misfortune, let the magistrate supply him with the remedy, and his wretchedness will come to an end.

The Greek views of suicide were related to their attitudes toward life,
death, and freedom. For Plato, death represented "the entry to the far superior world of Ideals compared to which earthly reality is a mere shadow."
Thus, suicide was never far from the surface, and attempts at suicide prevention were ambivalent. Man was the chattel of the gods or the state, but
when the state allowed it, suicide was permitted and even abetted.

HELLENISTIC PHILOSOPHERS

Although there was no single monolithic doctrine on suicide in the later
Graeco-Roman philosophical traditions, it is clear that suicide was widely
accepted as within the limits of normal options. We have already mentioned that some of the greatest names in Hellenistic philosophy are reported to have committed suicide. Let us discuss some of these.

Diogenes, the founder of the school of Cynicism, voluntarily held his
breath until he died (Diogenes Laertius, 6.76). Zeno, the founder of Stoicism, did the same after wrenching his toe (7.28). Cleanthes, Zeno's successor, was told by doctors to fast for two days for a tooth ailment, but he
continued his fast so that he could experience the entire passage to death
(7.176). It is usual in these accounts for suicide to seem an almost normal
response to discouraging circumstances or even to some relatively minor
imperfection. To fail to commit suicide seemed a display of bad character,

certainly a lack of heroism. Indeed, Zeno the Stoic counseled suicide as a reasonable end for a wise man (7.130).

This rash of philosophical suicides seems to have been associated with a generally pessimistic view of human existence. The human being is not an exalted or wonderful creation. The gods too are limited in power and not loving to man. Fear of the seemingly unavoidable changes in the cycle of life pushes man to destruction and oblivion, however great his accomplishments. There is a fatalistic preoccupation with the end of life in a hostile universe.

Plotinus: The Neoplatonist

Plotinus, the third-century (CE) neo-Platonist, agreed with Plato's view that death is to be welcomed by the philosopher but not sought before its proper time: "You should not expel the soul from the body. For in departing, it will retain something (of the more passive life), which is necessary in this case to its departure" (Plotinus, *On Suicide*, 1.9). Plotinus followed Plato in suggesting that there may indeed be times when suicide becomes necessary: "The soul is not to be separated from the body while a further proficiency is yet possible." Porphyry noted that when he himself was contemplating suicide, Plotinus convinced him that it was not a rational decision but was based on too much black bile.

The Cynics

Beginning with Diogenes of Sinope, the Cynic school taught the importance of living simply and renouncing all attachments. They lived as wandering beggars with no possessions of their own, maintaining the sparest of dress and diet.

Poor to begin with, or renouncing their property voluntarily, they lived as beggars. Possessing no houses of their own, they passed the day in the streets, or in other public places; the nights they spent in porticos, or wherever else chance might find them. Furniture they had none. A bed seemed superfluous. The simple Greek dress was by them made still simpler. . . . In scantiness of diet, they even surpassed the very limited requirements of their countrymen. (Zeller 1885, 317–318)

Diogenes undertook self-mortification when his teacher was not sufficiently severe. The Cynics tended to welcome reproaches from enemies, on the grounds that they teach man to know himself and to amend his faults. Should life become unsupportable, they reserved for themselves the right of suicide. When the seriously ill Antisthenes cried out, "Who will release me from these pains?" Diogenes answered, "This," and showed him a dagger. "I said," replied the other, "from my pains, not from life." Of this,

Diogenes Laertius commented, "It was thought that he showed some weakness in leaving his malady through love of life" (Diogenes Laertius, 6.18). Although there are contradictory accounts, Diogenes Laertius reported that Diogenes committed suicide through holding his breath (6.76), as did two later Cynics, Metrocles (6.95) and Menippus (6.100). Perhaps the most striking example of a Cynic suicide is that of Peregrinus, who cast himself into a pyre erected at the Olympic festival. Halliday (1970) has considered the death of Peregrinus as an instance of the same passion for martyrdom exhibited in early Christianity.

The Epicureans

The Epicureans operated according to a moderate pleasure principle. Epicurus, the father of Epicureanism, put it simply: "pleasure is the beginning and end of living happily" (Diogenes Laertius, 10.128). On the surface, Epicurus seems to have been indifferent to questions of death and suicide: "Death is nothing to us, since when we are, death has not come, and when death has come, we are not" (10.125). At times, he seems to have been opposed to suicide: "The wise man will not withdraw himself from life" (10.120).

Close examination indicates a somewhat more complicated position, however. Epicurus defined happiness in terms of internal rather than external states. Whereas Plato justified suicide under intolerable external circumstances, Epicurus seemed to do so in terms of avoiding internal suffering. Self-sufficiency does not consist of using little, but in needing little. One thereby gains freedom, which adds to the enjoyment of life. A self-sufficient person should have no reason to destroy himself but he might do so if there is no other way to avoid unendurable suffering (Cicero, *De Finibus*, 15–49). Still, Epicurus was no less severe with those who desired death than with those who feared it. Seneca (*Epistle*, 24.23) quoted Epicurus as saying, "It's ridiculous to run to death through weariness of life when it's by your manner of life that you've forced yourself to run to death." In another passage in the same epistle, he quoted Epicurus as saying, "Can anything be more ridiculous than to seek death when it's by fear of death that you've destroyed your peace in life?" To these, one may add a third saying: "Such is the blindness, nay, the insanity of death that some men are driven to death by the fear of it" (Seneca, *Ep.*, 24.24).

Unlike Epicurus, Hegesias of Cyrene concluded that life contains more pain than pleasure and that the only logical outcome is thus suicide. The "preacher of death" argued his viewpoint so well, according to Cicero, that a wave of suicides took place in Alexandria, and Ptolemy II had to banish Hegesias from the land (Cicero, *Tusc. Disp.*, 1.34.83).

The Stoics

The Stoics seemed to regard neither life nor death as very important. At the same time, they seemed almost obsessed with the idea of suicide as a way of overcoming their fear of death. In a sense, the Stoic attempted to conquer death by choosing it on his own terms. At best, the philosopher should commit suicide not to escape suffering but to avoid restrictions in carrying out life, since he should be as unaffected by suffering as by any other emotion.

A central problem prompting the Stoic view of life was a pervasive fear of a loss of control, ultimately over life itself. For the Stoic, cheerfulness was a philosophical duty, not an indication of natural optimism. The Stoic did not accept the idea of a caring and loving deity, and he was also too deep a thinker to place much permanent value on so limited a prospect as human success. He knew that he must fulfill his moral and social duty, but he could never desire reward, recognition, or love and could never even feel secure that his good acts would produce a good result.

Zeno, the founder of the Stoic school, defined the goal of life as living in agreement with nature (Diogenes Laertius, 7.87). If such an agreement exists, life is good; if it does not exist, suicide becomes the wise choice (7.130). Thus, Zeno was said to have killed himself out of sheer irritation (perhaps with imperfection itself) when he wrenched his toe by stumbling on his way home from the stoa. He held his breath until he died (7.20). His successor Cleanthes fasted, initially to cure a boil on his gum but ultimately, "as he had advanced so far on his journey toward death, he would not retreat," and he starved himself to death (7.176).

The Roman Stoics basically agreed with their earlier Greek counterparts — with one important shift. The question, as Alvarez (62) has suggested, was no longer whether to kill yourself when the inner compulsion became irresistible but how to do so in the right way. This attribute can be seen in a sampling of the writings of Cicero. Suicide, Cicero argued, is no great evil.

When a man's circumstances contain a preponderance of things in accordance with nature, it is appropriate for him to remain alive; when he possesses or sees in prospect a majority of the contrary things, it is appropriate for the wise man to quit life, although he is happy, and also for the foolish man to remain in life although he is miserable. . . . And very often it is appropriate for the wise man to abandon life at a moment when he is enjoying supreme happiness, if an opportunity offers for making a timely exit. For the Stoic view is that happiness, which means life in harmony with nature, is a matter of seizing the right moment. So that Wisdom her very self upon occasion bids the wise man to leave her. (*De Finibus*, 3.60 and 61)

According to Cicero, appropriate means is in accordance with nature, as is self-love. Thus, suicide is useful for the wise man.

In the *Tusculan Disputations*, Cicero depicted death as freeing man from chains. The gods in their benevolence have prepared for man a haven and refuge after the departure from worldly life (1.18). Some philosophers have disagreed with this, and some Stoics even felt that the soul is not immortal. Indeed, while earthly life is not wholly evil, the afterlife holds far more joy (1.84).

Cicero cited the deaths of Socrates and Cato as examples to show that suicide is permissible but only when the gods themselves have given a valid reason. One must not break the prison bonds except in obedience to the magistrate. The human soul should be dissociated from the body during life by means of philosophy and virtue, for such a life will best prepare the soul for the afterlife. It is highly desirable for one to quit the sorrows of this world to gain the joys of the next (1.71–75).

Much the same view can be seen in a sampling of the declamations of the elder Seneca (around 40 CE). These declamations were a series of arguments on a variety of subjects and were widely used as training for law students. Whatever may have been the various opinions in individual cases, it is clear that suicide was hardly shocking to either the speakers or the listeners.

A man whose wife and three children had died in a fire tried to hang himself but was cut down and saved by a passer-by. Was the passer-by guilty of an offense? The passer-by argued that one must have hope and that, in any case, if the man had truly wanted to hang himself, he ought to have done so immediately after the fire. The accuser argued that "It is a wrong done me if I have to die at your will when I should have died at mine." The one who attempted suicide was not accused, but rather the one who stopped him (Seneca, *Contraversiae*, 5.1).

Should a suicide be allowed burial? One speaker argued for burial on the grounds that "death should be undisturbed. There is equal cruelty in killing those who wish to live and forcing life on those who wish to die." The opposition argued that burial for a suicide is an outrage. "Some guilty conscience made him take refuge in death; one of his crimes is that he cannot be convicted. . . . One capable of killing himself might have dared anything" (Seneca, *Contraversiae*, 8.4).

In this case too, suicide was not criminal because it was immoral or because it destroyed human life. The criminal act was rather that the suicide upset the judicial processes or that it seemed to show bad character on the part of the suicide. For example, a tyrant ordered two sons to beat their father. One son leaped to his death. The other beat the father but later killed the tyrant. One opinion on this suicide was that, "This is not sparing one's father—it's sparing oneself." The discussion centered on the question of the extent to which one ought to obey a tyrant (Seneca, *Contraversiae*, 9.4).

A curious story appears in the preface to Book 10, in the form of a letter addressed by the elder Seneca to his sons regarding Titus Labienus, a writer whose books were burned by his enemies: "Labienus did not take this insult lying down, nor did he wish to outlive his genius. He had himself carried to the tombs of his ancestors and walled up. . . . he not only finished his life, he buried himself" (Seneca, *Contraversiae*, 10: preface).

Suicide was also a major topic in the letters of Lucius Anneaus Seneca, the brilliant Roman writer and statesman. The younger Seneca's writings show a deep concern and awareness of death. Man is always no more "than a moment ahead of the universal doom" (Seneca, *Ep.*, 71.15). Hope for the betterment of the human condition is false. "Truth doesn't grow and neither does virtue" (71.16). One must continue to try, but not because there is any hope of success. Pacurius held his own wake every night, believing that anyone who can say "My life is lived" rises daily from his bed to a sense of something gained (12.8–10).

One may hope for good but must always be prepared for the worst. People discover too late that they "stand in the shadow of death, of exile and suffering" (Seneca, *Ep.*, 24.12–15). The thinking man does well to feel terror before so dire a fate. Death provides a release from these horrors. Every day we stand nearer the end; every hour urges us toward the bank from which we must fall. One should not be afraid to quit the present field of action (120). Death is so far from being terrible that "by its grace all things lose their terrors." To Seneca, it seemed that it is life that is terrifying and death that provides release (24).

According to the younger Seneca, the events of earthly existence are paltry and not worth any emotional involvement. The questions of who wins the Battle of Pharsalus or an election are insignificant (Seneca, *Ep.*, 71). A man may leave the world if he feels that he has overstayed his welcome (120). The human body is an unpleasantness to be endured only as long as one wishes, and when one thinks fit, one may dissolve the partnership with this puny clay (65.22).

The Stoic felt bound by necessity and sought a sense of freedom and release. In this area, among others, the philosophy of Stoicism seems to suffer from a sort of constipation. One should escape from this life whenever one chooses, and he should die when the means are in hand: "Choose any part of nature and tell it to let you out" (Seneca, *Ep.*, 117.23–24). One should pick the means by which to quit life, for the option of suicide leaves the road to freedom open. To grumble is pointless, since life holds no man fast. "Do you like life, then live on. Do you dislike it? Then you're free to return to the place you came from" (70.15). The philosopher may choose his own mode of death just as he chooses a ship or a house. He leaves life as he would a banquet — when it is time (70.11; Plotinus, *On Suicide* 1.9).

Stoicism always emphasized duty and derogated pleasure and passion. Reason is good, while emotion is evil. Pleasure is best deferred. Apples taste sweetest when they are going rotten. The drinker drinks the last draft — the wave that drowns his senses — and puts the finishing touch on his drunken bliss. Every pleasure defers its most intense thrill to the last (Seneca, *Ep.*, 12).

Thus, death is not to be viewed as an evil, and suicide is suitable. Nonetheless, suicide should not be an act of passion or emotion. Whether one dies badly or well, in the manner of a philosopher, is the important point (Seneca, *Ep.*, 70.5–6). Seneca would not destroy himself merely to avoid pain, for the philosopher must be above pain: "I shall make my exit, not because of actual pain but because the pain is likely to prove a burr to everything that makes life worthwhile" (58.36). The man who dies because of pain is weak; the man who lives to suffer is a fool. Finally, man is not trapped:

You see that yawning precipice? It leads to liberty. You see that flood, that river, that well? Liberty houses within them. You see that stunted, parched, and sorry tree? From each branch, liberty hangs. Your neck, your throat, your heart are so many ways of escape from slavery. . . . Do you inquire the road to freedom? You shall find it in every vein of your body. (Seneca, *De Ira*, 3.15.3–4)

Seneca and his wife Paulina put these thoughts into action, calmly cutting their wrists at the order of his former pupil, the Emperor Nero.

This consistency between thought and action is also exemplified in the advice given to the incurably ill Marcellinus who was contemplating and ultimately committed suicide.

Be not tormented, my Marcellinus, as if you were deliberating any great matter. Life is a thing of no dignity or importance. Your very slaves, your animals possess it in common with yourself, but it is a great thing to die honorably, prudently, bravely. Think how long you have been engaged in the same dull course: eating, sleeping, and indulging your appetites. This has been the circle. Not only a prudent, brave, or a wretched man may wish to die, but even a fastidious one. (Seneca, *Ep.*, 77.6)

Epictetus, another major Roman Stoic writer, lived as a slave in the first century CE. He too did not view suicide as a criminal act.

If Thou dost send me to a place where men cannot live as their nature requires, I shall go away, not in disobedience but believing that Thou dost sound the note for my retreat. I do not abandon Thee, heaven forbid! But I recognize that Thou hast no need of me. (Epictetus, *Discourses*, 3.24)

A sufficient degree of unpleasantness in one's existence indicates that the gods no longer need him and that it is time to make one's departure (3.24). A man may simply decide that he "will not play the game anymore." Epictetus saw human life as of little account and hardly worth preserving.

"Thou art a little soul bearing about a course" (10.41). Still, suicide must not be performed frivolously:

Only let me not give up my heart faintheartedly or from some casual pretext. For again, God does not so desire; for he has need of such a universe and of such men who go to and fro upon earth. But if he gives the signal to retreat as he did to Socrates, I must obey him who gives the signal, as I would a general.[6] (1.29)

Marcus Aurelius, Emperor of Rome 162–181, CE, is famed for his *Meditations*, a classic text of Stoic thinking. To Marcus, the only evil in suicide is doing it in passion, emotionally. Indeed, "If you cannot maintain rationality, equanimity, magnanimity, . . . depart at once from life not in passion but with simplicity, freedom, modesty after doing this one laudable thing at least in thy life to have gone out of it thus" (Marcus Aurelius, *Meditations*, 10.8). If one is too restricted, "then get away out of life, yet so as if thou went suffering no harm. Why dost thou think that this is any trouble" (5.29). If circumstances cause the loss of one's self-control, then it is not worthwhile to live and it is in one's power to wipe out this judgment (8.47). If one cannot live as one wishes, then leave life. "This house is smoky, and I quit it" (5.29).

Roman Law

Suicide was not specifically mentioned in the fragments of the law of the Twelve Tables. Nevertheless, several later sources noted refusals to allow suicides to be buried and even of the crucifixion of their corpses (Pliny, *Natural History*, 36.24). Quintillian, however, claimed that the ban on suicide could be lifted in certain cases, given prior approval by the Senate (Quintillian, *Inst. Orat*, 7.4.39).[7] Motives were important in Roman law. Suicide, for example, was not punishable if caused by "impatience of pain or sickness" or "weariness of life, lunacy or fear of dishonor" (Justinian, *Digest*, 48.21.3.6). These laws tended to reflect both the earlier Aristotelian concept that man was a possession of the state as well as the suicidal pessimism of the later Roman Stoics. Thus, the suicidal pessimism exhibited in Greek thought and law was carried into Roman society as well. When the second-century philosopher Lucian realized that he was no longer able to take care of himself, he quoted: "Here endeth a contest awarding the fairest of prizes: time calls, and forbids us delay." Then, refraining from all food, he took his leave of life in his habitual cheerful humor. A short time before the end, he was asked, "What orders have you to give about your burial?" He replied, "Don't borrow trouble! The stench will get me buried" (*Lucian on Demonax*, 65, 66).

Demonax had an even more biting wit. Someone asked him what it was like in Hades. Demonax replied, "Wait a bit, and I'll send you word from there." Admetus, a poet, read him an epitaph that he had composed for himself. Demonax scornfully replied, "The epitaph is so fine that I wish it were already carved!" (*Lucian on Demonax*, 65, 66). Demonax's favorite quotation from the *Iliad* was: "Idler or toiler, tis all one to Death" (9.320).

NOTES

1. S. J. D. Cohen's (1982) list of suicides includes Xanthians, Cappadocians, Isaurians, Abydenes, Taochians, Sidonians, Gauls, Illyrians, and four instances by Spaniards, including the people of Sagantum, the Astapaeans, tribesman of Vaccaei, and citizens of Numantai.

2. The German classicist R. Hirzel (1908) attempted to impose order on some of these data. He suggested that the Homeric period was not especially plagued by suicide—this despite a strong sense of the heroic. Suicidal thoughts, argued Hirzel, did emerge as a problem during the times of political upheaval in the first millennium BCE. The 5th century BCE, however, produced a veritable epidemic of suicides. Hirzel suggested that this period combined pessimism with an extreme cult of individualism.

3. There seems to be no evidence for the historicity of this story. It appears to have been invented about 600 years after the purported event (Hooper 1967).

4. Is Plato here suggesting a relationship between suicide and unresolved Oedipal conflicts? This topic is taken up in chapters 8 and 9.

5. See I. F. Stone's *The Trial of Socrates* (1988).

6. Droge and Tabor (1992, 29–39) have found a precedent for rational suicide in this passage. Voluntary suicide is condoned when it is necessary (*anangke*) and rational; it is condemned when it is irrational. A rational suicide receives a divine signal that the time to die is at hand. "For the stoics the cosmic deity was the Logos of which human reason was a part. An individual's logos, therefore would allow him to determine the divinely (or more strictly, rationally) appointed time for his exit from life" (32). In other words, Zeno killed himself by holding his breath, not because he broke his toe, but because he thought that this event represented the divine signal to depart (31). While provocative, this line of historical reasoning is highly speculative. By their own admission, there is nothing in the account preserved by Diogenes Laertius that supports this theory explicitly. Furthermore, even if Droge and Tabor are historically correct, the psychological question remains as to why Zeno interpreted his broken toe as a divine signal to depart. After all, there is a very big leap between breaking one's toe and killing oneself. Zeno's decision, like Socrates', was likely provoked by a sense of loss of control. He attempted to regain control by his means of suicide—holding his breath. It presses the point to see Zeno's act as rational rather than as rationalized, masking underlying psychodynamic issues of gerophobia, depression, and feelings of hopelessness, helplessness, and loss of control.

7. See a more detailed discussion by Durkheim (1986, 331).

Chapter 3

Suicide in Jewish and Christian Thought

See I have put before you today life and death, blessing and curse, and you shall choose life so that you and your seed shall live.

Deut. 30.19

Then the Lord God formed man of the dust of the ground, and breathed into his nostrils the breath of life; and man became a living soul.

Gen. 2.7

Read not *harut* [carved] but *herut* [freedom]. One is not free unless he devotes himself to the study of Torah.

Avot, 6.2

This world is like a portico before the world to come. Prepare yourself in the portico so that you may enter into the banquet hall. An hour of repentance and good deeds in this world is better than all the world to come and better is one hour of the peace of spirit of the next world than all of this world.

Avot, 4.21–22

Many contemporary suicidologists (e.g., Fedden 1938, 30; Alvarez 1970, 51; Shneidman 1985, 30) have argued that there is no specific antisuicide teaching in the Hebrew Bible. Nevertheless, Hebraic thought in fact opposes not only suicide but also self-wounding. This chapter shall deal with the question of suicide and martyrdom first in Jewish and then in Christian thought. In both religions, the issue is placed in terms of the larger context of views of life versus death.

RABBINIC JUDAISM

The Talmudic tradition condemns suicide as a most heinous sin. The topic, however, evokes little discussion. The minutiae in laws of Sabbath observance or animal sacrifices in the Temple occupy far more space in the literature. For example, in the eight volumes of the *Aruch Hashulchan*, only one page pertains to suicide (*Yorah Deah*, 345).

The Biblical basis for the injunction against suicide has been derived from the Noahide laws: "For your lifeblood too, I will require a reckoning" (Gen. 9.5).[1] This statement has been seen as a prohibition not only against suicide but also against any form of self-mutilation (*Baba Kamma*, 91b).[2] The Hebrew Bible contains several additional prohibitions with regard to self-mutilation. For example, "Ye are the children of the Lord your God: Ye shall not cut yourselves, nor make any baldness between your eyes for the dead" (Deut. 14.1). Much the same prohibition is given specifically to the priests in Leviticus: "They shall not make baldness upon their head, neither shall they shave off the corners of their beard, nor make any cuttings in their flesh" (Lev. 21.5).

The prohibition against suicide is clear in Rabbinic law. A suicide, for example, is not given full burial honors. Rending one's garments, delivering memorial addresses, and certain other rites to honor the dead are not performed for a suicide victim. The definition of a suicide, however, requires intent, full wits, nondeficiency in behavior, and noninebriation (*Yorah Deah*, 345). There are also exceptions to the prohibition against suicide. According to the Talmud (*Sanhedrin*, 74a) one is obliged to accept death when the alternative is to be forced to commit adultery, murder, or idolatry. It should be stressed that this means allowing oneself to be killed under certain prescribed circumstances, not actively killing oneself.

But the Jewish law on suicide is only one narrow aspect of a far wider and more important idea: that God loves man without qualification and indeed created man in His own image. The Torah is thus given to man as a guide for living rather than merely as a preparation for death: "Ye shall therefore keep my statutes, and mine ordinances, which if a man do, he shall live by them: I am the Lord" (Lev. 18.5). The same idea is constant throughout the Bible and Rabbinic writings.

We shall discuss five central areas of this emphasis on life, based on Jewish sacred literature: (1) creation, (2) obligations and achievements, (3) choice and freedom, (4) the relationship between body and soul, and (5) suffering, pain, and martyrdom.

The Jewish View of Creation

Greek mythology held the view that the world preceded the Olympian gods, who, though immortal, were subject to fate and natural laws and were not omnipotent. Hesiod offered a theogony beginning with the mating of Gaea (earth) and Uranus (heaven) and ending with Zeus. Certainly the gods, whether Olympian or more local, were neither benevolent nor all-knowing. They were often in conflict with each other, and they were fundamentally selfish and capricious with no great love for man or the world.

The Hebrew Bible describes the Creator in a distinctly different manner. He is, in fact, the Creator of the entire universe and continues to be omnipotent over it. No other power can rival Him. Also, He created the world solely as an act of kindness and, in the highest expression of love and benevolence towards man, created him in the divine image. To destroy or damage any human being defaces the divine image, insults and diminishes the whole of God's creation, and reduces the divine plan of love in which the world was brought into being (Soloveitchik 1973).

To murder oneself or another is a grievous degradation of life. The individual does not belong to God in the sense of a chattel nor does he belong to himself. The notion of ownership implicit in the way the Greeks belonged to the state does not fit here. Instead, the human being, as the epitome of divine creation, has obligations commensurate with his central exalted position in the universe. To commit suicide destroys that position and scars the divine love on which the universe exists.

Not only is the world a continuing expression of the infinite love of the Creator, but the creation of man is an act of love as well (*Avot*, 3). The Hebrew Bible and Midrash regularly refer to man as the child of God, as the firstborn, as the precious son, and the like. God carries His people as an eagle carries his young (Exod. 19.4). The Song of Songs depicts this relationship in most tender terms as that of two lovers. Strikingly, this book has been viewed by Rabbi Akiba as the most sacred of the Bible. This sense of love is expressed by some of the leaders of the Hasidic movement, such as the rabbi of Berditchev whose affection for God, as well as his twitting of Him, are well known (though hardly unique) in Jewish literature. The importance of faith and trust in God is the subject of the fourth chapter of Bachya Ibn Pakuda's *Duties of the Hearts*, an important rabbinic work of the eleventh century. Bachya Ibn Pakuda defined faith as the sure confidence that God will help the individual in pure kindness and devotion. This is not an empty-headed notion that everything is wonderful, but a firm conviction that God's kindness and wisdom are total and that He is aware of all things and cares about them.

Man's role is to use those talents that God has given him to fulfill His commandments, including the general commandment to improve the world (Gen. 1.28). Success in one's work is possible, and one must work hard, but ultimately, one is in God's hands.

The Jewish View of Obligation and Achievement

A second important stopper of any urge to self-destruction in Jewish thought centers in the idea that the Creator has placed certain well-defined obligations on man, not as a sisyphean burden (see Chapter 6) but for the general purpose of affording each individual the means of coming close to God and living the most fulfilled sort of life. The demands made on man are not beyond the human ability to fulfill nor are they aimed at tricking man and keeping him subservient. They are a set of instructions given to him for his own benefit, just as a loving parent would instruct a small child. Man's purpose on earth is thus, at least on a working level, made clear. He need only do his human best to fulfill the divine dictates. He need not be disappointed at his failures to reach self-determined levels of success in any endeavor, whether intellectual or corporeal (*Avot*, 2.21). No self-proclaimed measure of success exists, except in a self-punitive mind, for man's obligations are set for him by the Torah.

It is highly significant within this system that the obligations are always completely purposive. The meaning or value of certain laws (e.g., the red heifer) is not explained, yet no law is capricious or arbitrary. Each is important and gives the human being a constant and profound obligation and purpose in life. Each moment and every human act can be rich with purpose.

In Plato's *Apology*, Socrates was portrayed as being in love with Athens and with wisdom. He took great joy from what he depicted as Apollo's mandate to him to seek wisdom, and he pursued it among the people of Athens for decades. According to Xenophon, however, Socrates' *joie de vivre* failed in the face of his fear of old age. Perhaps more than any other figure in Greek philosophy, Socrates came close to a life based on purposive obligation, yet there was nothing in his code to prevent suicide. His thought did not include the notion of a benevolent deity in whom he could trust all the way to the end. As the sense of hopelessness and helplessness grew within him, Socrates saw self-destruction as the easiest way. Apollo had given Socrates no message to the contrary. Therefore, feeling that he would soon begin to decline in physical and mental strength and to diminish in value, Socrates took the path to the hemlock, conducting a defense (according to Xenophon) that so irritated the jury that they would be certain not only to convict him but to sentence him to death as well. The Rabbinic system, in contrast, is not obsessed with the mysteries of birth, life, and death. The Mishna states rather that birth, life, death, and the final judgment all take place against man's will (*Avot*, 4).

Doctrinal explanations of the meaning of these events are not terribly important. One must have faith that each of these events is brought about by God and that He, in His omniscience and omni-benevolence, has planned them well. A Midrash states that among the first generations of human history, there was no old age in the world so that all adults looked young. The Biblical patriarch, Abraham, then prayed that signs of aging should appear on the elderly so that one could distinguish sons from their fathers (*Gen. Rabbah*, 58.9, 59.2, 65.9). God granted his prayer, and Abraham was the first to show marks of aging. This was seen as a sign of respect to the elderly.

The example of heroism is thus not the warrior facing his enemies on the battlefield but rather the "woman of valor" (*eishet chayil*) in Proverbs 31 who "laughs at the final day." She laughs not from a lack of understanding but from her deep faith in God's loving care. One further example of this view is the parable offered by Rabbi Elchonon Wasserman, one of the rabbinic giants of Eastern Europe between the world wars. Facing imminent death at the hands of the Nazis, Rabbi Wasserman explained the events around him in a parable. Perhaps it is not too far-fetched to view this as a sort of Rabbinic *Phaedo*.

Once a man who knew nothing at all about agriculture came to a farmer and asked to be taught about farming. The farmer took him to his field and asked him what he saw. "I see a beautiful piece of land, lush with grass, and pleasing to the eye." Then the visitor stood aghast while the farmer plowed under the grass and turned the beautiful green field into a mass of shallow brown ditches. "Why did you ruin the field?" he demanded.

"Be patient. You will see," said the farmer. Then the farmer showed his guest a sackful of plump kernels of wheat and said, "Tell me what you see." The visitor described the nutritious, inviting grain — and then once more watched in shock as the farmer ruined something beautiful. This time, he walked up and down the furrows and dropped kernels into the open ground wherever he went. Then he covered the kernels with clods of soil.

"Are you insane?" the man demanded. "First you destroyed the field and then you ruined the grain!"

"Be patient. You will see." Time went by, and once more the farmer took his guest out to the field. Now they saw endless, straight rows of green stalks sprouting up from all the furrows. The visitor smiled broadly. "I apologize. Now I understand what you were doing. You made the field more beautiful than ever. The art of farming is truly marvelous."

"No," said the farmer. "We are not done. You must still be patient." More time went by and the stalks were fully grown. Then the farmer came with his sickle and chopped them down as his visitor watched open-mouthed, seeing how the orderly field became an ugly scene of destruction. The farmer bound the fallen stalks into bundles and decorated the field with them. Later, he took the bundles to another area where he beat and crushed them until they became a mass of straw and loose kernels. Then he separated the kernels from the chaff and piled them up in a huge hill. Always, he told his protesting visitor, "We are not done, you must be more patient."

Then the farmer came with his wagon and piled it high with grain, which he took to a mill. There, the beautiful grain was ground into formless, choking dust.

The visitor complained again. "You have taken grain and transformed it into dirt!" Again, he was told to be patient. The farmer put the dust into sacks and took it back home. He took some dust and mixed it with water while his guest marveled at the foolishness of making "whitish mud." Then the farmer fashioned the "mud" into the shape of a loaf. The visitor saw the perfectly formed loaf and smiled broadly, but his happiness did not last. The farmer kindled a fire in an oven and put the loaf into it.

"Now I know you are insane. After all that work, you burn what you have made."

The farmer looked at him and laughed. "Have I not told you to be patient?" Finally the farmer opened the oven and took out a freshly baked bread — crisp and brown, with an aroma that made the visitor's mouth water.

"Come," the farmer said. He led his guest to the kitchen table where he cut the bread and offered his now pleased visitor a liberally buttered slice.

"Now," the farmer said, "now, you understand."

God is the Farmer and we are the fools who do not begin to understand His ways or the outcome of His plan. Only when the process is complete will we all know why all this had to be. Until then, we must be patient and have faith that every-thing — even when it seems destructive and painful — is part of the process that will produce goodness and beauty. (Sorasky 1982, 431)

The Jewish answer to Socrates' fear of old age is that man can only place himself in God's hands and must continue to do his best to obey God's purpose. Further, his existence is meaningful and significant to God. There-fore, decisions about his life and death should come not from his own limited mind and his own limited knowledge, but from God alone.

The Jewish View of Choice and Freedom

A third major aspect of Rabbinic thought concerns the concept of choice and freedom. Greek mythology is peppered with stories involving a Hob-son's choice, that is, a situation that appears to require a choice but in which there are in fact no livable alternatives.

The riddle of the Sphinx and Oedipus' response to it were a major theme of Greek mythology. The monstrous Sphinx — part lion, part eagle, and part woman — accosted travelers and asked her famous riddle: "What goes on four legs in the morning, two legs at midday, and three legs in the evening?" Travelers could not answer the riddle, and the Sphinx devoured them. Oedipus presented the Sphinx with the correct answer. It is man who walks (crawls) on four legs in the morning of his life, two in his matu-rity, and three (with a cane) in his later years. Oedipus slew the Sphinx; in so doing, however, he showed that he accepted the two bad choices offered him by the riddle. He could either surrender his life or accept the Sphinx's deterministic and highly pessimistic view of life as a cycle. In accepting this decremental view of aging, Oedipus expressed his agreement with the

Sphinx's philosophy of self-destruction and proceeded to live it out, fulfilling the self-destructive curse.

Comparing Greek and Biblical attitudes toward suicide is illuminating.
To the Stoic, there was a choice as to whether to continue one's life or end
it. Suicide is thus considered a viable option worthy of the philosopher's
careful consideration. Suicide is not a criminal act, as long as one's decision
is based on reason and not emotion; it is indeed more appropriate for the
philosopher than for the average citizen.

In the Rabbinic system, there is no thought of a decision about suicide.
Suicide is forbidden by the Torah and is not at all the act of a Talmudic
scholar. Indeed, it is considered a criminal act that should be punished by a
court, were it possible. Still the criminal-victim is seen as probably acting
under at least a temporary insanity and may therefore require pity and
compassion more than persecution.

In Rabbinic thought, the choice between life and death is not one to
mull over daily, in the way that talk of suicide filled the letters of Seneca
and other writings by Classical philosophers. It was a choice made once:
"See I have put before you today life and death, blessing and curse, and
you shall choose life so that you and your seed shall live" (Deut. 30.19).
The choice is not whether or not to destroy one's life but how best to live it.
The Stoics saw fate as a powerful force capriciously controlling human des-
tinies. Indeed, necessity was so strong that they sought to escape it. In particular, they sought to escape from the inevitability of death through the
illusion of gaining control over death through suicide. Knowing that he
could bring death by slitting his wrist gave Seneca the "feeling of freedom
in every vein." The option of bringing death seemed to give the Stoic an
illusion of control by which he could prevent death from striking him by
chance.

The Mishna is not concerned with fate. It asserts that real freedom always exists in the human realm, that is, the freedom to act righteously. The
Mishna does not posit illusory freedom or choice in matters beyond human
control. In this way, the rabbis disagreed with the Stoics. Where the Stoics
felt overwhelmed by necessity or fate in all things *except* the time and manner of their death, the rabbis argued that in such matters as death, there
was, in fact, no choice. "Against your will you are born, against your will
you live, against your will you die. Against your will you shall in the future
give account before the King of Kings" (*Avot*, 4.29).

The Stoics desperately sought a feeling of freedom that would offer them
at least a temporary illusion of control. The rabbis, by contrast, accepted
that God controls these matters of life and death. Feeling no need to take
these impossibly difficult decisions from the hands of the one omnipotent
and benevolent Deity, the human being gains the freedom to devote his
attention wholly to those tasks that are peculiarly his, that is, loving God
and man and studying and fulfilling God's commandments. The Mishna

goes on to offer its own statement on freedom. The Ten Commandments were carved (*harut*) on stone: "Read not *harut* but *herut* [freedom]. One is not free unless he devotes himself to study of the Torah" (*Avot*, 6.2). Freedom here means the freedom of the human spirit from fears and desires. When one's fears and desires run rampant, then one is dominated by them and there is no freedom. The Stoic sought freedom from the terror of death by choosing his own means of exit. The rabbinic Jew acknowledged God's total power over birth, life, and death. In so doing, he accepted the responsibility of his freedom to make important moral choices. Birth and death are events beyond human understanding, God alone will handle them. The individual is given freedom in terms of following the Torah.

The Stoic comparison of life to a banquet from which one may depart at will meets a striking antithesis in a second-century Mishnaic statement. "This world is like a portico before the world to come. Prepare yourself in the portico so that you may enter into the banquet hall" (*Avot*, 4.21–22). That is, prepare yourself in this world by living righteously so that you may merit the rewards of the next world. The two worlds are dissimilar in function. In this world, good deeds and repentance are appropriate and more beautiful than all the rewards of the next world. At the same time, the peace of spirit attainable in the next world is preferable to all of the joys of this world. Earthly life is therefore not a banquet that must inevitably end. It is a time for work and preparation. The contrast with Stoic views carries on to a second point. One must not assume that the next world is some sort of refuge from this one (*Avot*, 4). There is still awareness, and one must come before the King of Kings for a final judgment that will be beyond anything earthly man can comprehend. Both Earth and Heaven are thus important, but each in its own way.

The Relationship Between Body and Soul

From the rabbinic point of view, body and soul should function together harmoniously. Though the body supports the soul in their joint service of God, there is none of the Platonic sense that the body must die to liberate the soul. Body and soul are different but need not be in conflict.

Man must keep his body both physically and morally clean (Buchler 1922, 14–20). It is told that Hillel once left the house of learning with his students. They asked where he was headed, and he replied that he was going to perform a religious duty — to bathe in the bathhouse. A king appoints someone to keep his statue clean. Therefore, man, created in the divine image, must certainly keep his body clean (*Avot D'R Nathan*, 2.33). Hillel described the soul as a guest in the body; the body should keep itself fit in order to offer hospitality to so distinguished a guest. To Hillel, the body was neither an evil to be repressed nor a bastion of heroism to be glorified by Olympic victories. For him, both physical and spiritual activities were part of man's fulfillment of his obligation to God.

The Israeli scholar Ephraim Urbach has pointed to the fact that *nefesh*, the Hebrew word for soul, is used in a number of places in the Hebrew Bible to refer to the whole human being. Urbach has supplied a number of references to support this view (e.g. Exod. 4.19, 1 Kings 19.10) and specifically distinguished the term *nefesh* from the Greek word *psyche* or *anima*, which connotes a disembodied soul (Urbach 1979, 214–215).

Suffering, Pain, and Martyrdom: A Jewish View

Jewish thinkers were as aware as anyone of the inescapable pains that life has presented to man after he knowingly rejected the physical and spiritual beauty of Eden. One of the great Talmudic teachers of our century was at times so darkly depressed that he could not lecture for weeks.[3] There is an account of another great Talmudist (Berlin 1943) who was thrown into a state of terror while watching a sunset from the balcony of a hotel room. Still, there is never the feeling that human suffering was desired by a capricious divinity. Man is not a plaything but a deeply beloved child.

In this post-Edenic state, each human personality has its own strengths and weaknesses, and man feels fear, struggle, and pain. The Talmud tells the poignant story of Rabbi Elazar (*Berachot*, 5b):

R. Elazar fell ill and R. Johanan went to visit him. He noticed that he was lying in a dark room, and he bared his arm and light radiated from it. Thereupon he noticed that R. Elazar was weeping, and he said to him: "Why do you weep? Is it because you did not study enough Torah? Surely we have learned: The one who does much and the one who does little have the same merit, provided that the heart is directed to heaven. Is it perhaps lack of sustenance? Not everybody has the privilege to enjoy two tables. Is it perhaps because of the lack of children? This is the bone of my tenth son!" He replied to him: "I am weeping on account of your beauty that is going to rot in the earth." He said to him: "On that account you surely have a reason to weep," and they both wept. In the meanwhile he said to him, "Are your sufferings welcome to you?" He replied "Neither they nor their reward." He said to him: "Give me your hand," and he gave him his hand and he raised him.

The Hebrew Bible refers often to the suffering of man. The Psalms deal with human sadness, and Naomi stated openly that God had given her a bitter load. Nevertheless, whatever their hardships, however depressed their emotional state, suicide was not a viable answer. A Talmudic debate is often cited as to the basic value of life itself:

Our Rabbis taught: For two and a half years were Beth Shammai and Beth Hillel in dispute, the former asserting that it were better for man not to have been created than to have been created, and the latter maintaining that it is better for man to have been created than not to have been created. They finally took a vote and decided that it were better for man not to have been created than to have been created, but now that he has been created, let him investigate his past deeds or, as others say, let him examine his future actions. (*Eruvin*, 13b)

This passage has often been cited to illustrate the basic pessimism in the rabbinic view of life. Even in the most pessimistic interpretation, however, suicide is not permitted. The rabbis themselves had a brighter view of this debate. They saw it as referring only to the wicked who make poor use of their lives, whereas for the righteous, life is indeed a benefit (Tosafot on *Eruvin*, 13b). This view stands in marked contrast to the pessimism with regard to human creation expressed by Hesiod.

Let us examine the understanding of pain and suffering that appears in the traditional Jewish attitudes towards martyrdom. These attitudes were put to the acid test for the rabbis of the Roman period; they had to decide to what extent a Jew might break the law of the Torah if threatened with death by persecutors. They decided that one could break any law under threat of death, except for three: adultery, murder, and idolatry, or unless public disgrace to the Torah was involved (*Sanhedrin*, 74a). Thus, under the severe persecutions of the Roman Era, there were many cases in which people were punished or put to death for trying to uphold the Law. Death *per se* was never a desired solution, however, nor was martyrdom sought for its own sake. For example, Rabbi Akiba was tortured cruelly by the Romans when they found him teaching the Torah during the period of persecution that followed the Bar Kochba War (135 CE). As the story is told in the Babylonian Talmud (*Berachot*, 61b), a Roman officer saw Rabbi Akiba smiling and asked him why. Rabbi Akiba responded that he was in great agony, and he knew he would soon die. He was glad only that in his last moment, he could still sanctify God's name by reciting the Shema: "Hear Oh Israel, the Lord our God is one." Rabbi Akiba did not seek martyrdom and felt no beatific joy at his pain. Rather, he continued to express his faith in God.

This story remained the model for Jewish martyrs facing marauding crusaders and other Jew-hating mobs through the Middle Ages. It is better to live and not to seek martyrdom, but if one must die, then let it be in the best possible manner. It is significant that the Jews typically preferred peace and quiet to a martyr's death. Moreover, within their limited means, they often fought back. Death was to be avoided if possible. One chronicle reports the story of a young Talmudic student in the Middle Ages, who, when faced with torture, suddenly grabbed the sword from his torturer and killed him (Haberman 1946, 74). A second case is reported in which Rabbi Simon Ben Abraham slew some Jewish children when they were in danger of forced baptism. A second rabbi called him a murderer and stated that he should be punished with a horrible death. Then the persecutors began to skin the survivors and pour sand into their bodies. Suddenly, the torture was halted, and the victims survived, except for those whom the rabbi had killed. Clearly, the rabbi's actions in killing the children were not condoned (*Daat Zekenim* on Gen. 9).

Questions of self-defense also arose. Some groups of people allowed themselves to be slaughtered by Seleucid soldiers rather than desecrate the Sabbath by defending themselves. This was a new problem, and the Jews had to decide how to handle it. According to the Talmud, the religious leaders proclaimed that Jews not only must defend themselves if attacked on the Sabbath but also *must attack* if the situation seemed to require offensive action (*Eruvin*, 45a; *Shulchan Aruch; Orach Chaim*, 329. 6, 7). This has remained standard in Jewish law.

Exceptions to the Rule: Jewish Suicides

Despite these injunctions, a number of suicides are reported in Jewish writings. There are only six suicides in the entire Hebrew Bible and none in the Pentateuch. Chronologically, they are as follows: the self-stabbing of Abimelech (Judg. 9.54); the crushing of Samson (Judg. 16.30); the self-stabbing of Saul (1 Sam. 31.14; 2 Sam. 1.6; 1 Chron. 10.4) and his armor bearer (1 Sam. 31.15, 1 Chron. 10.5); the hanging of Ahitophel (2 Sam. 17.23); and the burning of Zimri (1 Kings 16.18). Significantly, the Hebrew Bible also portrays some cases of suicide prevention, involving individuals who expressed suicidal wishes but were helped by God's therapeutic intervention (e.g., Elijah, Jonah, Job, and Jeremiah).

Other suicides have been reported in nonrabbinic writings of the Second Temple period as well. In the Apocryphal First Book of Maccabees, for example, Eleazar sacrifices himself by darting beneath the elephant of an enemy general and running his sword into it (1 Macc. 6.46). In the Second Book of Maccabees, two acts of suicide are recorded—first, that of Ptolemy, and second, that of Ragesh (Razis). Ptolemy, an advocate of the Judeans at the Syrian Court of King Antiochus Eupator, poisons himself after being accused of treason (2 Macc. 10.12). Ragesh first attempts unsuccessfully to die on his sword rather than fall into the hands of the Syrians (2 Macc. 14.41–42). He subsequently succeeds in disemboweling himself after throwing himself from a wall (2 Macc. 14.43–46). The historian Flavius Josephus also mentioned a number of suicides in his work *Wars of the Jews*, including the mass suicides at Jotapata in 69 CE and Masada in 73.

No Talmudic passage can be taken as praising suicide or glorifying heroism in the Greek sense, nor is there an obsession with death as the solution to life's problems or with the issue of control. Nevertheless, according to the Talmud, suicide can be permissible and even preferred in select instances in which a person is faced with forced apostasy or tortures that might be more horrifying than death.

The great scholar Rabbi Hanina ben Teradion, who was burned to death by his Roman persecutors with a Torah scroll wrapped around him, would not even open his mouth so as to breathe in the flames and die more quickly: "Let him who gave me my soul take it away, but no one should injure himself." In other words, he refused to advance his own death actively.[4] The Roman executioner, impressed by the personal greatness of Rabbi Hanina and the terrible awe of the moment, wanted to be joined to him (*Tosefot Avodah Zarah*, 18a; *Maharsha*). He offered to end Hanina's torture by removing the wet sponges from around his heart, which had artificially prolonged his life. This Rabbi Hanina approved, assuring the executioner of a portion in the world to come.[5] The executioner then removed the sponges, and, knowing that he himself would now be severely punished by the Romans, he leaped into the fire. Both were assigned a place in the world to come (*Avodah Zarah*, 18a; *Sifre* and *Yalkut Shimoni* on Deut. 32:4).[6]

The story of the 400 boys and girls who leaped into the sea rather than be sent to lives of prostitution in Rome is comparable (*Gittin*, 57b; and a similar story in *Lamentations Rabbah*, 1.45). The basic principle here is that "they feared lest idol worshippers force them to sin by means of unbearable tortures, then it is commanded to destroy oneself" (*Tosafot, Avodah Zarah*, 18a; *Gittin*, 57b; also Rabbi Jacob Emden, *Hagahot*). At such a point, it may be more desirable to sanctify God's Holy Name by suicide than to sin. Again, this is not an approbation of suicide *per se* in any sense nor an obsession with issues of control, as in many of the Greek suicides. Human life remains an object of great importance. It should be noted that the young people in Gittin 57 and the elders in the parallel story in *Lamentations Rabbah* asked for a rabbinic opinion before leaping into the sea so that they would not lose their share in the world to come. Gittin also describes the suicide of Hannah after the martyrdom of her seven sons,[7] and *Avodah Zarah* 18b recounts the suicide of Beruria, the wife of Rabbi Meier. Other Talmudic suicides include the Hasmonean princess who was loved by her former slave Herod (*Baba Batra*, 3b), a Roman officer who saved the life of Rabban Gamliel (*Taanit*, 29a) and the suicides of a father and mother after the father threw their son from the roof for receiving food from a guest without permission (*Hullin*, 94a). Another suicide involved a student whose name was falsely besmirched by a harlot (*Berachot*, 23a). The Talmud (*Semachot*, chap. 2 and 5) also relates two incidents of childhood suicide, the first involving the son of Gornos of Lydda, who ran away from school, and the second, that of a child in Bnei B'rak, who broke a bottle on the Sabbath. Each child killed himself after his father threatened to punish him. Neither was ruled an intentional suicide.

Two more suicides are mentioned in the *Midrash Rabbah*. The first (*Ecclesiastes Rabbah* 10.7) describes a pagan eunuch of the emperor of Rome who attempted to embarrass Rabbi Akiba. When the eunuch was shamed in return, he killed himself. The second (*Genesis Rabbah* 65.22) describes the suicide of Jakum of Tzeroth who, after taunting Rabbi Joseph Meshitha, inflicted as self-punishment the four modes of execution typically sentenced by the courts. He stoned, burned, strangled, and decapitated himself.

There are a number of significant suicides in later Jewish history as well, including 500 Jews at York in the twelfth century, hundreds in Verdun, France, in 1326, and many more in response to the Spanish Inquisition. While it is not our intention to create a laundry list here, there have been periods of external persecutions throughout Jewish history that have put Jews in the position of choosing apostasy or suicide (Haberman 1946). Durkheim's aforementioned observation on the comparatively higher rate of suicide among Jews in late nineteenth-century Bavaria and the suicides among Jews in Central and Eastern Europe in the 1930s and during World War II are also clearly connected to external forces. The importance of the theme of suicide in modern Yiddish literature has been explored in a new work by Janet Hadda (1988), who has focused largely on suicidogenic family themes. Famous Jewish suicides in modern times include that of Otto Weininger, the self-hating Jewish intellectual, who in 1903 shot himself in Ludwig von Beethoven's apartment; Ernst Toller, a playwright and revolutionary who killed himself in New York in 1939 in despair after the fall of Madrid to Francisco Franco, and Samuel Zygelbojm who in 1943 committed suicide in London to protest the indifference of Polish, British, and other authorities to reports of the Holocaust and the savage destruction of the Warsaw Ghetto. According to some accounts, Sigmund Freud, who was suffering from a painful and incurable illness, also took his own life.

It is obviously incorrect, then, to claim that there are no suicides in Biblical and later Jewish history. Individual suicides have occurred despite the injunctions against them. Nevertheless, suicide is strongly prohibited in Biblical and later Jewish thought, and when it has appeared within the culture, it may represent individual idiosyncrasies, impossible external situations, or profound Graeco-Roman influences. The basic Jewish preference for life over death as expressed in the Hebrew Bible has never changed nor has suicide ever been idealized as an end in itself.

When suicidal forces have emerged, they have typically represented an alien influence on Jewish life. For example, the family dynamic pinpointed by Hadda (passionate women, passive men) follows more of a Greek than a Biblical family pattern. The thinking of Weininger represented Hellenic polarities of thought with regard to sexuality and to life in general (see chapters 4 and 7).

Jotapata and Masada: Two Speeches on Suicide

There are glaring differences between Josephus' accounts of the mass Jewish suicides at Jotapata and at Masada. The story of the defense of Masada against the Romans and the mass suicide of its Jewish defenders in 73

CE has gained a new celebrity in our day, spurred on by the archeological findings of Israeli archeologist Yigael Yadin. The fortress of Masada was the only Jewish outpost not yet conquered by the Romans. It was defended by 900 Sicarii nationalists led by Eliezer Ben Yair.

Indeed, Masada has become a symbol of bravery in modern Israel and around the world. Curiously, it is never once mentioned in rabbinic literature and for years was known only through the account of Josephus, a Jewish historian in Rome. Any mention of suicide is conspicuously absent in *Yosippon*, a later Hebrew account of the Jewish revolt; here the defenders fought against the Romans to the death (Ben Gurion, *Sefer Yosippon*, ch. 87). Numerous scholarly articles have debated the meaning and the veracity of Josephus' account. For our purposes, the story is useful in that it offers some insight into Josephus' own views on suicide. While Josephus obviously had his own agenda, one thing is clear — he viewed suicide as completely alien to Jewish intellect, spirit, and law. By now, the speech of Eliezer Ben Yair to his followers at Masada (at least the version in the account of Josephus) ranks as one of the famous orations of antiquity. No less important for understanding Josephus' approach is an earlier speech of his own.

Earlier in the Roman-Jewish war, Josephus was the commander of the Jewish garrison of the town of Jotapata in Galilee. As Josephus described it, he saw little chance of holding out against the powerful Roman army of Vespasian and urged his people to surrender. The defenders would not give up, however, and they held out against the Romans for some weeks. Finally, the city fell. Josephus fled to a cave where he found forty of his soldiers already in hiding. Soon the Romans too found the cave and demanded their surrender. The Jewish soldiers favored a mass suicide but Josephus strongly disagreed (*Wars of the Jews*, 3.514–516). In his speech, he sought to dissuade the other fighters from suicide, offering a traditional Jewish set of arguments that opposed Graeco-Roman philosophical thinking on several points. First, in contrast to the Socratic view, body and soul are the best of friends, and they should remain together. It may be glorious to die for freedom in battle but not to die at one's own hand. Suicide is an act not of bravery but of the utmost cowardice and foolishness. Self-murder is contrary to natural instinct but, even more, it is impiety to God, who is angry when he sees his gift of life treated with contempt. The body is entrusted to the soul by God for safe-keeping.

Josephus was the only survivor of the group in the cave so we have no second account by which to verify the authenticity of his speech or whether he even gave it. For our purpose, however, what is important is that Josephus had the chance to write the speech that he would have liked to have given and, in truth, may have given. And the speech represents a good pious sermon of which a rabbi might have been proud, a strong tirade against suicide.[8]

Josephus' subsequent portrayal of Eliezer Ben Yair's speech at Masada (*Wars of the Jews*, 7.598–603) presents a very different view of suicide. Scholars have debated whether Ben Yair ever gave the speech at all or, if he did, what he actually said. It is quite likely that Josephus followed the practice accepted by classical historians since Thucydides of reporting not a verbatim account of an oration but rather an account of what could have or seemingly ought to have been said.

In the speech at Masada, Josephus, who hated the Sicarii, may well have put into Ben Yair's mouth ideas that Josephus himself deplored. The speech contains several parts. In part one (600–601), Ben Yair argued that God had given the Sicarii freedom to choose their own sort of death. The revolt against the Roman Empire failed because God had sentenced the Jewish race to extinction. Let the defenders of Masada therefore take their own lives. Many of Ben Yair's arguments seem more suitable to Greek than to Jewish thinking—for example, the idea that man displays personal freedom in its highest form by choosing how and when to die. Further, as for the Greeks, life has no meaning because God has forsaken His people.

When his followers did not respond enthusiastically to this call for a mass suicide, Ben Yair tried a second, even more explicitly Greek argument: "*We should not fear death, because it is not death, but life which is the calamity. Death gives freedom to the soul which then returns to a wonderful abode where it dwells with God. Death is much like sleep*" (emphasis added, 601–602). At this point, one wonders where Ben Yair studied his Plato (*Phaedo*, 68d) or his Seneca (*Ep.*, 24). Of course, it is hardly likely that a Judean nationalist revolutionary like Ben Yair knew much of Plato or Stoicism. Josephus probably did, however, and he has put into Ben Yair's mouth a most extreme dualism between body and soul in an argument for suicide. He then portrayed Ben Yair as citing as a good example the Indian Brahmins who bring on their own deaths with great pleasure and courage in their desire for death and immortality (602). It is noteworthy that Ben Yair is portrayed as using examples from a clearly non-Jewish philosophy to support his argument for suicide.

Ben Yair's harangue now entered a third stage. His references to freedom, the imprisonment of the soul, and the Brahmins had made no impression on his followers who, although misled, were still loyal Jews. He now turned to the great suffering of the Jews during the war, the immense trauma of the destruction of Jerusalem, and reached a peak of intensity in depicting a man watching his wife and children being carried off by heartless enemies (602–603). Here at last Ben Yair spoke to the heart of the Jew his love for his homeland and his family. The listeners responded with deep emotion to his plea, and the mass suicide was carried through. Josephus thus showed that the Jew was essentially a good family person, even though some few had been duped by the wicked Sicarii, who were the foes both of everything Jewish and of the benefits of Roman civilization.

Comparison of the Jotapata and Masada speeches reveals more about Josephus' agenda than a concentration on either speech alone. It also reveals a dramatic contrast between Jewish and Greek attitudes toward suicide. Josephus seemed obviously interested in portraying himself positively and Ben Yair negatively. He went about this in several ways: (1) Ben Yair was portrayed as both anti-Jewish and anti-Roman. He was anti-Roman in that he refused to surrender to Rome. He was anti-Jewish in that he argued for suicide on anti-Jewish grounds. He cited Indian rather than explicitly Graeco-Roman philosophers in support of these views, so that he would in no way be appealing to the Romans. Josephus also emphasized throughout the story that the Sicarii fought bravely. It was not their lack of courage but their lack of Jewishness and/or Romanitas that brought about their fall.[9] (2) Josephus, in contrast, portrayed himself as loyal both to Judaism and to Rome. He found favor with Rome in that he argued for capitulation and accommodation rather than for pointless resistance. At the same time, Josephus was also a good Jew who had strongly defended his people's abhorrence of suicide. Josephus may have hoped that his rebuttal of the Stoic's doctrine of suicide would serve to increase his stature in Roman eyes, since the Stoics had declined in popularity among the Flavian emperors at that time (69–96 CE).

To return to our original point, many Jewish suicides may have been carried out for Graeco-Roman reasons. Suicide is completely alien to Jewish intellect, spirit, and law. It is a damnable act of fools, cultists, and traitors. The mass suicides at both Jotapata and Masada, for Josephus, were carried out for largely non-Jewish, indeed for Graeco-Roman, reasons and were not to be used as models or examples of Jewish behavior.

CHRISTIANITY

Christianity is called the daughter religion of Judaism and is based partially on the same Hebrew Bible. One would thus expect it to demonstrate the same life-centeredness, belief in a loving God, and general repugnance toward suicide. And in a sense it does, especially in its more modern forms. At the same time, Christianity grew up within the Graeco-Roman world, and its leaders were influenced by the Platonic ambivalence toward life and death and even by the Stoic elevation of suicide disguised as a type of martyrdom.

Suicides and Martyrs in the Early Church

Only one suicide occurs in the Christian New Testament — that of Judas Iscariot, who hangs himself on the branch of an olive tree after his betrayal of Jesus (Matt. 27.3–5). Significantly, no condemnation of his suicide occurs in the New Testament or in the writings of the early church fathers.

Indeed, martyrdom was a fact of life for the early Christians, who felt a sort of apocalyptic intensity and excitement that has little role in the mainstream Western churches of the twentieth century. Some early Christian writers—Mark is a good example—spent more time discussing exorcism, faith healing, miracles, and the end of days and less time on ethics than most modern churchmen. It should be remembered that Christianity in its first years grew up among pagan cults and was greatly influenced by Jewish pietistic, apocalyptic, and ascetic groups, such as the Essenes and that it soon absorbed strong elements of Greek thought as well. Thus, intense eschatological excitement blended with the chronic depression of Greek philosophy.

A number of Christian thinkers have seen the death of Jesus as voluntary. How could it not be if He was both divine and human? Tertullian, for example, held that Jesus Christ on the cross gave up the ghost freely and of His own volition before death by crucifixion overtook Him (*To the Martyrs*, 4). Origen supported this point of view (*Exhortation to Martyrdom*). Even St. Augustine agreed on the voluntary aspects of the death of Jesus: "His soul did not leave His body constrained, but because He would and where He would and how He would" (Augustinus, *The Trinity*, 4).

Centuries later, St. Thomas Aquinas argued very much the same thing in his discussion of whether Christ was slain by another or by Himself (*Summa* 3.47.1). Aquinas began by offering three "objections" to the idea that Christ was slain by another. First, he offered the citation from John: "No man takes my life from Me, but I lay it down of myself [my own initiative]" (John 10.18). Second, he cited Augustine: "Those who were crucified were tormented with a lingering death"; this did not happen in Christ's case,[10] since "Crying out, with a loud voice, He yielded up the spirit" (Matt. 27.50). Third, Aquinas again cited Augustine's view that Christ willed His soul to leave His body. At the same time, Aquinas pointed to a seemingly contradictory passage in Luke (18.33): "After they have scourged Him, they will put Him to death."

Aquinas attempted to resolve this seeming contradiction by distinguishing between direct and indirect causes. Christ's persecutors were a *direct* cause of His death. Christ was an *indirect* cause of His death, however, by not preventing this: "Therefore, since Christ's soul did not repel the injury inflicted on His body but willed His corporeal nature to succumb to such injury, He is said to have laid down His life, or to have died voluntarily" (*Summa*, 3.47.1).[11]

The New Testament itself focuses on the mystery and passion of the sacrificial death of Jesus as part of a divine plan to save mankind: "For God so loved the world that he gave His only begotten son, that whoever believes in Him should not perish but have eternal life" (John 3.16). Furthermore, this act is seen as representing the epitome of martyrdom: "Greater love has no one than this, that one lay down his life for his friends" (John 15.13).

Love and sacrifice are thus closely intertwined throughout the New Testament: "We know love by this that He laid down His life for us and we ought to lay down our lives for the brethren" (1 John 3.16).

There is also a theme of ascetic withdrawal, which deemphasizes attachments in this world and concentrates on the superiority of the next. Several quotes bear this out:

Do not love the world nor the things in the world. If anyone loves the world, the love of the Father is not in him. (1 John 2.15)

If anyone comes to me and does not hate his own father and mother and wife and children and brothers and sisters, yes, and even his own life, he cannot be my disciple. (Luke 14.26)[12]

He that hates his life in this world, shall keep it onto life eternal. (John 12.25)

Jesus' last utterance on the cross (Matt. 27.46 and Mark 15.34) — "Eli, Eli, Lama Sabachtani," that is, "my God, my God, why hast thou forsaken me?" — expresses a feeling of abandonment atypical of the suicide-preventive narratives in the Hebrew Bible and among God-fearing Jews at the time of Jesus.

St. Paul's epistle to the Philippians is explicit in its almost Platonic praise of death over life. The statement, "For to me to live is Christ and to die is gain" (Phil. 1.21), reflects a certain perturbation as Paul considered both life and death, unsure as to which would be the better way to serve. Clearly, though, the true "commonwealth" or *politeuma* (Phil. 3.20) was in heaven, and Paul played down the seeming materialism of Judaism as opposed to the spiritual mystery of Christianity. The epistle states that Jesus will "change our vile body that it may be fashioned like unto his glorious body" (3.21) and Paul will stay at his appointed post, although he longs to depart: "For I am in a strait betwixt the two, having a desire to depart, and to be with Christ, which is far better. Nevertheless to abide in the flesh is more needful for you" (Phil. 1.23–24).[13] This strong dualism between body and soul and the preference for the next world over this one is reflected even more clearly in Paul's second epistle to the Corinthians: "Therefore, we are always confident knowing that whilst we are at home in the body, we are absent from the Lord. . . . We are confident, I say, and willing rather to be absent from the body and to be present with the Lord" (2 Cor. 6–8).

Let us place these citations in perspective. The New Testament, like all religious works, is subject to a variety of interpretations. Suicide is not advocated in blunt, unmistakable language. Still, it is easy to see an impatience and disdain for life in many New Testament passages, and certainly the next world is considered preferable to this one. Man is thought to be closer to Jesus Christ in that next world when he has shed the diversions of the flesh. This is much closer to the Platonic vision than to the Rabbinic one that values life in both this world and the next.[14]

Martyrdom was a major issue in the early church. In general, the Romans were little interested in anyone's religious beliefs, but the Christians seemed to be political troublemakers, if not saboteurs or rebels. The belief in a man-god was understandable enough in an empire that deified its own rulers, but the Romans could easily feel suspicious of a cult that met secretly (in the Catacombs, for example), that proselytized among women and slaves, and that rejected the worship of the divine Caesars and the empire itself. Moreover, in the beginning at least, the Christians were associated with the Judeans, who had their own foreign beliefs and ways of life and who had often revolted against their Roman overlords. By the late first century, the Roman government had begun to feel that force should be used to make Christians behave like good Romans and particularly to show a patriotic respect for the government, including the offering of sacrifice to the emperor. A correspondence between the Emperor Trajan and Pliny, his governor in Bithynia, discussed the Christian problem (Pliny, *Letters*, Bk. 10).

Many Christians responded by refusing to compromise their faith in any way, and gave up their lives as martyrs (the Greek term for witnesses) for their faith. Martyrdom was often the only choice for the Christian, but, there was not only the acceptance of martyrdom as unavoidable, but also a desire — and indeed an active pursuit — of death.

One of the earliest martyrs was Ignatius of Antioch who was fed to the beasts in the arena in Rome around 107. Little is known of his life, but he left some thoughts on religion and martyrdom in a series of letters written while a prisoner on the way from Antioch to Rome. Many of his ideas show the influence of classical Hellenism.

Martyrdom was already a central theme in Christianity. Ignatius begged his influential friends in Rome not to intervene to save him. He could be "an intelligible utterance of God, but if your affections are only concerned with poor human life, then I become a mere meaningless cry once more" (*Epistle to the Romans*, 1). The Christian martyr actively sought death, for only through death could his life be more than a meaningless cry.

He seemed to feel an urgent need to prove his nothingness: "Pray leave me to be a meal for the beasts, for it is they who can provide my way to God . . . ground fine by the lion's teeth to make pure bread for Christ. . . . let them not leave the smallest scrap of my flesh" (Ignatius, *Epistles*, 4). Ignatius called himself a useless burden, who desired to be demolished and devoured to the last particle, "so that I need not be a burden to anyone after I fall asleep." His desire for martyrdom was active and uncompromising: "I am yearning for death with all the passion of a lover" (Ignatius, *Epistles*, 9). Ignatius removed himself, as did the later ascetics, from any interest in physical life: "In me there is left no desire for mundane things, but only a murmur of living water that whispers within me, 'come to the Father.' . . . I want no more of what men call life."

Ignatius displayed the Greeks' pervasive and absorbing interest in death. Through Christian devotion, however, he believed that he could overcome death. By touching the resurrected Christ, the disciples "came by their contempt for death and proved themselves superior to it" (Ignatius, *Epistle to the Smyrneans*, 3). "His death . . . is the very mystery which has moved us to become believers and endure tribulation to prove ourselves pupils of Jesus Christ" (Ignatius, *Epistle to the Magnesians*, 8). In addition, the Greek dichotomy between soul and body that is so foreign to Judaism now appeared in Christian terms: "When there is no trace of my body left for the world to see, then I shall truly be Christ's Disciple" (*Epistle to the Romans*, 4). The accomplishments of this world meant nothing: "Suffer me to attain light pure and undefiled, for only when I come thither shall I be truly a man." Perhaps the most striking passages in these letters are those depicting the need for total self-obliteration: "How good it is to be sinking down below the world's horizon." In his mind, a man is lowly and insignificant until by dying, he rises above death.

To Ignatius, martyrdom seemed to offer the hope of meaning in a life that otherwise has no inherent worth. There was thus a pressure to offer up one's life both because of the Christians' uncomfortable political status in the Roman Empire and also because of the themes of death and martyrdom so central in the New Testament. Still, as much as Ignatius might long for martyrdom, he seemed more to wish not to avoid it rather than to seek it as actively as many others did.

Christians were still being persecuted in the middle of the third century when Bishop Cyprian of Carthage was executed for his faith by the Roman officials. The church was now larger, however, and its adherents more militant. Martyrdom was no longer unusual, and many staunchly devout Christians went to their deaths before crowds in the arenas or, more privately, in prisons. Cyprian's letters and essays reflect the mood of a new age and also the personality differences between him and Ignatius. Many of his letters deal with events during the persecutions under the Emperor Decius. Cyprian was a great believer in martyrdom, although ironically, he was strongly criticized for absenting himself from Carthage for some time to avoid arrest.

Several themes appear repeatedly in Cyprian's writings. First, he discussed how much the world hated the Christians. There was of course much ill-feeling between Christians and pagans in the third century. For Cyprian, however, the theme of hatred appeared to be a theological concept. He quoted Luke (6.22): "Blessed are ye when men shall hate you." Cyprian went on: "if the world hates you, remember that it hated me before you. You can neither desire martyrdom till you have first hated the world, nor attain to God's reward unless you have loved Christ. And who loves Christ does not love the world." Between Christ and the world there had to be antagonism. Likewise between Christian and pagan there could be only hatred. Second, Jesus' crucifixion brought salvation to the world. His act of self-sacrifice and suffering was so immense, however, that it must now be "a great matter to imitate him who in dying convicted the world" (*On the Glory of Martyrdom*, 29); "what He exhorts man to suffer, He Himself first suffered for us" (Cyprian, *Letters*, 55.3). The crucifixion set the example of the highest possible moment toward which man must strive, since the world of the body is evil and should be scorned: "Consider what glory it is to set aside the lusts of life. . . . What then is martyrdom, the end of sins, the limit of dangers" (*On the Glory of Martyrdom*, 54). Moreover, "Death makes life more complete, death rather leads to glory." Pontius, a friend and biographer of Cyprian, indicated in his work *A Life and Passion of Cyprian* that he too was elated by a passion for "the consummation of martyrdom" (Pontius, 7). One must therefore not condemn the cruel executioners but rather "pray for the salvation of those that persecute him" (9); one "must forgive and forgive and again frequently forgive" (10). It was the general wish of the Christians who witnessed Cyprian's execution "that the entire congregation should suffer at once in the fellowship of a like glory" (18): "Much and excessively do I exalt his [Cyprian's] glory; but still more do I grieve that I remained behind."

Clearly a passionate desire for martyrdom invigorated Christianity during these years of persecution. This is not to say that all Christian thinkers of this period were suicidal. Lactantius, in his description of the last great persecution early in the fourth century, gave full honor to the martyrs (*Divine Institutes*, 89, 90) but castigated the persecutors, seeing them as enemies rather than as helpers who brought glory to martyrs. The era of persecution ended under the Emperor Constantine who accepted Christianity. Martyrdom was replaced by ascetic monasticism, which became the major beneficiary of Christianity's eschatological energies.

St. Augustine and After

Despite his insistence on the voluntary aspects of the death of Jesus, Saint Augustine (354–438) strongly condemned suicide in the *City of God* as "a detestable crime and a damnable sin" (1.27). He based this prohibition on his interpretation of Deuteronomy 5.17: "Thou shalt not kill"[15] (1.20). Even the suicides of Judas Iscariot (1.17) and of the Roman matron Lucretia (1.19) were seen as evil, and he portrayed Jesus as urging flight from persecution rather than self-murder (1.22). One must not commit suicide out of magnanimity (1.22), because of physical violation of chastity (1.19), or to avoid future sin (1.27). Augustine stated his preference for the saintly Job over the suicidal Cato (1.24).

Augustine's attitudes toward suicide were tested in his controversies with

the heretical Circumcelliones and Donatists. Augustine first argued that
the Donatists tended to engage in waves of martyr suicides, often seeking
to provoke and even invite their own persecution. After the battle of Bagai
in 347, the two rebel leaders, Donatus of Bagai and Marculus, were ar-
rested and died. According to the Donatist account, they were executed,
Donatus being thrown down a well and Marculus from a rock. Saint Optatus suggested that the Donatists caused their own downfall, but Augustine
went even farther by questioning whether they were thrown down or actually threw themselves down and stating that such self-precipitation was a
common practice among the Donatists, which they attempted to justify by
the example of Razis as narrated in 2 Maccabees 14 (Willis 1950).

Both Optatus and Augustine condemned the dominant Donatist passion
for quasi-martyrdom by suicide. Whole companies threw themselves from
rocks (they despised hanging, since Judas the traitor had died that way).
The Donatists did not kill themselves if they could persuade the authorities
to do it, however. One device was to attack magistrates on the road. Sometimes ordinary travelers were stopped and invited to kill them and were
threatened with murder themselves if they did not comply.

Despite his condemnation of suicide, Augustine still wrote to a Roman
soldier stationed at a frontier outpost that he should not defend himself
against barbarians lest it give rise to sinful intentions in his heart (Augustinus, *Epistles*, 185.2.7).

Christian thinking on suicide after Augustine reflected the political and
legal changes from the Roman empire to medieval Christendom. With the
success of Christianity, martyrdom or dying for the faith was no longer an
issue within the old Roman empire (though it remained so for Christian
missionaries who sought to convert pagan tribesmen outside the boundaries of Christian civilization).

The second Council of Orleans (533) produced the Church's first official
disapproval of suicide[16] by denying funeral rites to suicides accused of
crimes. The Council of Braga (563) extended this ban to all suicides. In
590, the Council of Antisidor forbade the church to accept offerings for the
souls of suicides (see also Donne 1608; Sullivan 1984).

Aquinas came out strongly against suicide in his *Summa Theologica*.
Despite his argument that Jesus was the voluntary indirect cause of his own
death (*Summa*, 3.47.1), Aquinas attempted to demolish pagan prosuicide
arguments. Aquinas (2.2.64.5) reiterated Augustine's argument that asso-
ciates suicide with murder (*City of God*, 1.20). Aquinas then added three
arguments of his own. First, suicide is unnatural. Every man bears an in-
stinctive charity toward himself and should thus desire to do himself no
harm. Suicide, being both unnatural and uncharitable, is a mortal sin.
Second, an individual is a member of a social unit. Thus, Aquinas echoed
the Aristotelean argument that suicide is antisocial. Third, life is the gift of
God. Though given, it remains His property, so only God can pronounce

the sentence of life and death: "I will kill and I will make to live" (Deut. 32.39).

Of all later Christian thinkers, John Donne (1572–1631) was unique in seeing the implications for a Christian tolerance of suicide in the voluntary death of Christ. For Donne, Christ's death was brave and voluntary: "it is a heroic act of fortitude, if a man when an urgent occasion is presented, expose himself to a certain and assured death as he did" (*Biathanatos*, 3.4.5). Donne thus viewed the passion of Christ as a Greek altruistic suicide. He was a martyr who gave his life to redeem man; many of the early Christian martyrs also seemed suicidal in nature: "And that Apollonia and others, who prevented the fury of the executioners, and cast themselves into the fire, did therein imitate this act of our Savior, of giving up his soul, before he was constrained to do it." This behavior certainly stands in marked contrast to that of the Jewish martyrs for faith who tried to avoid death if at all possible and to live in a way that did not compromise their faith.

In summary, then, the Christian Church slowly but surely formalized its opposition to suicide. This can be seen in the statements of Augustine, the church councils, and Aquinas. Nonetheless, Donne pointed to the potentially suicidal strain in the passion of Jesus Christ, which is the foundation of Christianity. One strand of Christian thought has emphasized the altruism of the story of Jesus while still opposing suicide. A second strand bears much of the obsession with death inherent in early Graeco-Roman heroism.

NOTES

1. Curiously, the prohibition against suicide actually precedes the injunction against homicide that God gives to Noah: "Whoever sheds the blood of man, by man shall his blood be shed" (Gen. 9.6).

2. While most commentators (e.g., Rashi) have derived their prohibition against suicide from this source, at least one commentator, Ibn Ezra, made somewhat different arguments to the same conclusion. An article by the Israeli Supreme Court Justice, Haim Cohen (1976) has discussed these issues.

3. Private communication from one of his disciples.

4. This refusal, while highly commendable, cannot be expected from most people in such extreme circumstances.

5. Rabbinic law has never interpreted this story as encouraging active or assisted suicide. Remember that Rabbi Hanina refused his disciples' advice to open his mouth to take in the fire. Rabbi Hanina's allowing the executioner to remove the sponges from around his heart can be seen instead as a refusal to continue measures that artificially prolonged his torture.

6. A. J. Droge and J. D. Tabor (1992, 102) have suggested a parallel between Rabbi Hanina's position that God is the one who takes away life and the statements of Plato and Cicero that one is not to depart except at the bidding of the gods. There is no indication whatsoever, however, that Hanina saw his torture as a divine

bidding, nor was there any love of death *per se* or concern with personal control. He was faced with unbearable pain, rather than a relatively minor annoyance like Zeno's broken toe. Similarly, the pagan executioner was not awarded a place in the world to come because he committed suicide but because he participated in the awe of Hanina's final moment and performed an act of great compassion. The essential difference between the Jewish and Greek positions is this: Judaism is basically attracted to life rather than to death even when external circumstances may make one's life unbearable. Greek thought, in contrast, was basically attracted to death, even when life is quite bearable (see also the work of Orbach, Millstein, Har-Even, Apter, Tiano, and Elizur, in press).

7. An alternate version portrays Hannah as "falling" rather than "jumping" off a roof (*Lamentations Rabbah*, 1.50).

8. Droge and Tabor (1992, 94) have followed a different line of interpretation, deriving Josephus' argument against voluntary death in his Jotapata speech from Plato's discussion in the *Phaedo* of when one ought to choose death.

9. Droge and Tabor (1992, 94), in contrast, have argued that Josephus was attempting to portray both Ben Yair and himself as "philosophically" astute.

10. It is reasonable to assume that Jesus' short survival on the cross may have been occasioned by a weakened physical condition.

11. Droge and Tabor (1992, 21, 46) have pointed to the similarity between the deaths of Jesus and of Socrates. Socrates drank the poison voluntarily, in response to some necessity sent by the gods, in addition to having received the death penalty.

12. Augustine anticipated the suicidal implications of this phrase but denied that it could be used to justify the self-homicide on the part of the Donatists (Donne, *Biathanatos*, 3.4.6).

13. Droge and Tabor (1992, 122)have argued that Paul "lusts after death." Although he finally rejects the "gain" of death, it is clearly death that he prefers.

14. On this point, we disagree with Droge and Tabor. They have suggested a tolerance for certain types of suicide among Jews, Christians, Greeks, and Romans. We contrast the antisuicidal strain in Judaism with the fascination with death apparent in the Graeco-Roman world. The other-worldliness of the New Testament seems more Graeco-Roman than Judeo-Christian.

15. The Hebrew phrase *lo tirtsach* (Exod. 20.13, Deut. 5.17) is more accurately translated as "thou shalt not murder" than "thou shalt not kill" and is so interpreted in rabbinic literature.

16. The first antisuicide legislation in canon law was actually passed at the Council of Arles in 452. These measures were not directed against suicide in general but were simply a repetition of the earlier Roman economic legislation forbidding the suicide of slaves (see also Fedden 1938, 115).

II

INDIVIDUAL CASE
STUDIES

Chapter 4

Cycle versus Development: Narcissus or Jonah

Narcissus had played with her affections, treating her as he had previously treated other spirits of the waters and the woods, and his male admirers, too. Then one of those he had scorned raised up his hands to heaven and prayed: "May he himself fall in love with another as we have done with him! May he too be unable to gain his loved one!" Nemesis heard and granted his righteous prayer.

Ovid, *Metamorphosis*, 3.366–475

Now the word of the Lord came unto Jonah, the son of Amitai, saying, "Arise, go to Nineveh, that great city and proclaim against it: for their wickedness is come up before me." But Jonah rose up to flee unto Tarshish from the presence of the Lord. . . . So they took up Jonah, and cast him forth into the sea; and the sea ceased from its raging. . . . And the Lord had prepared a great fish to swallow up Jonah. . . . Then Jonah prayed unto the Lord his God out of the fish's belly. . . . and the Lord spake unto the fish, and it vomited out Jonah upon the dry land.

Jonah, 1–2

The Greek and Hebrew worlds offered widely divergent concepts of cycle and development, and these were linked closely to their attitudes toward life and death. The assumptions underlying the Greek and modern Western attitudes seem to be as follows: First, the course of life is filled with irreconcilable alternatives, a series of Hobson's choices. Second, tragic-heroic man attempts to deal with this dilemma by hopeless cycles through opposing alternatives. Third, there is no way out of this trap, so the cycles become more helpless, hopeless, and suicidal.[1]

The assumptions underlying Biblical and later Jewish thought are quite different. First, the world is not filled with irreconcilable conflicts. Second, Biblical and rabbinic man avoids the tragic-heroic trap. Third, meaningful development is possible; there is the potential to escape the dialectical-cyclical vacillation leading nowhere. This sense of development is purposive, hopeful, and suicide-preventive.[2]

SISYPHUS AND THE CONCEPTION OF CYCLE

Cyclical themes have appeared in literature from earliest antiquity, first in the concept of fertility cycles that were intertwined with the pagan beliefs in gods who die in autumn and return to life in spring (e.g., Thammuz, Osiris, Persephone). Greek thought was pervaded by the notion of cycle: A man rises up only to be overcome by *hubris* (pride) and cast down into *nemesis* (retribution), the nadir of the cycle.

Historians have tended to see the story of nations in terms of a cycle. Primitive peoples conquer established civilizations, become civilized themselves, and are, in their turn, conquered by other primitive, warlike invaders. Ibn Khaldun, Edward Gibbon, G. W. F. Hegel (with his construct of thesis, antithesis, and synthesis), and Arnold Toynbee (one might also add Karl Marx) have exhibited this trend of thought.

The common element in all of the tragic cycles is that man lives in the face of an inevitable end. He is alone and his activities are, in the long run, futile. The best for which he can hope, the most admirable state, is that of the tragic hero, the individual who struggles against overwhelming odds with no real hope of effecting any change. He is Prometheus or the Man of La Mancha, with his "impossible dream." His efforts, as Aristotle pointed out in the *Poetics*, lead to misfortune and arouse pity; the very greatness of his heroism lies in its complete uselessness.

An important treatment of the idea of cycle appears in Albert Camus' great existentialist work, *The Myth of Sisyphus* (1975). In the ancient Greek myth, Sisyphus, a clever fellow and the father of the illegitimate and crafty Odysseus, was condemned, for various crimes and tricks against the gods, to push a boulder up to the top of a hill and over. Each time, just before he reached the top, however, the boulder rolled back down, and Sisyphus had to push it up all over again — surely an utterly futile existence.

For Camus, Sisyphus as a tragic hero represents an existential model. The picture is horrifyingly stark and uncompromising. The hero must accept only that the world is totally absurd, and he must refuse any sort of consolation, hope, or reliable principles (19). Halfway measures are meaningless and unworthy. Everything or nothing must be explained (20), although, in truth, "any principle of explanation is useless" (75). "Between everywhere and forever there is no compromise" (61). Camus saw the only true human achievement in the ability of the individual to struggle, even when he has realized and accepted that there is neither earthly achievement nor life after death. The overwhelming misery of Sisyphus' existence can be elevated only by the painful consciousness of ultimate futility that touched him each time he pushed the stone to the top of the slope and saw it roll back down again. In this moment of thought lies Sisyphus' tragic magnificence, his most meaningful and lucid insight into the human condition.

Since man learns nothing new, the cycle must repeat. In fact, tragic man, basing his sense of worth in his imperfect achievements, perhaps has as strong an urge toward failure as toward success. In the *Poetics*, Aristotle wrote that the arousal of fear and pity in the audience in response to the hero's suffering is a chief feature of drama. The grandeur of the lost cause arouses much attention and is a very attractive notion, whatever its impracticality. There is no resolution to this pattern, and the individual must fail in his search for ultimate achievement. He may, however, try to maintain some illusion of mastery, by resorting to indifference (Camus 1975, 69) and accepting the totality of absurdity. Sisyphus personifies Blaise Pascal's famous statement, "Man is but a reed, the weakest in Nature, but he is a thinking reed. . . . he is great because he knows that he is miserable" (*Pensées* 1958, 6.347 and 397).

The protagonist in the tragic cycle, as portrayed from the ancient Greek playwrights down to Camus, is also burdened by his grandiose need to avoid accepting any limitation on his power or freedom. The world seems alien and threatening, and only by means of his heroic achievements can the hero become worthy to surpass or transcend these limitations. Again, this effort can end only in failure. No amount of achievement can prevent the onset of nemesis. It is noteworthy, too, that Sisyphus pushes his burden alone. He has no companion, no fellow, no kin with him. Camus wrote: "There is only one truly serious philosophical problem and that is suicide. . . . The fundamental subject of *The Myth of Sisyphus* is this: it is legitimate and necessary to wonder whether life has a meaning; therefore it is legitimate to meet the problem of suicide face to face" (11 and 7).

KOHELETH (ECCLESIASTES) AND THE CONCEPT OF DEVELOPMENT

The Biblical book of Koheleth rejects the pattern of the cycle that is inherent in *The Myth of Sisyphus*.[3] Koheleth asks searching questions, as does Camus, but here the cycle is merely a problem with which to deal, not the all-determining basis of human existence. Koheleth's world is neither meaningless nor absurd, and in it man may work, learn, and be happy. Let us view Koheleth's rejection of the cycle design, which was an approach shared by later rabbinic thought. Koheleth does indeed speak of cycles:

> What profit hath man of all his labor wherein he laboreth under the sun?
> One generation passeth away, and another generation cometh, And the
>   earth abideth for ever.
> The sun also ariseth, and the sun goeth down,
> And hasteth to his place whence he ariseth.
> The wind goeth toward the south, and turneth about unto the north. It
>   turneth about continually in its circuit,
> And the wind returneth again to its circuits.
> All the rivers run into the sea, yet the sea is not full. Unto the place
>   whither the rivers go, thither they go again (1.3–7)

This is the cycle of seasons; one might call it the ecological cycle. It is not, however, a deterministic cycle of nations or of human lives and not the product of some mystical fate. It is the same pattern that God established to reassure Noah after the great flood, a gracious gift to man and not a chafing burden. This pattern sets certain parameters for human activity and wisdom, but it does not foredoom the individual or greatly limit his ability to be useful, productive, or content. There is no indication that Koheleth sees this natural cycle as nefarious or threatening.

The famous third chapter seems to indicate a concept of development with regard to human affairs:

> To everything there is a season, and a time to every purpose under the
>   heaven:
> A time to be born, and a time to die;
> A time to plant, and a time to pluck up that which is planted;
> A time to kill, and a time to heal;
> A time to break down, and a time to build up;
> A time to weep, and a time to laugh;
> A time to mourn, and a time to dance;
> A time to cast away stones, and a time to gather stones together;
> A time to embrace, and a time to refrain from embracing;
> A time to seek, and a time to lose;
> A time to keep, and a time to cast away;
> A time to rend, and a time to sew;
> A time to keep silence, and a time to speak;
> A time to love, and a time to hate;
> A time of war, and a time of peace.[4] (3.1–8)

The above passage does not describe life as a cycle. Rather, it advises that there is a time for everything. Some situations may require planting, and other situations uprooting. There is a time to be born, and a time to die. Indeed, many things that come from God are beyond human reach, but man need not feel helpless or doomed. To recognize mortal limitations and to accept divine omnipotence does not threaten the individual with annihilation.

Koheleth faces a dilemma, as does the Greek tragic hero, but the key question is not whether the individual should go on living in a world that has no use for him. Koheleth is not touched by suicidal doubts. Rather, since the world functions so well, he wonders what is left for man to improve or create. "What profit hath man of all his labor where-in he laboreth under the sun. . . . There is nothing new under the sun. Is there a thing whereof it is said: See this is new? It hath been already in the ages which were before us" (1.3–10). This is not a mere academic exercise; it is a deeply troubling question. Yet, while an ultimate answer is not to be found, there is enough to do in the meantime, and Koheleth seeks to learn, to understand, and to do. "And I applied my heart to seek and to search out by wisdom concerning all things that are done under heaven" (1.17). Wisdom can indeed increase both man's sensitivity and his pain: "For in much wisdom is much vexation" (1.18). But wisdom is still a good thing: "Then I saw that wisdom excelleth folly as far as the light excelleth darkness" (2.13). There is no suggestion, as in Sophocles' *Oedipus*, that human wisdom's truest value lies in making man feel his misery (1.335). Misery is miserable, not sublime. Man need not feel impelled toward a pitiable fate; he need not live in the rarefied yet horrifying pattern of the tragic hero, of Prometheus and Antigone. He can enjoy life, and God sees this as good. "There is nothing better for a man than that he should eat and make his soul enjoy pleasure for his labor. This also I saw that it is from the hand of God" (Eccles. 2.24).

In contrast to Sisyphus, Koheleth contends that a man ought not to live alone. Association with others can be frustrating, yet "See life with the woman whom thou lovest" (9.9) and "The three-fold cord is not quickly severed" (4.12). One cannot be totally egocentric. Koheleth opposes many aspects and implications of the cyclical-heroic view. Camus rejected a belief in God and any notion of human immortality; indeed, he saw in this rejection the basis of human freedom. Koheleth avers that man is, by nature, morally free and able to reach some sort of accommodation with God. The problem is not God nor the universe nor man. There exists instead the practical question of what man may do that will make a difference. Camus saw Sisyphus' realization of his misery as his nirvana, the whole meaning of his being. Koheleth prizes wisdom but not as the sole value or as effective without the body. Koheleth is troubled by the very real dilemma of misery that is caused by factors beyond man's power. This is not the only issue in life, however, and one need not despair totally if one cannot resolve it. In any case, some miseries are within human power to remedy. Koheleth does not depict the world as alternating starkly between the two poles of hubris and nemesis, success and failure, all or nothing. The question is not life versus suicide, "to be or not to be." Granted that there is life and there is death, the question is how man should react. There is no fencing with the illusion of a final answer. Rabbi Tarfon stated very succinctly centuries later: "It is not thy duty to complete the work but neither mayest thou desist from it" (*Mishna Avot*, 2.16).[5]

The difference between these two points of view is graphically illustrated in the stories of Narcissus and Jonah, which offer contrasting models of individual development. The myth of Narcissus depicts a chilling tale of wasteful self-disintegration. The book of Jonah, in contrast, offers a compelling analysis of the struggle toward self-integration and maturation.

NARCISSUS AND JONAH

The Myth of Narcissus

The earliest sources of the myth of Narcissus have long since been lost. Our most complete account from antiquity is in Ovid's *Metamorphosis* (ca. 43 BCE to 17 CE). Although physically beautiful, Narcissus leads a life full of precarious oscillation, and ultimately he ends up a suicide. His story develops thus:

1. A seer prophesies that the handsome Narcissus will live to a ripe old age, provided that he never knows himself (30.347–359). Narcissus' life thus begins with a riddle that presents him with an insoluble conflict. He is filled with primordial guilt and fear. Narcissus must avoid self-knowledge or die.

2. Although many fall in love with Narcissus, he heartlessly rejects lovers of both sexes. His lack of inner knowledge is masked by a stubborn pride (hubris) in his own beauty (3.359–378). Among these lovers is Echo, who has no voice of her own and can only reflect back what Narcissus says (3.379–392).

3. One of those Narcissus has scorned raises his hands to heaven and prays: "May he, himself, fall in love with another, as we have done with him; may he, too, be unable to gain his loved one!" (3.405–406).

4. Nemesis, hearing this righteous prayer, causes Narcissus to seek shelter from the sun near a pool and to fall in love with his own reflection in it. At first, Narcissus unsuccessfully tries to embrace and kiss the beautiful boy who confronts him (3.414–454).

5. Subsequently, he recognizes himself and lies gazing at his image for hours. Desiring to separate his soul from his body, he seeks a "joint death."

   Alas! I am myself the boy I see. . . . I am on fire with love for my own self. . . . My very plenty makes me poor. How I wish I could separate myself from my body! I have no quarrel with death, for in death I shall forget my pain: but I could wish that the object of my love might outlive me: as it is, both of us will perish together when this one life is destroyed." (3.463–475)

6. Grief is destroying him, yet he rejoices in the knowledge that his other self will remain true to him. Saying "alas" (which Echo repeats), Narcissus pines away unto death, mourning the boy he loves in vain.

   His last words as he gazed into the familiar waters were "Woe is me for the boy I loved in vain!" and the farewell, "Farewell!" said Echo too. He laid down his weary head on the green grass, and death closed the eyes which so admired their owner's beauty. (3.497–502)

Conon's account of the myth ends with Narcissus plunging a dagger into his breast (*Narrations*, 24).

The Book of Jonah

Consider, in contrast, the Book of Jonah in the Hebrew Bible. Jonah is confused and in conflict several times during the narrative. In fact, he expresses suicidal ideas on several occasions, but he does not commit suicide. Here is an outline of his story:

1. Jonah is ordered by God to go warn Nineveh of its wickedness. Jonah attempts to avoid God by running away to Tarshish (Jonah 1.1–3).

2. God sends a great wind after him, endangering his ship. When asked his identity by his shipmaster, Jonah admits to being the cause of the storm. Jonah asks his shipmates to throw him into the sea so as to spare them: "And he said unto them, 'Take me up, and cast me forth into the sea; so shall the sea be calm unto you: for I know that for my sake this great tempest is upon you' " (1.4–16).

3. They do so and Jonah is saved by a great fish prepared by God. While Jonah is in the belly of the fish he prays to God. After three days, the fish vomits Jonah out safely onto dry land:

   Then Jonah prayed unto the Lord his God out of the fish's belly. . . . "For Thou didst cast me into the depth, in the heart of the seas; and the flood was round about me; All Thy waves and Thy billows passed over me. And I said: 'I am cast out from before Thine eyes': yet I will look again toward Thy holy temple. . . . That which I have vowed I will pay. Salvation is of the Lord." And the Lord spake unto the fish, and it vomited out Jonah upon the dry land. (2.2–11)

4. Once again, God commands Jonah to go to Nineveh. This time Jonah goes and gives the people of Nineveh God's message. They repent and are saved (3.1–10).
   Jonah is angry, however, and desires to die: "But it displeased Jonah exceedingly, and he was angry. . . . 'Therefore now, O Lord, take, I beseech thee, my life from me; for it is better for me to die than to love' " (4.1–4).

5. Jonah leaves the city to sit on its outskirts. There he is shielded by a gourd plant prepared by God. "And the Lord God prepared a gourd and made it come up over Jonah, that it might be a shadow over his head, to deliver him from his evil. So Jonah was exceedingly glad because of the gourd" (4.6).

6. God then destroys the plant with a worm, exposing Jonah to the sun. Jonah again expresses the wish to die: "And the sun beat upon the head of Jonah, that he fainted, and requested for himself that he might die, and said: 'It is better for me to die than to live' " (4.7–8).

7. God again intervenes, asking Jonah "Art thou greatly angry for the gourd?" When Jonah admits that he is, God uses the opportunity to explain the meaning of divine mercy:

"Thou hast had pity on the gourd, for which thou has not labored, neither madest it to grow, which came up in a night and perished in a night; and should not I have pity on Nineveh, that great city wherein are more than six score thousand persons that cannot discern between their right hand and their left hand, and also much cattle?" (4.9–11)

The method that God uses to implant this teaching is a deeply important part of the lesson. Rather than rebuke Jonah directly and impatiently, as would seem fitting at this point, God makes use of a parable about a gourd. This type of intervention avoids wounding Jonah and enables him to meet God halfway, a clear step in his development (4.9–11).

The ideas of cycle and development appear quite vividly in the life stories of Narcissus and Jonah. The myth of Narcissus has been employed in classic psychoanalytic thinking to refer to an individual who is totally self-absorbed — that is, one who is narcissistic rather than object-invested (Freud 1914; Hartmann 1964). Close examination of this myth, however, suggests a cycling between seemingly opposing alternatives.

Table 4.1 divides the narrative into three phases. In the first part of the narrative, Narcissus tends to be self-absorbed and filled with hubris, treating his lovers as mere extensions of himself. This trend becomes accentuated in his relationship with Echo, who becomes a perfect mirror for Narcissus, reflecting everything Narcissus says. Narcissus is self-absorbed and egoistic, in Durkheim's terms, insufficiently connected with his environment (a C position of detached individuation in Figure 1.2), but he is not yet suicidal. Then, a rejected suitor prays that Narcissus himself will experience unrequited love. Nemesis answers this prayer, seducing Narcissus with a false sanctuary — a clear beautiful pond to provide shelter from the heat. Nemesis employs the pool to cause Narcissus to fall hopelessly in love for the first time. Narcissus is infatuated with the face in the pond, not realizing that it represents his own reflection. Narcissus is now other-absorbed or altruistic in Durkheim's terms, insufficiently differentiated from his environment (an A position of deindividuated attachment, in Figure 1.2).[6]

Now, however, Narcissus recognizes that the face in the pond is his.[7] Narcissus is not self-invested but empty of self, striving to grasp his missing self, which has now been projected onto the outside world. Such a psychotic juxtaposition splits Narcissus apart (A/C, Figure 1.2) and he takes his life, either passively or actively (depending on the version). As Ovid put it: "How I wish I could separate myself from my body." This is schizophrenia. In Durkheim's terms, Narcissus is anomic, experiencing confusion about the boundaries between himself and the outside world.[8]

Narcissus kills himself or allows himself to die because he is unable to resolve successfully his individuation–attachment dilemma; he is trapped along the AC axis. He cycles between hubris (C) and nemesis (A). First, he is individuated at the expense of attachment (i.e., the egoistic or C posi-

Table 4.1
Individual Development for Narcissus and Jonah

Narcissus

Act	Move	Outcome
Narcissus mirrors and abandons Echo.	C	Mirroring Narcissim
Narcissus idealizes and is absorbed by face in brook.	A	Idealizing Narcissism
Narcissus recognizes face in brook as his own. He idealizes his own mirror and commits suicide.	A/C	Suicide

Jonah

Act	Move	Outcome
Jonah runs away in confusion from God's command to go to Nineveh. He asks to be thrown overboard but God sends fish to save him from drowning.	$A/C \rightarrow B_1$	Level One Regression and Suicide Prevention
Jonah becomes stronger. God causes fish to vomit Jonah out on dry land.	E_1	Level One Emergence
Jonah goes to Nineveh but latter expresses disagreement with God.	D_1	Level One Dialogue
Jonah sits outside Nineveh in confusion and again expresses suicidal desire. God shields him from the sun with gourd.	$A/C \rightarrow B_2$	Level Two Regression and Suicide Prevention
Jonah becomes stronger. God causes worm to eat gourd.	E_2	Level Two Emergence
God teaches Jonah the message of mercy: to help others without being absorbed by them.	D_2	Level Two Dialogue

tion); then he is attached at the expense of individuation (i.e., the altruistic or A position). Finally, overwhelmed by his conflicts on both of these issues (i.e., the anomic or A/C position), he murders himself.

In the story of Jonah, the idea of cycle is missing. Jonah is presented with a difficult dilemma at the beginning of the story. Nineveh is a symbol of evil to him, and he thinks that it should not be spared through God's mercy; at the same time, Jonah does not want to defy God. Jonah rejects the Hobson's choice between the altruistic (A) and egoistic (C) pitfalls of Narcissus (see Table 4.1).

Jonah takes a ship to Tarshish. A storm comes, and Jonah tells his shipmates to throw him overboard. The story could thus end in his virtual suicide but it does not. God intervenes like a protective parent, securing Jonah in the stomach of a great fish (position B_1 in Table 4.1). As he becomes stronger, he prays to God and the fish spits Jonah out on dry land (E_1). Finally Jonah agrees to bring God's message to the people of Nineveh (D_1). Antithetical thinking between individuation and attachment is avoided. These life forces are not seen as mutually exclusive opposites requiring dialectical resolution and suicide. God provides the stopper to allow Jonah to develop in a manner that integrates individuation and attachment.

Jonah's journey is not complete, however. He does not yet fully grasp God's higher purpose and thus becomes angry when the people of Nineveh repent and are saved. He is still in opposition to God (the AC conflict), although at a higher stage of development. He runs away and sits outside the walls of Nineveh where he once more expresses the wish to die. God again intervenes, providing a second stopper or protective wall for Jonah — this time a gourd plant to shield Jonah (position B_2). The wall is removed a second time, through the destruction of the gourd by a worm (E_2). Jonah once more expresses suicidal thoughts but God again intervenes, this time engaging Jonah in a mature dialogue as to the meaning of repentance and ending Jonah's confusion with regard to integrating individuation and attachment (*Yalkut Shimoni*).

The suicide-preventive element in this story is the convenantal stopper that allows Jonah to regress out of a polarized dichotomy between individuation and attachment. Under God's protection, Jonah is able to grow and avoid the conflictual logic that leads to the demise of Narcissus.

THE SUICIDE OF OTTO WEININGER

The tragic end of the self-hating Jewish intellectual, Otto Weininger, exemplifies the threat of suicide to one torn between individuation and attachment. Weininger shot himself to death in 1903 at the age of twenty-three in the very apartment where Beethoven had died some seventy-six years earlier. Weininger became famous posthumously for his brilliant but erratic book *Sex and Character* (1903), which is noteworthy for its

Jewish self-hatred, its misogyny, and its strongly Platonic elevation of logic and ideal form.

In this work, Weininger argued that woman does not act from principle as she has no continuity. Woman does not need logical support for her mental process. Man, by contrast, feels the obligation to keep the logical standard that he has set up for himself, but woman resents any attempt to require that her thoughts be logical. She may be regarded as "logically insane" (149). Weininger equated women and Jews with the lack of any genuine self-being or integrity of self-definition. Woman believes in others. She has a center of gravity, although it is outside her own being. The Jew believes in nothing, either within or outside himself (320–321).

Weininger projected his own inadequacies on women and Jews. Nazi ideologues cited his ideas to elevate Aryanism and masculine strength. Weininger's ravings reveal much about his emotional condition. He regarded attachment and individuation as contradictory. This conflict was directly expressed by Weininger in letters regarding his own life. In one of his most poignant confessions, he wrote:

That is the worst; not being able to love when one is loved and knows one is loved, with hatred toward that bitter feeling of a desire to love deep down in the heart. This petrification, this barrenness! An olive tree on the hardest granite! My soul cannot free itself and enter into that of another who loves me. (Weininger, *Condemnation*, 1902)

Weininger, though ethnically a Jew, followed the pathological pattern of the Greek Narcissus. He rejected those who would love him, and his soul remained aloof and barren. It is as if he perceived loving as weakness, yet he felt frozen and alone as a result.

This conflict in itself is potentially suicidal. The psychiatrist David Abrahamsen (1946) has added, however, that Weininger did not simply reject the advances of others but indeed accepted them. The very acceptance of life gave birth to his loneliness and rejection of life. Abrahamsen has put it this way:

He [Weininger] seems to have sought to establish relations with others, to join with the crowd. Yet to think he enjoyed being in the crowd would be a mistake. When he was part of a group, he was with the others only superficially. He wanted to belong to them, to share with them in youthful activity, so strong was his longing for life. And yet he was freezing within, alone. His earnest desire for life evolves into hatred and fear of it. The stronger the longing, the stronger the fear. The division within him appeared in many contradictory and irreconcilable attitudes in the form of ambivalency and splitting. This affective ambivalency became gradually apparent in his attitudes toward women and toward Jews. (Abrahamsen 1946, 21–22).

Weininger was a prime example of an anomic personality (A/C). He was simultaneously drawn and repelled by the irreconcilable alternatives of individuation and attachment[9] and of life and death.[10] Weininger was not simply conflicted *between* individuation and attachment but conflicted within each of these drives as well. He craved attachment yet feared it. He needed individuation yet feared it as well. Suicide became his only way out.

NOTES

1. Neuringer and Lettieri (1982, 31) have noted a relatively long history for the observation that suicidal individuals display a narrow, highly focused, dichotomous and fixed thinking style. Westcott (1885) first observed the suicidal situation as one in which the person perceives only two alternatives of which the least odious is suicide. Cavan (1928) described the suicidal quality as a "fixity of ideas." The suicidal trap of wanting mutually exclusive opposites is expressed in Sylvia Plath's *The Bell Jar* (1986, 78). In this autobiographical novel of mental breakdown and suicide, the talented young poet Esther Greenwood laughs scornfully to her boyfriend: "If neurotic is wanting two mutually exclusive things at one and the same time, then I'm neurotic as hell. I'll be flying back and forth between one mutually achieving thing and another for the rest of my days."

2. Curiously, it has become almost a truism of modern Western thought to view dialectical thinking, whether that of Hegel, Marx, or Jung, with admiration and Talmudic "hairsplitting" with disdain. Hairsplitting is seen as, at best, a clever but ultimately trivial attempt to avoid life's tragic irreconcilabilities. Biblical and Rabbinic thought, however, do not see the world as tragic. Further, it is the very "hairsplitting" attacked by the Western world that offers an alternative to suicidally polarized thinking. Indeed, it offers the possibility of therapeutic development by avoiding irreconcilable extremes. Shneidman (1985, 179) has argued for the suicidal implications of irreconcilable extremes in his essay on *Moby Dick*.

3. See Albert Camus, *The Myth of Sisyphus* (1955). Camus altered some of these ideas in his other works; for example, *The Plague* (1948).

4. The translations from Koheleth are from Robert Gordis, *Koheleth: The Man and His World* (1955).

5. Rabbinic literature does, in fact, contain the notion that the world was not created in a perfect state and that man may and should improve it; for example, "Everything that was created in the first six days needs improvement" (*Pesikta Rabati*, 23). See also J. D. Soloveitchik, *Halakhic Man* (1983).

6. Kohut has termed these two phases "mirroring" and "idealizing" narcissistic configurations. For Kohut (1971), unlike Freud, narcissism is defined not by the target of the instinctual investment (i.e., whether it is the subject himself or other people) but by the nature or quality of the instinctual charge" (26). Thus, an idealizing configuration whereby one invests his energy in the "omnipotent other" is seen by Kohut as narcissistic, as is the withdrawal of psychic energy inward into the "grandiose self" (i.e., the mirroring configuration). The intent behind the idealizing position is as inherently self-serving (you are perfect, but I am part of you) as is that behind the mirroring position (I am perfect). Narcissus cycles between Kohut's

mirroring and idealizing narcissistic configurations, but he is still not actively suicidal.

7. The theme of the double or *doppelgänger* has been very popular in European literature. It typically involves the attempts of a hero to reunite with his missing double, often a reflection (see Rank 1971). In Kohut's terms, the mirror has become the ideal.

8. In Shneidman and Farberow's (1957) terms, Narcissus represents an example of "suicidal logic" or the inability to integrate one's personal self (I_s) and one's social self (1_o). For such persons, one can be obtained only at the expense of the other.

9. Kalman Kaplan (1988) has developed an Individuation Attachment Questionnaire (IAQ) to assess individuation and attachment. The IAQ assumes an inherent ambiguity in our traditional definitions of near and far and attempts to separate out the often fine distinctions found in relation to these dynamics. For example, agreement with the statement "It is important for me to take other people's needs into account" may indicate a *need for attachment*. At the same time, agreement with the statement "It is important for me to meet others' expectations of me" may indicate a *fear of individuation*. Likewise, agreement with the statement "Other people's judgment of me seldom determines how I feel about myself" may indicate a *need for individuation*, while agreement with the statement "A person does not need involvement with others to be fulfilled" may indicate a *fear of attachment*. Weininger's personality indicates high needs and high fears on both individuation and attachment; hence, his suicidal conflict.

10. Israel Orbach and his colleagues (1983) have developed instruments for separately assessing attraction and repulsion with regard to both life and death. This procedure generates four measures: *attraction to life, repulsion from life, attraction to death*, and *repulsion from death*.

Chapter 5

Suicide in Greek Tragedy

> But now prostrate beneath so great a woe, not tasting food nor drink, he sits among the sword-slain beasts, motionless where he sank. And plainly he meditates some baleful deed. For so portend his words and lamentations. . . . Some scheme let me devise which may prove to my aged sire that I, his son, at least by nature am no coward, for 'tis base for a man to crave long life who endures never-varying misery.
>
> Sophocles, *Ajax*, 317–328, 471–475[1]

Leading figures, usually heroic ones, in the fifth-century dramas of Sophocles and Euripides often saw no way but suicide to free themselves from what they perceived as no-win life situations. These plays were familiar to educated Greeks and Romans of antiquity and were frequently quoted in the writings of that time.

An immensely important aspect of the Greek literary tradition is that the hero has basic flaws that drive him to destruction. He devotes himself to winning honor, and it is disgraceful for him to do less than strive to be a champion. So strong a drive may easily involve violence, harshness, or uncontrollable temper. To achieve heroism is more important than life itself, and this goal often demands the sacrifice of one's own life. The tragic hero is also typically trapped in a Hobson's choice. No matter what he does, the Greek hero moves inexorably toward his doom. There is no stopper. Prophets in Greek drama often use what should be freeing knowledge to taunt or lead the hero to self-destruction through a series of vague riddles that present information in a concealed or inaccessible way.

The great tragedy of Oedipus exemplifies all these patterns. The characters feel trapped between the need to save Thebes and the need to protect or pacify Oedipus, who finally, in the truest heroic manner, sacrifices himself to save the city of Thebes. He accepts the classic Hobson's choice—the cyclical riddle of the Sphinx with all its destructive implications, and he finds no stopper in a grim and hostile world.

This sense of hopelessness is expressed powerfully in Sophocles' *Antigone.* Greatness in human life brings doom (613), and a doomed man cannot even accurately distinguish good from bad (622). The house of Oedipus is utterly without hope (598), with no possibility of cure (1342) or of prayer to a concerned deity to extricate the family from its fate. Creon is told this very thing by the chorus at the end of *Antigone:* "Pray thou no more, for mortals have no escape from destined woe" (1336). Finally, the riddles of Tiresias only confuse and antagonize Oedipus, who has been a good and devoted king of Thebes. Why is the riddle form used rather than that of the Biblical parable, like the one that Nathan presented to David (2 Samuel 12)? Perhaps the riddle enables Tiresias to keep control of the situation; he gains his security through presenting himself as an indispensable source of knowledge. In any case, he gives Oedipus no clear information whereby he may improve his situation—in fact, he makes matters worse.

Characters in Greek tragedy are trapped in no-win cyclical situations not entirely of their own making.[2] There is no way out of the cycle nor is there much chance of seeing the alternatives clearly. Their prophets, like Tiresias, speak in riddles that are meant to be misleading and unhelpful. Indeed, prophecy in Greek tragedy is completely deterministic: *Consequence Y will occur no matter which antecedent X_1 or X_2 the tragic hero attempts.* Oedipus has no saving answers to the riddle of the Sphinx, for there are none. Answering "correctly" or "incorrectly" will lead to the same self-destruction of the house of Labdacus. There is neither hope nor prayer. The deities themselves, as products of the natural world, are both too powerless and too preoccupied with their own affairs to intervene (Kaufmann 1972, chapter 2). The entire tragic context is a breeding ground for suicide. An excellent study by M. D. Faber (1970) has noted sixteen suicides and self-mutilations in the twenty-six extant plays of Sophocles and Euripides. There is also a seventeenth—Jocasta in the *Phoenissae* by Euripides.[3] Many of these suicides, however, especially those in Euripides, fall into a pattern of ritual murder, in which the person does not actually raise a hand against himself.

In these dramas, character after character is led to a suicidal end. Faber has employed Durkheim's three categories of suicide to argue that the suicides in Sophocles tend to be primarily egoistic (initially outward destructive tendencies that are turned inward) while those in Euripides tend to be primarily altruistic (basically inward destructive tendencies that are sometimes disguised as outwardly heroic or martyr-like acts). Some cases for both playwrights may fall into Durkheim's anomic type (Table 5.1).

Table 5.1
Self-Destruction in Greek Tragedy

Character	Gender	Source	Method	Type
Oedipus	M	Oedipus Rex(Sophocles)	Self-blinding	Anomic
Jocasta	F	Oedipus Rex(Sophocles)	Hanging	Egoistic
Antigone	F	Antigone(Sophocles)	Hanging	Anomic
Haemon	M	Antigone(Sophocles)	Stabbing	Egoistic
Eurydice	F	Antigone(Sophocles)	Stabbing	Egoistic
Ajax	M	Ajax(Sophocles)	Stabbing	Egoistic
Deianeira	F	The Trachinae(Sophocles)	Stabbing	Anomic
Heracles	M	The Trachinae(Sophocles)	Burning	Egoistic
Phaedra	F	Hippolytus(Euripides)	Stabbing	Anomic
Menoeceus	M	The Phoenissae(Euripides)	Jumping	Altruistic
Jocasta	F	The Phoenissae(Euripides)	Stabbing	Altruistic
Evadne	F	The Suppliants(Euripides)	Burning	Anomic
Iphigenia	F	Iphigenia in Aulis(Euripides)	Hanging	Altruistic
Macaria	F	The Heracleidae(Euripides)	Stabbing	Altruistic
Polyxena	F	Hecuba(Euripides)	Stabbing	Altruistic
Alcestis	F	Alcestis(Euripides)	Unspecified	Altruistic
Hermione	F	Andromache(Euripides)	Attempted Stabbing	Anomic

SOPHOCLES

Oedipus Rex

Suicide is a major theme in four of Sophocles' seven surviving plays: *Oedipus Rex, Antigone, Ajax,* and *The Trachinae. Oedipus Rex* contains one egoistic suicide (Jocasta) and one anomic self-mutilation (Oedipus himself).

The play begins with the priest of Zeus telling King Oedipus of the ravages of plague upon the city of Thebes (24–48). Creon announces that the plague is due to the unavenged murder of Laius and describes the circumstances surrounding that unresolved crime (114–131).

Oedipus volunteers to reopen the search for the murderer of Laius (133–140), cursing the killer to a life of misery and solitude (224–251). Oedipus seems obsessed with past familial connections that, at least on the conscious level, are not his (259–264). There is no stopper to lighten the heroic burden of excessive responsibility that Oedipus takes on.

The unfolding of the terrible secret continues in earnest. Tiresias, the blind oracle, is summoned. Like the seer in the legend of Narcissus, he speaks in unfathomable riddles and points to the dangers in self-knowledge: "Alas, how dreadful to have wisdom where it profits not the wise!" (316–317). He tries to leave (320–321), but Oedipus will not permit it (326–327). Once again, Tiresias speaks but in riddles so maddening that even when he finally and bluntly accuses Oedipus of being the killer, he is not understood (350–368). Oedipus becomes furious, accusing both Tiresias and Creon of lying and plotting against him (431). At the same time, however, Oedipus wants to know more. Tiresias again resorts to riddles, reminding Oedipus of his prowess in deciphering the riddle of the Sphinx (432–440).

This same pattern continues through the play. Oedipus becomes more and more obsessed with the need to get at what the audience knows will be a most unwelcome truth. One reluctant party after another is called in, all given the same Hobson's choice of revealing to Oedipus the awful truth about his past or incurring his wrath by withholding information. Still, Oedipus insists on charging full speed ahead to obtain the knowledge that will prove to be his undoing, first with Jocasta (725–860), then with a messenger (925–1045), and finally with the herdsman (1125–1185). Again, like the seer in the Narcissus story, Jocasta tries to stop Oedipus in his search both for the murderer and for self-knowledge: "For the gods' sake, if thou hast any care for thine own life, forbear this search! My anguish is enough" (1060–1061); she further warns: "Ill-fated one! Mayest thou never come to know who thou art" (1069).[4] Then the herdsman begs him to stop (1165). But Oedipus offers the herdsman the same Hobson's choice on penalty of death: "Thou art lost if I have to question thee again" (1166). Oedipus forces the herdsman to reveal the last piece in the horrible puzzle and finally sees his position clearly. He himself murdered Laius, his father, and married Jocasta, his mother. He is now determined to kill Jocasta, feeling that through her, he was cursed from his birth on: "Oh, oh! All brought to pass — all true! Thou light, may I now look my last on thee — I who have been found accursed in birth, accursed in wedlock, accursed in the shedding of blood!" (1182–1185).

Oedipus then rushes into the palace. There he finds that Jocasta has hanged herself and puts out his eyes:

For he tore from her raiment the golden brooches wherewith she was decked, and lifted them and smote full on his own eye-balls, uttering words like these: "No more shall ye behold such horrors as I was suffering and working! Long enough have ye looked on those whom ye ought never to have seen, failed in knowledge of those whom I yearned to know — henceforth ye shall be dark!" (1265–1270)

When the full truth is revealed, Jocasta's first impulse is to call out the name of the long-dead Laius and then to blame Oedipus. Laius is at fault for fathering Oedipus, and Oedipus to blame for murdering his father and causing her such misery. Only after this egoistic reaction does she hang herself (Durkheim's position C). The suicide is filled with anger toward Laius and Oedipus who have brought her such pain, isolation, and shame.

The self-blinding of Oedipus follows this same basic pattern. His first impulse upon learning the truth is apparently to commit not suicide but homicide against Jocasta. She becomes not his wife but the ultimately betraying and abandoning mother, and he wants to kill her: "To and fro he went, asking us to give him a sword — asking where he should find the wife who was no wife, but a mother whose womb had borne alike himself and his children" (1255–1257). Only when he sees that Jocasta is dead does he turn his aggressive impulses inward. Significantly, he puts out his eyes with the golden brooches from her dress, rather than with the sword. He is finally paying his debt to the devouring earth-mother. More than even suicide, self-blinding may serve to shield Oedipus from an overwhelming world. If he cannot see the world, he can diminish his contact with it. Further, his eyes have proved to be his undoing: "Why was I to see, when sight could show me nothing sweet?" (1335). Self-blinding also protects Oedipus from a feared reunion with his accursed parents in the place of the dead (1370–1375). Oedipus' lethal combination of disengagement and enmeshment fits Durkheim's anomic (position A/C) pattern of self-destruction.

Antigone

Sophocles' *Antigone* contains three suicides, those of Antigone, Haemon, and Eurydice. Antigone is the daughter of Oedipus and Jocasta. She has long been viewed in Western thought as a sterling example of a highly individuated and idealistic woman who senses strongly the conflict between the higher moral law and the wickedness of an earthly ruler.[5] When faced with Creon's decree that her brother Polyneices should remain unburied, she invokes the authority of the law of the gods and buries him (450–456). Closer scrutiny reveals a far more complex character, however. She is over-identified with her family of origin and with the opinion of the community at large; she is also obsessed with death. Antigone's idealism masks the driving force of her life, which is the fulfillment of the curse of the house of Labdacus with which the play begins.[6] Her hopelessness is so profound it can lead only to self-destruction (1–3).

This theme echoes throughout the play. After she has been condemned by Creon to be buried alive, Antigone reiterates her depressive obsession:

Thou hast touched on my bitterest thought, — awaking the ever-new lament for my sire and for all the doom given to us, the famed house of Labdacus. Alas for the horror of the mother's bed! Alas for the wretched mother's slumber at the side of her own son, — and my sire! From what manner of parents did I take my miserable being! And to them I go thus, accursed, unwed, to share their home. Alas, my brother, ill-starred in thy marriage, in thy death thou hast undone my life! (859–871)

But Antigone has already expressed her thoughts of a noble death (72–73), and this theme develops as the play proceeds. Antigone now sees death as preferable to life, as freedom from life's miseries.

Die I must, — I knew that well (how should I not?) — even without thy edicts. But if I am to die before my time, I count that as a gain:[7] for when anyone lives as I do, compassed about with evils, can such a one find ought but gain in death? (458–462)

Slightly later, she notes: "Be of good cheer, thou livest; but my life hath long been given to death, that so I may serve the dead" (560–561).

Antigone links her death with the fulfillment of the curse on her family: "From what manner of parents did I take my miserable being! And to them I go thus, accursed, unwed, to share their home" (869). She seems to strive to fulfill the curse on the house of Labdacus by bringing about her own death without offspring. She goes "living to the vaults of death" to join her dead brother (916–920). Antigone even uses the image of being wed to Acheron, the "Lord of the Dark Lake" (808–814).

That this preoccupation is not just resignation with regard to her sentence can be seen by her expression of a greater, even an incestuous allegiance to her dead family of origin than to the living, even at the very beginning of the play. She sees marriage through the metaphor of death. She defies Creon's order to leave Polyneices unburied because "I know that

I please where I am most bound to please" (89). She sees herself as lying with her brother in love: "I shall rest, a loved one with him whom I have loved, sinless in my crime" (74). An even more definitive example of this over-allegiance to her family of origin at the expense of present relationships is her striking statement that she would not feel compelled to bury a husband or child as she would a brother. The former are replaceable while the latter is not:

Never, had I been a mother of children, or if a husband had been mouldering in death, would I have taken this task upon me in the city's despite. What law, ye ask is my warrant for that word? The husband lost, another might have been found, and child from another, to replace the firstborn: but, father and mother hidden with Hades, no brother's life could ever bloom for me again. (909–918)

Antigone also seems totally indifferent to Haemon, her fiancé, remaining strangely silent in the face of Creon's attacks on him. Indeed, most manuscripts give Ismene line 572:[8] "Haemon beloved! How thy father wrongs thee." Antigone is unable to relate to anyone. She rejects her sister Ismene roughly (69–72). Antigone also seems to go out of her way to insist that her deed be made public, while Ismene wishes to keep it quiet (84–85), and to be exceptionally insolent in her confrontation with Creon (481–483). Yet she later laments that she will die alone, forlorn, and friendless (919).

Her embeddedness with her family of origin is further expressed in her method of suicide, which mimics that of her mother: "We described her hanging by the neck. . . . While he was embracing her with arms thrown around her waist" (1220–1223). In her vacillation between enmeshment and isolation and her confusion between self and other, Antigone proceeds to an anomic suicide (the A/C position).

Haemon, son of Creon and the fiancé of Antigone, enters midway through the play (628–630) "grieving for the doom of his promised bride Antigone." What develops is an accelerating step-by-step struggle between father and son. Creon questions whether Haemon will remain loyal to him, given his (Creon's) sentencing of Antigone: "Art thou come in rage against thy father? Or have I thy good will?" (635). Haemon's first response is quite mild, submitting to his father's authority (636). To be sure, Haemon then skillfully attempts to present his own deeply felt views and defends Antigone strongly, far more strongly than she defended him (699). Creon responds by invoking the authority of age over youth (727–728). At this point, the quarrel intensifies until Haemon threatens suicide openly (728–763).

The leader of the chorus warns Creon of Haemon's suicidal state, but Creon chooses for too long to ignore it (768–769). When he at last relents, it is too late. Haemon's emotions reach a peak when Creon interrupts his mourning for the dead Antigone. Creon's attempts at intervention are useless at this point and, in all likelihood, seem to Haemon another effort by his father to reestablish control. Haemon reacts violently, attempting to stab his father. After this fails, he turns his murderous wrath inward and falls on his own sword (1219–1239):

But his father, when he saw him, cried aloud with a dread cry and went in, and called to him with a voice of wailing: . . . But the boy glared at him with fierce eyes, spat in his face, and, without a word of answer, drew his cross-hilted sword: — as his father rushed forth in flight, he missed his aim; — then, hapless one, wroth with himself, he straightaway leaned with all his weight against the sword, and drove it, half its length, into his side. (1225–1239)

Haemon's suicide is egoistic (position C). He feels controlled by his father, and his resultant rage, like that of Oedipus, is first projected outward against his father before it is inverted. Once again, there is the horrible image of marrying in death. "Corpse enfolding corpse he lies, he hath won his nuptial rites, poor youth, not here, yet in the halls of Death" (1240–1241).

The final suicide in Sophocles' *Antigone* is that of Eurydice, the wife of Creon and the mother of Haemon. She enters late in the play and has only one speech (1183–1190). She has heard of the family disaster and asks the messenger to repeat the story. Upon hearing of Haemon's suicide, Eurydice silently returns to her house (1243). Her silence rightly arouses concern from both the leader of the chorus and the messenger (1245–1257).

At this point, the messenger reports that Eurydice too has killed herself:

Sire, thou hast come, me thinks, as one whose hands are not empty, but who hath store laid up besides; thou bearest yonder burden with thee; and thou art soon to look upon the woes within thy house. . . . Thy queen hath died, true mother of yon corpse — ah, hapless lady! — by blows newly dealt. (1279–1287)

The messenger's further description reveals Eurydice's rage toward her husband, blaming him not only for the death of Haemon but also for the death of her other son, Megareus, as well. This hostility is characteristic of egoistic suicides (position C).

There, at the altar, self-stabbed with a keen knife, she suffered her darkening eyes to close, when she had wailed for the noble fate of Megareus who died before, and then for his fate who lies there, — and when, with her last breath, she had invoked evil fortunes upon thee, the slayer of thy sons. (1297–1300)

Ajax

A prime example of Sophoclean egoistic suicide is the Greek warrior Ajax in the play bearing his name. Ajax has gone mad with jealousy because Achilles' armor has been given to Odysseus. In a frenzied state, he attempts to murder Odysseus. He is prevented in this by the goddess Athena, who deflects his anger so that he slaughters a herd of sheep instead (40–55). The text makes clear that Athena desires not simply to restrain Ajax but to humiliate him deeply and mock him in his madness in front of Odysseus (91–117). Ajax's hubris has provoked Athena's anger:

Then boastfully and witlessly he answered, "Father, with heaven's help a mere man of nought might win victory, but I, albeit without their aid, trust to achieve a victor's glory." . . . By such words and such thoughts too great for man did he provoke Athena's pitiless wrath. (759–777)

The very intensity of Athena's wrath sets the stage for Ajax's subsequent suicide. As his rage passes, it is replaced by a potentially self-destructive depression. This is not uncommon among egoistic suicides:

Yet hope we: for ceased is the lightning's flash: His rage dies down like a fierce southwind. But now, grown sane, new misery is his, for on woes self-wrought he gazes aghast, wherein no hand but his own had share; and with anguish his soul is afflicted. (256–262)

His defenses are overcome, and he cries for the first time, refusing food or drink (317–328). Ajax first contemplates murdering Odysseus (391) and then himself (393).

The suicidal aims of Ajax are even more clearly articulated in his ruminations about his lost honor in the eyes of his father. An honorable suicide may be his only solution:

With what face shall I appear before my father Telamon? How will *he* find heart to look on me, stripped of my championship in war that mighty crown of fame that once was his? No, that I dare not. . . . Some scheme let me devise which may prove to my aged sire that I, his son, at least by nature am no coward, for 'tis base for a man to crave long life who endures never-varying misery. (463–467, 471–475)

The egoistic nature of Ajax's suicide is already hinted at in his initial inclination toward homicide (also shown by Oedipus and Haemon), in his rejection of tears as cowardly, and in his excessive concern with honor in his relationship with his father. In his final talk with his young son, Ajax reveals his own sadly erroneous views of human development. The childhood years are sweet in their innocence, before a man must prove his manliness in facing life's tragic tribulations (545–559). The pattern that Ajax prescribes for his son appears to describe his own childhood. Ajax himself was broken to his father's "stern rugged code" and plucked early from his mother's embraces. This premature rupturing of Ajax's bond with his mother has impelled him toward an egoistic suicide (position C). The need for his mother's attention appears in Ajax's daydream of her grief at his death: "She, woeful woman, when she hears these tidings will wail out a large dirge through all the town" (848–849). Immediately after this refrain, Ajax falls on his sword and dies (865).

Ajax's friends do not know how to deal with his problem. He certainly does not disguise his suicidal intent, yet those around him allow him to go off by himself, something clearly not recommended for suicide prevention. In fact, the only step toward suicide prevention is taken by Ajax's brother, Teucer, who sends a messenger from the Greek chieftains ordering that Ajax not be left alone (748–755). The messenger arrives too late, but the common-sense suicide-preventive message is clear: Do not leave a suicidally depressed man alone!

The behavior of Odysseus, the rival of Ajax, is quite sensible throughout this play, an unusual pattern among characters in classical drama. At the beginning of the play, Odysseus is appropriately afraid to confront the crazed Ajax when Athena proposes to summon him (74–82). Later, however, it is the same Odysseus who pleads with Agamemnon for the burial of Ajax's corpse. Agamemnon finds this incomprehensible, given Odysseus's previous hatred of Ajax. Odysseus responds maturely. Although it is the sign of a wise man to adjust to changing situations, Agamemnon sees it differently, accusing Odysseus of instability and impulsiveness:

Odysseus: Then listen: For the gods' sake, venture not thus ruthlessly to cast forth this man unburied.
Agamemnon: Thou, Odysseus, champion *him* thus against *me?*
Odysseus: Yes; but I hated him while hate was honorable.
Agamemnon: Shoulds't thou not also trample on him when dead? . . .
Odysseus: This man was once my foe, yet was he noble . . .
Agamemnon: Unstable of impulse are such men as thou.
Odysseus: Many are friends now and hereafter foes. (1332–1359)

The Trachiniae

Two suicides occur in *The Trachiniae* — the anomic self-stabbing of Deianeira, the unhappy wife of Heracles, and Heracles' own egoistic self-burning. In her first speech, Deianeira expresses tremendous conflict between her gratitude toward Heracles for fighting for her hand and delivering her from dangers and her anger at his prolonged absence from her after the marriage (26–37). She feels abandoned and resentful toward him but seems able to express these feelings only through excessive concern (41–47). Deianeira goes on to chide her son, Hyllus, for not having looked for his father (65–66).

Her uncertainty toward Heracles surfaces in her hesitancy to accept what should be the good news of Heracles' safety and indeed triumph

(178–190). Even after she comes to believe this news, her joy is short-lived, rapidly followed by a desire to know why he was away so long and by great misgivings over the future. These fears are natural to one raised with the Greek understanding of cycle (233–247): "Yea, have I not the fullest reason to rejoice at these tidings of my lord's happy fortune? To such fortune, such joy must needs respond. And yet a prudent mind can see room for misgiving, lest he who prospers should one day suffer reverse" (300–304).

Deianeira's misgivings are borne out as she learns the truth about the love affair of Heracles and his mistress Iole, whom Deianeira has already befriended and welcomed into her house (313–327). It is the pursuit of this love that has kept Heracles so long away. Deianeira's unrealistic and idealized self-expectations seem to prevent her from openly expressing a well-justified anger and hurt (Faber 1970, 56). She seems bewildered and hapless (379–380), going so far as to excuse Heracles and Iole, at least on the conscious level (448–452), and she will not say a harsh word about either of them (461–465).

At the same time, however, Deianeira struggles with an inner fury that threatens to break out of control (547–548), but she cannot accept her own anger (549–557). Finally, she determines to send Heracles a robe that she had dipped in the blood of the centaur Nessus many years earlier after he was mortally wounded by Heracles' poisoned arrow. As he lay dying, Nessus had instructed Deianeira to take some of the blood from around the wound and to use it as a charm so that her husband would never look at another woman (569–572).

Nessus' response contains a riddle in the style of Tiresias. Might he not have meant that Heracles will die before he looks at another woman? Deianeira seems to ignore the hints of danger in the gift, treating it only as a love potion (577–580), but she has hinted at a far more sinister intent slightly earlier (576, 665–675, 710–715). On the one hand, she cannot accept responsibility for having done any wrong, even when she is accused of this by her son Hyllus (804–808). On the other, Deianeira walks away rather than defend herself (787), because she knows or fears at some level that she has done something wrong. It is this smallness, timidity, and excessive concern with others' opinion of her, that distinguishes her from a more actively aggressive figure such as Medea. These characteristics were no doubt accentuated by the total failure of her father to protect her from the sexual advances of the river god Achelous. Indeed, her treasured Heracles saved her from this ravage as well (1–13).

This embedded, altruistic quality surfaces along with egoistic anger turned inward. Deianeira's vacillation and confusion about the boundaries between self and other are typical of an anomic (position A/C) suicide. At this point, Deianeira resolves to take her own life: "Howbeit, I am resolved that, if he is to fall, at the same time I also shall be swept from life; for no woman could bear to live with an evil name, if she rejoices that her nature is not evil" (718–720). She cannot go on living with a feeling of being seen as less altruistic than she has always seemed to herself. There is no expression of sympathy or remorse toward her husband.

One can only wonder how Deianeira could have been so naive all along, unless her naiveté was purposely aimed at providing an acceptable way to express her murderous hostility toward Heracles. Both the anger and embeddedness in Deianeira's suicide are evident in the fact that she stabs herself in her own marriage bed, presumably the one Heracles intended to share with Iole:

"Ah, bridal bed and bridal chamber mine, farewell now and forever; never more shall ye receive me to rest upon this couch." She said no more, but with a vehement hand loosed her robe, where the gold-wrought brooch lay above her breast, baring all her left side and arm . . . she had driven a two-edged sword through her side to the heart. (925–935)

Deianeira is not a larger-than-life tragic figure like Medea or Antigone. She is in many ways a repressed, somewhat average homebody, confronted with an unfaithful husband. Deianeira is not basically crazy, yet she is made mad by events and by a structure that does not allow her to express normal anger in a healthy way. Rather, her anger is bottled up, until it explodes first against Heracles and then against herself.

The second suicide in this play is Heracles, who seems an unsympathetic brute. Racked with pain from the burning robe, his first reaction, like that of Oedipus, Haemon, and Ajax, is the urge to murder Deianeira, not himself (1109–1112). Only after Heracles learns from Hyllus that Deianeira has already killed herself does he ask Hyllus to help in his suicide as he is now too incapacitated to complete the act:

Thither, then, thou must carry me up with thine own hands, aided by what friends thou wilt; thou shalt lop many a branch from the deep-rooted oak, and hew many a faggot also from the sturdy stock of the wild-olive; thou shalt lay my body thereupon, and kindle it with flaming pine-torch. (1193–1196)

This transformation from homicide to suicide has the earmarks of yet another egoistic suicide — aggression first turned outward and then rotated 180 degrees inward. The extremely egoistic (position C) and controlling quality of Heracles is made even more manifest by his almost incredible command to Hyllus to marry Iole, whom Hyllus views as responsible for his mother Deianeira's death. Heracles nearly drives his own son to suicide (1221–1232, 1247–1248).

The illness in the classical Greek family is never more apparent than in this complicated and brilliant play by Sophocles. First, the quite average Deianeira is driven to suicide. Second, Hyllus blames his mother Deianeira for Heracles' death. Next, he blames Iole for his mother's death. Finally, his dying father Heracles orders Hyllus to marry Iole, despite Hyllus' warning of his own suicide. Average people too can be pathologized by such an unhealthy structure.

EURIPIDES

Suicides in the plays of Euripides are very different. Many seem like ritual deaths or martyrdoms in which the victims submit passively to group demands. These are mostly altruistic people with insufficient boundaries in relation to the outside world; some are anomic, with confused boundaries. Suicides appear in seven of Euripides' nineteen extant plays: *Hippolytus, The Phoenissae, The Suppliants, Iphigenia in Aulis, The Heracleidae, Alcestis,* and *Hecuba.* An eighth play, *Andromache,* contains an attempted suicide.

Hippolytus

In *Hippolytus,* Phaedra, the wife of King Theseus of Athens, is caught in a miserable family situation and at the same time has unrealistic expectations of herself. She falls madly in love, by Aphrodite's design, with her stepson Hippolytus. Although she resists her passion in great misery, her servant betrays her secret to Hippolytus. Phaedra then hangs herself, leaving behind a note that falsely charges Hippolytus with raping her. Theseus believes the note and pronounces a curse of death upon his son. The curse is soon fulfilled, and the truth is revealed too late.

According to this play, the gods are selfish and cruel, utterly without compassion toward man. Aphrodite plots to destroy Hippolytus for living in chastity. She has filled his stepmother Phaedra with passion for him, and the heart of his father will be turned against him (7–52).

Phaedra mixes an exaggerated sense of honor and guilt with a tendency toward self-punishment: "My hands are pure, but on my soul there rests stain" (317). She must hide her passion to save her honor: "Alas for thee! My sorrows, shouldst thou learn them would recoil on thee" (327) — even if it means suicide: "out of shame I am planning an honorable escape" (331). The nurse accuses her of trying to be better than the gods: "O cease, my darling child, from evil thoughts, let wanton pride be gone, for this is naught else, this wish to rival gods in perfectness" (474–475). There is no stopper in Phaedra's rush toward suicide. She is too overwrought to remain silent, Aphrodite works against her, and her nurse betrays her by spilling the secret of her passion to Hippolytus (593–594).

When discretion and good sense fail, death seems the only cure: "And last when I could not succeed in mastering love hereby, me thought it best to die; and none can gainsay my purpose" (397). As she puts it, "I know only one way, one cure for these my woes, and that is instant death" (599).

Phaedra's punitive conscience is accompanied by low self-esteem engendered by her fears of misogyny and her unhappiness and helplessness at being a woman (406–409). This view is echoed by the chorus and by Hippolytus who delivers a particularly sharp attack on women. Women are vile (650) and filth (653): "I can never satisfy my hate for women, no! Not even though some say this is ever my theme, for of a truth they always are evil. So either let some one prove them chaste, or let me still trample on them forever" (665–667).

Phaedra suffers under the burden of a family background that rivals that of Oedipus. Her mother had slept with a white bull, her sister had been raped by Dionysus, and she herself is the "third to suffer" (337–340): "That 'love' has been our curse from time long past" (343). She fears most that her passion for Hippolytus will become known and she will be seen as a traitor to her husband and children. She would rather die: "This it is that calls on me to die, kind friends, that so I may ne'er be found to have disgraced my lord, or the children I have borne" (426–427). Phaedra struggles to free herself and her children from her family pattern, but she is too enmeshed to succeed and destroys both herself and Hippolytus (714–720).

Hippolytus, too, in his last breath, laments that he is bound by a miserable family past that cannot be expiated: There is neither repentance or forgiveness (1366–1371). The gods remain unhelpful to the end. Hippolytus is special to Artemis, but she cannot help him in his final pains. She leaves before his death, the sight of which would be a pollution to her: "And now farewell! 'tis not for me to gaze upon the dead, or pollute my sight with death scenes, and e'en now I see thee nigh that evil" (1432–1433).

Phaedra lives in a world in which her gods and her family have been at best uncaring, in which her individuality and womanhood are despised, and in which error cannot be corrected. Caught in a conflict between Aphrodite and Artemis, she sees no way out but suicide. Phaedra destroys herself because, much like Sophocles' Antigone, she is embedded in a miserable situation. At the same time, she has an unrealistic expectation of herself. Vacillating between the altruistic and egoistic positions leads Phaedra to an anomic suicide (position A/C). All Euripides' suicides are either anomic or altruistic, not egoistic.

The Phoenissae

Euripides treats the story of the family of Oedipus quite differently in *The Phoenissae*[9] from the way that Sophocles does in his trilogy. Antigone is portrayed as a bright-eyed Gidget anxious to sneak a look at the attacking army (127–192). Jocasta is still living, and Oedipus sits shut up in a house in Thebes, commiserating with himself over his misfortunes and cursing his sons who put him there. There are two altruistic suicides in *The Phoenissae* — Menoeceus,[10] the son of Creon, and Jocasta.

The seer Tiresias informs the Thebans in his usual taunting way that Thebes can be saved from the invaders only by the death of a young unmarried man to repay the earth for the slaying of Ares' dragon. This is the very essence of a Hobson's choice, an apparent pressure to destroy either one's own life or that of one's city (935–939). Menoeceus pretends to be persuaded by Creon to flee the city, but secretly goes to the appropriate site and stabs himself (1086–1088).

Menoeceus genuinely believes that he must give precedence to the city over his own private needs and offers his life as a gift. His suicide is thus altruistic (position A):

Now I go to make the city a present of my life, no mean offering, to rid this kingdom of its affliction. For if each were to take and expend all the good within his power, contributing it to his country's weal, our states would experience fewer troubles and would for the future prosper. (1013–1016)

The second suicide, Jocasta, has failed to reconcile her two sons, Eteocles and Polyneices, with each other. They are greedy and ambitious, and Oedipus himself is predictably pessimistic. Jocasta is certain that one will kill the other in their duel (1072–1081). She warns her daughter Antigone, "daughter, thy brothers are in danger of their life" (1268). Jocasta then links her sons' imminent deaths with her own: "If I can forestall the onset of my sons, I may yet live; but if they be dead, I will lay me down and die with them" (1281–1282). She kills herself after discovering that her sons have indeed killed each other:

So both at once breathed out their life of sorrow. But when their mother saw this sad mischance, in her o'er mastering grief she snatched from a corpse its sword and wrought an awful deed, driving the steel right through her throat, and there she lies dead with the dead she loved so well, her arms thrown around them both. (1465–1469)

The suicide of Sophocles' Jocasta is egoistic, emerging from introjected anger. Euripides' Jocasta is altruistic and kills herself from "o'er mastering grief." She has never freed herself from her oppressive family mythology (position A). As Creon says: "Ah! woe is thee, Jocasta! What an end to life and marriage hast thou found the riddling of the Sphinx! But tell me how her two sons wrought the bloody deed, the struggle caused by the curse of Oedipus" (1350–1352).

The gods bring about much of the human misery in *The Phoenissae*. Oedipus says: "For nature did not make me so void of understanding, that I should have devised these horrors against my own eyes and my children's life without the intervention of some god" (1611–1613). Earlier he notes: "So today, father, the god, whose'er this issue is, has gathered to a head the sum of suffering for our house" (1579–1580).

Creon, Menoeceus, Antigone, and Jocasta all show genuine good character, but the gods are narcissistic and human beings are stuck. Both suicides in *The Phoenissae* are caused by a lack of knowledge of a better way to live. The Greek world offers no stoppers and no outlets for a man like Menoeceus — it puts him in an unresolvable Hobson's choice. It offers neither end nor resolution in the curses of dragons and sphinxes that destroy the family of Oedipus.

The Suppliants

Euripides' *The Suppliants* treats the story of Oedipus' children from a different angle. Here the families of the seven champions who fought against Thebes come to seek help from Athens and Theseus, its king. *The Suppliants* depicts the different mentalities of Theseus and Evadne. Theseus is open, flexible, confident, and at the same time serious. Evadne is uncommunicative, flighty, and lacking confidence both in herself and in the world around her. She is without a stopper and ultimately an anomic suicide (an A/C position).

While many Euripidean characters are heavily embedded in their life patterns, Theseus is a clear-thinking, balanced man who sizes up situations well (232–237), can recognize flaws in his own character (337), and can treat others empathetically (284) and considerately (946). His optimism is unusual among Euripidean characters: "For there are who say, there is more bad than good in human nature, to the which I hold a contrary view, that good o'er bad predominates in man, for if it were not so, we should not exist" (197–198). He displays a religious faith that is both serious and realistic without being morbid. Although Theseus appears to accept the prevalent Greek idea of mother earth, he is not overly burdened by it — perhaps because he sees the gods as benign (596–597). The gods, especially Athena, are portrayed as friendly and encouraging to Theseus (1183–1184). Are the gods good to Theseus because he has a positive approach to living, or is his approach to living positive because the gods are good to him? In any case, Theseus stands in marked contrast to Evadne, the wife of the champion Caponius.

Evadne is not caught up in an inescapable destructive environment. Rather it is largely personal problems that impel her to jump into the funeral pyre of her husband. Morbid and depressed, she is "resolved not to save her life, or to prove untrue her husband" (1028). She seeks some recognition or notice, especially from her father, and will "leap from this rack in honor's cause" (1015). She tries to hide her purpose from her father, but she clearly also wants attention. She resorts to riddles: "It would but anger thee to hear what I intend, and so I fain would keep thee ignorant, my father" (1050); again, "Thou wouldst not wisely judge my purpose" (1053). Yet, at the very same time, Evadne, like Sophocles' Antigone, wants her deed to be a model for all Argos (1067).

The final challenge of Evadne to Iphis, her father, before she leaps on her husband's funeral pyre, is worth examining: "Tis all one; thou shalt never catch me in thy grasp, lo! I cast me down, no joy to thee, but to myself and to my husband blazing on the pyre with me" (1070–1071). Indeed, it seems less important for her to burn with her husband than that he burn with her. The father then commences a long soliloquy on his own troubles in old age (1080–1113), showing little concern for Evadne herself. Perhaps her father's indifference is the root of Evadne's anomic behavior and her suicide as she vacillates erratically between a desire for symbiosis and fear of any human contact (position A/C).

Iphigenia in Aulis

Iphigenia, daughter of Agamemnon, is an altruistic suicide in Durkheim's terms. She accepts willingly, almost gladly, the order of a seer that she must be sacrificed before her father's army will be able to sail for Troy. This is ritual murder, not suicide in the twentieth-century use of the word. In this play, however, there is no real distinction. The characters of *Iphigenia in Aulis* are encumbered with the same problem as so many other characters of Hellenic drama — the general cheapness of human life in the heroic view of man.

There is the usual foreboding of calamity. Agamemnon states this very clearly at the beginning of the play. Hubris will be followed by nemesis (23–25), and every man is born to his grief (35–45). Agamemnon laments: "Woe's me for mortal men! None have been happy yet" (162–163). All must go as the fates will; again in Agamemnon's words: "Woe, woe is me, unhappy, caught by fate, outwitted by the cunning of the gods" (442–445). Nevertheless, Agamemnon still feels compelled to slaughter Iphigenia, even when Menelaus relents in his demands for her sacrifice (505–512).

Indeed, Iphigenia herself seems to avoid any active attempt to evade her death. She grasps for a freedom that she does not have by trying to make her death seem voluntary instead of obligatory: "I have chosen death: it is my own free choice. I have put cowardice away from me. Honor is mine now. O mother, say I am right" (1375–1377). Iphigenia is a dependent young girl who attempts to ingratiate herself with her father by offending her mother: "O mother, blame me not! Let me go first/And put my arms about my father's neck" (633–634). Yet the theme of abandonment is constant (637–638, 664): "Mother, my father has gone, Left me, betrayed and alone" (1317–1320).

Iphigenia is at first horrified at the suggestion of her sacrifice. She finally accepts her situation bravely, however, as suits a woman from a heroic family. In addition, she wishes to defend her father against what she perceives as the anger of her mother toward him, "Oh, hate him not — my father, and your husband" (1453). Agamemnon, weak and indecisive, will not commit himself to any course of action that will preserve his daughter's life. The success of the expedition to Troy, his own prestige, and his fear of an attack on his own city seem more important to him.

These problems seem serious enough, but the biggest difficulty again is that classical Greek society offers no stopper — no way out. What is Iphigenia to do? Who is to explain to her that this situation is another Sphinx riddle that offers only a road to obliteration? It seems normal to Iphigenia that she should die in a heroic attempt to help the army and thereby salve her father's feelings, win his approval, and fulfill her family's tradition. This negation of self shows Iphigenia's suicide to be altruistic (position A). She is unable to free herself from the group pressure around her.

The Heracleidae

The Heracleidae begins after the death of Heracles. The family of Heracles seeks refuge in Athens from his old enemy, King Eurystheus of Argos, who wishes to kill them. Demophon of Athens is willing to help the fugitives, but an oracle pronounces that a girl of noble descent must be sacrificed to the goddess Persephone in order for him to defeat the Argives (412–414).

Once again, the characters are faced with a Hobson's choice — the safety of the family versus an individual life. Macaria, the daughter of Heracles, learns of the trouble from Iolaus, her father's old friend. She seemingly takes total responsibility for her brothers while neglecting herself (478–480). Iolaus takes advantage of this self-sacrificing streak in Macaria to pressure her, not very subtly, to resolve the state's perplexity by offering herself as a victim (482–491). Macaria takes the bait, revealing a willingness to let herself be sacrificed for others. Death is welcome to her, as long as it is glorious and freely chosen (510–532).

Iolaus is greatly moved by Macaria's altruistic gesture, praising her as a true daughter of Heracles. He suggests a fairer method — a lottery involving Macaria and her sisters (541–546). Macaria will have none of this! Her sacrifice for others has no meaning if it is imposed through a lottery, nor does she seem to want to avoid the sacrifice through winning the lottery: "My death shall no chance lot decide, there is no graciousness in that peace, old friend. But if ye accept and will avail you of my readiness, freely do I offer my life for those, and without constraint" (541–543). She wishes to protect her sisters, but it is also possible that an altruistic suicidal urge underlies this dramatic gesture in the name of others (position A). She echoes Seneca in stating that one fulfills one's purpose in life most fully by the way in which one leaves it: "For I, by loving not my life too well have found a treasure very fair, a glorious means to leave it" (532–533). This wins the approval of those around her: "Who can speak more noble words or do more noble deeds henceforth for ever?" (534–535), and again: "Daughter, thou art his own true child, no other man's but Heracles; that godlike soul" (539).

She travels the high road of heroism as her fathers did before her. Through her self-sacrifice, Macaria likewise fulfills the way of her father Heracles; perhaps more importantly, she seeks his approval. She must do it freely, however: "Stand by and veil my body with my robe, for I will go even to the dreadful doom of sacrifice, seeing whose daughter I avow myself" (563–564). This seems the epitome of altruistic suicide. She must die to fulfill her father's glory but she must have the heroic sense that she has chosen it freely.

Hecuba

Polyxena, prisoner of the Greek conquerors after the fall of Troy and the last surviving daughter of Queen Hecuba, is another altruistic suicide. Her sense of *noblesse oblige* makes it impossible for her to escape the ritual death demanded of her. The play commences with the Greek fleet ready to return home after sacking Troy. The ghost of Achilles appears and demands that a virgin be sacrificed on his tomb before the fleet can sail. Primal terrors horrify the protagonists: "O'er the summit of his tomb appeared Achilles' phantom, and for his guerdon he would have one of the luckless maids of Troy" (97); the ghost demands: "Whither away so fast, ye Danai, leaving my tomb without its prize" (114). At the very moment of Polyxena's sacrifice, Achilles' son raises the knife and invites his dead sire to come drink the black blood of a pure virgin (536–537).

Euripides' characters seem laden with a sort of primal guilt simply because they exist. For them, the pristine simple world of nature is not to be reworked or improved by man's labors or even by his mere existence. Its virginity is not to be disturbed. Man can expiate the innate foulness of his existence only by returning something in its virgin state to the monstrous and hellish earth that demands its due. What better sacrifice than a young virgin who will now be devoted only to earth and to no one else.

This overwhelming sense of primal guilt adds to the daily pressures of life in captivity to push Polyxena to her death. First, there is her sense of ruin and outrage: "For my own life, its ruin and its outrage, never a tear I shed; nay, death is become to me a happier lot than life" (210–211). The duty of the hero is to act heroically (379–380). Indeed she prefers death to unheroic behavior (348–351).

Rather than rebuke her executioners for murdering her, she forgives them. Like Iphigenia and Macaria, she seeks to create the illusion of control over her own death: "Of my free will I die; let none lay hand on me; for bravely will I yield my neck" (559–562). The Greeks are impressed with the bravery of their Trojan captive, and they unbind her. Polyxena then voluntarily tears open her robe, sinks to her knee, and bares her breast (562–565). Her heroic sense of *noblesse oblige* leads her on to altruistic suicide: "Young prince, if 'tis my breast thou'dst strike, lo! here it is, strike home! or if at my neck thy sword thou'lt aim, behold! that neck is bared" (563–565).

From Polyxena's point of view, this becomes altruistic suicide or martyrdom (position A). She needs to feel that she is dying freely because she cannot confront her captors with their injustice.[11] From the point of view of the Greeks, her ritual sacrifice is a necessary evil, part of the Hobson's choice with which they confronted themselves. Achilles' son is torn emotionally over the necessity of killing a girl so heroic and brave, "half glad, half sorry in his pity for the maid, cleft with the steel the channels of her breath" (560). He seems almost to want not to kill Polyxena, but there is no stopper, no way out!

Alcestis

In one of Euripides' most puzzling plays, King Admetus of Thessaly is told that the fates demand his death unless he can find someone who is willing to die in his place. His aged parents sharply refuse his request, but Alcestis, his young beautiful wife, offers herself (1–27). Both general and personal motives seem to be prompting Alcestis in her decision.

The demands of the gods of the underworld are inexorable and horrifying. Not even the Olympian gods can overrule them. In the opening scene, the god/death meets Apollo in a deadly serious debate for the life of Alcestis (52–55). Man does not really have a right to enjoy his life on the earth. Who he is or what he has accomplished mean nothing. In the end, the netherworld demands. All of this means that one of the characters must die. Alcestis is the one who will satisfy Death's claims. Man's situation is, in its deepest sense, cheerless and hopeless (146–147). He may be met at any moment by the cruel demands of mysterious forces that show him neither mercy nor understanding. Alcestis accepts this view: "But these things are a god's doing and are thus" (297–298). It is perhaps more natural for an intelligent, concerned woman like Alcestis to accept these demands than for a selfish, hypocritical coward like Admetus.

On the personal level, Alcestis' motives for substituting her life for Admetus' are quite complex. She is not a heroic or epic figure, nor does she speak of her debt to heroic ancestors. Rather, she is a lady of the noblest sort (152–154). When the day of her death arrives, she bathes, dresses in her best finery, and prays to the goddess of the earth to watch over her children (158–170). She seeks to comfort each servant in the house individually as they weep sorrowfully over her (192–196).

She bewails, as do so many Greek heroines, the loss of intimacy in her marriage bed (180–182). She puts Admetus first, even before her own life, and seems unable to fulfill herself unless she gives her unworthy husband her entire existence. Admetus' only concern at the death of his wife for him is his own abandonment (277–280).

A puzzling line seems to reveal another aspect of Alcestis' psyche. To Admetus, she says: "But, torn from you, I would not live with fatherless children, nor have I hoarded up those gifts of youth in which I found delight" (283–285). On the surface, this statement makes no sense. Why are the children better off losing Alcestis than losing Admetus? Alcestis appears to be one of those women who must always cover up for a miserably inferior husband. She feels totally responsible for him and can never consider looking at her situation in any other way, whether it kills her in one blow, as here, or makes her life miserable for many years, day by day. Perhaps she fears showing her own weakness or dealing decisively with an unrewarding marriage. Perhaps, simply disillusioned, she is leaving the field and abandoning a totally dependent husband.

The choice here is not the classical Hobson's dilemma of Greek drama. Other protagonists who are offered a chance to die in Admetus' place refuse. This is not the heroism that proves so destructive to Ajax or the house of Atreus. It is rather a false sense of responsibility rooted in an over-idealized conception of herself and an insufficient differentiation from her environment. Alcestis is clearly an altruistic martyr-suicide (position A).

Andromache

The complex plot of Euripides' *Andromache* includes one surrender to be murdered (Andromache) and one attempted anomic suicide (Hermione), both unsuccessful. Andromache, the widow of the Trojan hero Hector, is now a slave concubine of Neoptolemus, son of Achilles. While Neoptolemus is away at Delphi, his jealous wife, Hermione, and her father, Menelaus, threaten to kill Andromache's son unless she surrenders herself to them to be put to death in his stead. When she does so, Menelaus announces that both will be killed. They are saved only by the timely arrival of old Peleus, father of Achilles. As much a coward as a bully, Menelaus withdraws, leaving his prisoners to Peleus. Hermione goes into a panic upon her father's departure (865–868).

She is deeply afraid of what her husband Neoptolemus will say when he hears about her plotting. She might be sent away in a scandal. This leads her to thoughts of suicide (808–810). She will be abominable in the eyes of all men for her deeds (834–839). Only the quick action of her servants restrains her from hanging and later stabbing herself (811–813).

The suicide attempt by Hermione is anomic (position A/C). It is initiated by Menelaus' cowardly abandonment of her in conjunction with her over-dependence on him. In that family, troubled relationships have been passed down from one generation to the next (614–616, 638–639). Yet Hermione's suicide seems to be prevented by her returning home to her father's house, with its seeming protection. Orestes enters her life to rescue her from her immediate difficulty (983–989).

The arrival of a father figure twice saves characters in this play. First, Peleus arrives to save Andromache and her son from Menelaus and Hermione. Second, Menelaus' home, as despicable as he himself may be, provides a suicide-preventive haven for Hermione.

SUMMARY

The world of the Greek drama offers no protection to an individual confronted with a Hobson's choice. The gods are uninvolved and capricious, and they do not intervene to limit the effects of a suicidal cycle. All the narratives resemble the myth of Narcissus, in that they involve fixation and oscillation (the AC axis). Individuation is obtained at the expense of attachment and attachment at the expense of individuation. Suicide is an all too frequent result.

NOTES

1. This quotation and all subsequent quotations from Greek tragedies come from W. J. Oates and E. O'Neill, Jr., *The Complete Greek Drama*.

2. Aristotle offered what has been regarded as the classic definition of tragedy "as an imitation of an action that is serious, complete, and of a certain magnitude; in language embellished with each kind of artistic ornament, the several kinds being found in separate parts of the play; in the form of action, not of narrative, through pity and fear effecting the proper purgation of these and similar emotions" (*Poetics*, Chap. 6). The tragic hero is "a man who is highly renowned and prosperous, but one who is not preeminently virtuous and just, whose misfortune, however, is brought upon him not by vice and depravity but by some error of judgment or frailty" (*Poetics*, chap. 13).

3. Only one possible act of self-destruction occurs in the seven surviving plays of Aeschylus, the third great Greek tragedian. It is the death of Eteocles in *Seven Against Thebes* (692–715). It is not definitively a suicide, however, as opposed to a reckless disdain for life *per se*, and thus will not be treated as such in the present chapter. It will be treated subsequently with regard to the curse of Oedipus.

4. This constant discouragement of Oedipus' and Narcissus' search for self-knowledge seems to contradict the dictum of the Delphic oracle — "Know Thyself." The Delphic dictum actually enjoins that man be aware of his loneliness and powerlessness before the gods and does not in fact command a search for self-knowledge.

5. Indeed, this point of view was invoked by the prosecution at the Nuremberg trials as an argument that German citizens were obligated to disobey Hitler's racist and genocidal laws.

6. Faber (1970, 84) has made exactly this same point about Antigone. "Is it

possible that Antigone, who is often singled out as the most individualistic of Greek heroines, is, in reality, one of the least individualistic? For I believe that what we have here is a person whose own integration into the family unit and whose deep preoccupation with the opinion of the community at large have prevented her from achieving the autonomy, the sense of individual worth, which is usually accorded her." Indeed, it is remarkable that Western thought has idealized Antigone and ignored the pathological curse of the house of Labdacus that underlies her heroism. Clearly Sophocles himself did recognize it.

7. See also Philipians 1.21: "For me to live is Christ and to die is gain" and related discussion in Chapter 3.

8. The noted translator Elizabeth Wyckoff has written that this line is Ismene's in almost all manuscripts. The only traditional evidence for giving this line to Antigone is that the Aldine edition (1502) and Turnebus (1553) gave it to her (1960, 227–228).

9. This play is named after the Phoenissae, a group of Phoenician women who represent the point of view of outsiders and who view the events occurring in Thebes from an uninvolved point of view.

10. Megareus, the other son of Creon, was one of the Theban champions who defended a gate of the city, in Aeschylus' *Seven Against Thebes*. Euripides in *The Phoenissae* calls him Menoeceus and presents another version of his death.

11. Contrast the altruistic Greek heroine with Rabbi Akiba who at the moment of death recited the Shema ("Hear O Israel, the Lord is our God, the Lord is one"). Akiba reconfirmed his faith in God and in life and did not need to seek illusory control by pretending to die willingly.

Chapter 6

Suicide and Suicide Prevention in the Hebrew Bible

But he [Elijah] himself went a day's journey into the wilderness, and came and sat down under a broom tree; and he requested for himself that he might die, and said, "It is enough; now O Lord, take away my life; for I am not better than my fathers." And he lay down and slept under a broom tree; and behold, an angel touched him, and said unto him, "Arise and eat." . . . And he arose, and did eat and drink, and went on the strength of that meal forty days and forty nights unto Horeb the mount of God.

1 Kings 19.4–8

The relative infrequency of suicide in the Hebrew Bible is striking when compared to Greek narratives. The entire Tanach presents only six cases (Ahitophel, Zimri, Abimelech, Samson, Saul, and Saul's armor-bearer). More significant for our theme are several additional figures who express a wish to die or to kill themselves yet do not carry it through (e.g., Elijah, Moses, David, Job, and Jonah). There seem to be two major reasons for this. First, the basic Biblical thought pattern rejects the pressing necessity of constantly making Hobson's choices (the A–C choices in Figure 1.2). Second, in trying situations, God acts as a positive parent or therapist protecting his confused children and providing the necessary stopper to support the individual in his time of need (See Figure 1.3).

Not all the Biblical suicides conform to Shneidman's definition of suicide as "a conscious act of self-induced annihilation." L. D. Hankoff (1979, 6) has suggested that the six suicides have the following characteristics in common. "All of the self-destructive behaviors were plausible having clearcut precipitants or situations which offered the reader an understandable explanation for the self-destruction. All were males in a state of physical stress or apt to be in mortal danger at the hands of enemies very shortly, and in the midst of a turbulent, rapidly moving situation. All but one, Saul's armor-bearer, were prominent people whose positions of leadership were seriously damaged or threatened."

Durkheim's typology can be applied once again to these suicides. Three of the six suicides (Ahitophel, Zimri, and Abimelech) seem egoistic, one (Saul's armor-bearer) is altruistic, and none are anomic. Two (Samson and Saul) can be termed "covenantal." (See Table 6.1.)

The Bible is not obsessed with the sense of heroism so endemic to the Greek world, nor is there the Greek dualism between body and soul. The Biblical God is a strong and nurturant parent, not a capricious deity. Man's highest goal is thus to be obedient to God's will rather than to liberate the soul from the body. Freedom is toward something rather than merely away. Man does not have to earn love through fame or achievement, for it comes unconditionally from God, nor is there the same sense of the tragic that exists in the Greek world. Man is free to choose good over evil. There is no belief in doom, and there is always the possibility of prayer, repentance, atonement, and genuine change. A person's life is not warped beyond cure or without hope. Prophecy in the Hebrew Biblical world typically aims at social intervention. *Consequence Y will occur unless some antecedent X intervenes.* The people of Nineveh will be destroyed, unless they repent (Jonah). But it is the possibility of the saving antecedent X that gives the Hebrew Bible an inspiring therapeutic vision rather than a tragic one, and this possibility makes the prophet a concerned messenger of God rather than a taunting actuary. If the Biblical prophet is successful in his endeavors, then his dire predictions will not come to pass.

Finally, Biblical characters do not face the same Hobson's choices that Greek heroes do. They are not presented with riddling sphinxes and oracles that distort their sense of judgment. Even when they do seem to be mired in no–win situations, there is typically a stopper — an opportunity to return to their covenant to deepen their relationship with God. *In short, the Hebrew Bible is not a Greek tragedy.*

EGOISTIC SUICIDE

Ahitophel, a counselor of King David, joins Absalom's rebellion. Seeing that Absalom has been tricked into following a foolhardy plan certain to lead to David's victory, Ahitophel sets his house in order and strangles himself:

And when Ahitophel saw that his counsel was not followed, he saddled his ass and arose, and got himself home unto the city; and set his house in order, and strangled himself; and he died and was buried in the sepulcher of his father. (2 Sam. 17.23)

Table 6.1
Suicide in the Hebrew Bible

Character	Gender	Source		Method	Type
Ahitophel	M	2 Sam.	17:23	Strangled	Egoistic
Zimri	M	1 Kings	16:18	Burning	Egoistic
Abimelech	M	Judges	9:54	Sword	Egoistic
Samson	M	Judges	16:30	Crushing	Covenantal
Saul	M	1 Sam.	31:4	Sword	Covenantal
		2 Sam.	1:6		
		1 Chron.	10:4		
Saul's Armor Bearer	M	1 Sam	31:5	Sword	Altruistic
		1 Chron.	10:5		

One of several reasons, all egoistic, probably prompt Ahitophel's suicide. First, he now fears that Absalom's attempt to overthrow David is doomed and that he will die a traitor's death. Second, and less likely, is Ahitophel's disgust at Absalom's conduct in setting aside his counsel, thus wounding Ahitophel's pride and disappointing his ambition. Third, David's curse may have prompted Ahitophel to hang himself (*Makkot*, 4a). Finally, rabbinic writers have also argued that since Ahitophel is a suicide, his family inherits his estate. If he were to be executed as a rebel, his possessions would be forfeit to the king. Ahitophel thus seems to be an egoistic suicide (position C) and is listed in the Mishna (*Sanhedrin*, 10.2) as among those who have forfeited their share in the world to come.

The wicked Zimri is an egoistic suicide (position C) with no redeeming qualities. King Elah of Israel passes his days drinking in his palace while his warriors battle the Philistines. Zimri, a high-ranking officer, takes advantage of the situation, assassinates Elah, and mounts the throne. His reign, however, lasts only seven days. As soon as the news of King Elah's murder reaches the army on the battlefield, General Omri is proclaimed King and lays siege to the palace. When Zimri sees that he is unable to hold out against the siege, he sets fire to the palace and perishes in the flames: "And it came to pass, when Zimri saw that the city was taken that he went into the castle of the king's house, and burnt the king's house over him with fire, and he died" (1 Kings 16.18).

Abimelech, strictly speaking, is an assisted suicide. After carving out a principality for himself in Israel by various brutalities, he receives a mortal wound from a stone thrown by a woman from a fortress that he is besieging. Realizing that he is dying, Abimelech asks his armor-bearer to finish him off so that it will not be said that a woman has killed him. This act of hubris qualifies him as an egoistic suicide (position C).

And a certain woman cast an upper millstone upon Abimelech's head, and broke his skull. Then he called hastily unto the young man his armor-bearer, and said unto him: "Draw this sword, and kill me, that men not say of me: A woman slew him." And his young man thrust him through and he died. (Judges 9.53–57)

COVENANTAL SUICIDE

Samson, the great defender and leader of the Israelites, has been blinded and publicly mocked by the Philistines. Faced with torture and death, he asks God for the strength to take as many Philistines with him as possible and pulls down the central pillars of the temple of Dagon, killing thousands in one last blow:

And Samson called unto the Lord and said: "O Lord God, remember me, I pray thee, and strengthen me." . . . And Samson took fast hold of the two middle pillars upon which the house rested, and leaned upon them, the one with his right hand, and the other with his left. And Samson said: "Let me die with the Philistines." And he bent with all his might, and the house fell upon the lords, and upon all the people that were therein. (Judges 16.23–31)

It is tempting to see Samson as a Biblical equivalent of Sophocles' Ajax. Samson, like Ajax, has fallen from his previous state of leadership. Is Samson too employing suicide to restore his lost image in the eyes of others? Closer examination indicates that Samson's suicide is not egoistic like that of Ajax. Samson is not alienated from his society, but rather very much a part of the people of Israel. His uncut hair is part of his Nazarite consecration to God, not a symbol of macho heroism. He loses his strength when he abandons his consecration by cutting his hair. His death is not an attempt to restore his own lost honor at the expense of his people, but comes about in his effort to strike a telling blow against the enemies of Israel.

Is then Samson's suicide altruistic and self-sacrificing? This interpretation too must be rejected. Samson does not suffer from a failing sense of his own personality. Rather, he calls upon the Lord God to strengthen him in his final attempt to destroy the Philistines. His purpose is not self-annihilation but the carrying out of his divinely ordained mission to free Israel from the Philistines. Thus, Samson's suicide seems to be neither egoistic nor altruistic but may be labeled covenantal (position B), in the sense that it is in the service of the Biblical God, with neither over-isolation (position C) nor over-integration (position A) in his boundaries with his society. Significantly, his action leads to a long period of peace (Judges 13).

A second covenantal suicide is that of King Saul. Rabbinic literature has regarded King Saul as a man of great stature, the anointed of the Lord. Yet his reign is marked by series of mistakes, ending with his suicide during a losing battle against the Philistines on Mount Gilboa. Here, Saul sees three sons and many of his fighters slain and is himself severely wounded. Surrounded by enemies and not wishing to be taken prisoner and exposed to the mockery and brutality of the Philistines, King Saul entreats his armor-bearer to kill him. The latter refuses and Saul falls on his own sword: "Then said Saul to his armor-bearer: 'Draw thy sword, and thrust me through therewith; lest these uncircumcised come and make a mock of me.' But his armor-bearer would not; for he was sore afraid. Therefore Saul took his sword, and fell upon it" (1 Samuel 31.1–4).

The suicide of Saul has been taken by commentators in different ways. The Midrash Rabbah (on Genesis 9.5) has pointed to Saul as an example of a permissible suicide (see also *Midrash Rabbah, 34.13* and *Shulchan Aruch, Yoreh Deah*, 345.3). One commentator has considered Saul as a special case because, before the final battle with the Philistines, he receives a message from the witch of Endor that he will die. By taking his own life, he is therefore not defying Providence. Other commentators have viewed Saul as an example of a suicide who takes his own life in order to avoid greater profanation of the divine name. In this view, Saul fears that if he is captured alive by the Philistines, they will desecrate his body, either by torture or by forcing him to commit idolatrous acts. This interpretation means that suicide may be permissible if it is committed in order to prevent dishonor to God's name rather than for personal reasons. As such, Saul's suicide can be classified as covenantal rather than as either egoistic or altruistic.[1]

Two of Saul's earlier actions place him in conflict between excessive altruism and egoism (Kaplan and Schwartz 1990). King Saul provokes God's rejection of his kingship over Israel because, in his attack on Amalek, he fails to destroy all the livestock and also spares the life of King Agag (1 Sam. 15.7–9). God then reveals to Samuel that he has rejected Saul's kingship because Saul has not fulfilled the divine intention of completely obliterating the nefarious Amalek (1 Sam. 15.10–23). Here Saul is being overly altruistic (position A).

In the second case, Saul orders the murder of the priests of Nob and accuses them of siding with the innocent David, the newly anointed one of God, in his flight (1 Sam. 22.13). Ahimelech, a priest of Nob, protests the innocence of the priests, but Saul orders his servants to kill them. When they refuse to kill "the priests of the Lord," Saul turns to the informer Doeg the Edomite who carries out the murderous job, killing not only the priests but all their livestock (1 Sam. 22.18–19). Eventually, God departs from Saul and will no longer answer him (1 Sam. 28.6). In this case, Saul is being overly egoistic (position C).

In neither situation does Saul's response fit the precipitating event, and

God strongly disapproves of his actions. In fact, the two decisions can be seen as polarities along the counter-normative AC axis. First, Saul spares King Agag. This act is too altruistic (position A) and does not maintain a sufficiently impermeable defensive wall for Saul against the very dangerous and aggressive King Agag. In the second case, he attacks the sanctified priests of God. This act is too egoistic (position C) and represents an overly impermeable wall against people who have not harmed him. Vacillating, he first *underreacts* against the real threat of the Amalekites and then *overreacts* against the innocent priests of Nob for helping David.

The rabbis of the Talmud have described a voice coming from heaven after the incident of Amalek, saying "Be not overly righteous." After the Nob incident, the voice again comes, saying "Be not overly wicked." The point is that one who pities the wicked will eventually be cruel when he should be merciful (*Babylonian Talmud, Yoma*, 22b; Rosenberg 1976).

ALTRUISTIC SUICIDE

The suicide of Saul's armor-bearer can be classified as altruistic because of his seeming lack of differentiation from Saul (position A): "And when his armor-bearer saw that Saul was dead, he likewise fell upon his sword and died with him" (1 Sam. 31.5). The Biblical passage relates that the armor-bearer first refuses to kill Saul and then falls on his sword in response to Saul's suicide. An Amalekite comes to David and reports that he assisted in Saul's suicide. For this, David orders him killed (2 Sam. 1.9–10, 14–16). Commentaries have seen David as behaving correctly in condemning the Amalekite to death, even though the Amalekite was simply following Saul's orders in assisting Saul to die (Ralbag on 2 Sam. 1.14).

There is no example of Durkheim's anomic suicide in the Hebrew Bible. The six suicides seem to be either egoistic, altruistic, or covenantal. The most sympathetic rabbinic treatment is given to the covenantal suicides (Samson and Saul). The harshest judgments are applied to suicides that seem clearly egoistic (Ahitophel, Zimri, and Abimelech).

BIBLICAL SUICIDE PREVENTION

In contrast to the cycles of heroism and suicide so endemic to Greek narratives, the Hebrew Bible recounts a number of interventions that prevent situations of despair from becoming full-blown suicide attempts. The Jewish sacred literature completely prefers living to suicide.

The Hebrew Bible portrays God as intervening, much as a good therapist might, to deflect the death wishes uttered by one Biblical character or another. Two themes stand in marked contrast to Greek literature. First, the Biblical characters are not typically under pressure to make a decision that will destroy them. Second, God provides a stopper, offering the characters a chance to overcome their problems (Table 6.2).

Table 6.2
Suicide Prevention in the Hebrew Bible

Character	Gender	Source	Method employed by God
Elijah	M	I Kings 18-19	Protected Withdrawal and Nuturance
Moses	M	Numbers II	Support and Practical Advice
David	M	Psalms 22	Renewal of Faith
Job	M	Job	Renewal of Relationship
Jeremiah	M	Jeremiah	Punishment of Evil
Rebecca	F	Genesis 27-28	Appropriate Matchmaking
Jonah	M	Jonah	Protected Withdrawal and Guidance

Elijah

Elijah reaches a peak of triumph (1 Kings 18.41) when he gains a stunning moral and political victory over the priests of Baal in their confrontation on Mt. Carmel. Even King Ahab supports Elijah, and now God has sent rain to end the long drought in Israel. Queen Jezebel, Ahab's Phoenician wife, remains recalcitrant, however. She threatens to kill Elijah, and he flees for his life to the desert of Be'er Sheva. There he sits alone under a bush and asks God to take away his life for "he is no better than his fathers."

But he himself went a day's journey into the wilderness, and came and sat down under a broom tree; and he requested for himself that he might die, and said, "It is enough; now O Lord, take away my life; for I am not better than my fathers." (1 Kings 19.4)

Does this express the same serious suicidal wish that we are accustomed to seeing in Greek stories? Perhaps not. Had death been Elijah's true objective, he could have let himself be killed by Jezebel. Instead, he flees to Judah, which is not under her rule, to seek safety. Nevertheless, Elijah is exhausted and deeply disappointed at the failure that has followed so soon after his moment of seeming victory. Elijah falls into despair, questioning the very value of his own life. This is consistent with the Greek cyclical plunge from hubris into nemesis. By contrast, however, his suicidal outburst is treated by God as a call for help. Elijah is first given rest, and then, unlike Sophocles' Ajax or Euripides' Phaedra, is twice provided with food and drink by an angel of God to prepare him for the work that remains to be done (1 Kings 19.5–8):[2]

And he lay down and slept under a broom tree; and behold, an angel touched him, and said unto him: "Arise and eat." . . . And he arose, and did eat and drink, and went on the strength of that meal forty days and forty nights into Horeb the mount of God. (1 Kings 19.5–8)

Elijah eats and drinks and then walks for forty days to the desert of Sinai to the cave (Metsudat David on 2 Kings 19.9) where Moses had received the Torah from God. Elijah goes back to the roots (position B) of Israelite thought and prophecy in order to regenerate himself and overcome his despair and self-doubt (movement ahead on the BED axis). God provides the stopper that is so missing in the Greek narratives by confronting Elijah in a mighty but loving theophany, discussing Elijah's problems with him, and providing him with guidance in carrying on. The potentially suicidal crisis overcome, Elijah is then assigned several new tasks, including the job of training Elisha as his successor (1 Kings 19.9–14).

Moses

Deeply disappointed over the complaints of the Hebrews, Moses cries out to God that the responsibilities of leading the people are too great and that God should kill him:

And Moses said unto the LORD, "Wherefore hast thou dealt ill with thy servant? And wherefore have I not found favor in Thy sight, that Thou layest the burden of all this people upon me? Have I conceived all this people? Have I brought them forth, that Thou shouldest say unto me. 'Carry them in thy bosom as a nursing-father carrieth the sucking child, unto the land which Thou didst swear unto their fathers?' Whence should I have flesh to give unto all this people? For they trouble me with their weeping saying 'Give us flesh that we may eat.' I am not able to bear all this people myself alone, because the burden is too heavy for me. If Thou deal thus with me, kill me, I pray Thee, out of hand, if I have found favor in Thy sight, and let me not look upon my wretchedness." (Num. 11.11–15)[3]

Moses is expressing his weariness and frustration with regard to going on alone (position C) with his burden (position A). His complaint to God may thus be seen as a message, a bargaining point, rather than as a serious desire for death. If you do not help me with my burden, then go ahead and kill me. Nevertheless, suicides do occur in frustrating situations such as this, even when the original intent is not death. God, the divine therapist, does listen and intervenes with a stopper (position B), a positive, practical solution. Let Moses select seventy elders to help him lead the Israelites (Num. 11.16–19).

David

Feelings of despair, abandonment, and even suicidal thoughts are apparent in many of David's psalms, but the psalmist renews his faith with God and overcomes these feelings of heavy self-doubt. An example of this process can be seen in the famous twenty-second psalm. It begins in despair over the psalmist's perception of his complete and utter abandonment by God (position C).

> My God, my God, why hast Thou forsaken me
> And art far from my help at the words of my cry?
> O my God, I call by day, but
> Thou answerest not.
> (Psalms 22.1-3)

Indeed this first verse is cited in the Gospels as the last words of Christ upon the cross (Matt. 27.46).

Psalm 22 continues, however, with a return by the psalmist to roots of his faith — to the earliest stages of trust (Erikson 1968). He overcomes the reproach of mockers and, like Elijah at Sinai, recovers his faith and overcomes his despair (position B).

> For Thou art He that took me out of the womb;
> Thou madest me trust when I was upon
> my mother's breasts.
> Upon thee I have been cast from my birth,
> Thou art my God from my mother's womb.
> (Psalms 22.9-11)

God provides the stopper. He has been the rock of the psalmist's faith since the primal experiences of birth and nursing. This basic trust that the psalmist has established with God is sufficient to overcome the writer's doubts and fears of abandonment:

> Neither hath He hid His face from him;
> But when he cried unto Him, He heard.
> (Psalms 22.24)

Job

The Book of Job is, of course, an immense topic all on its own. A just man, Job is assailed by a series of awesome misfortunes — the loss of his wealth, his family, and his health (AC axis). He is deeply grieved by these events, but his existential faith in God and life is not destroyed. He searches for reassurance that God has not forsaken him. Pat answers will not do for Job, nor a simple glorification of suffering. Job is strong, questioning, and unrelenting in his demands in his relationship with God. He does not turn to suicide as an answer but drives his way through to a deepened affirmation of life.

Job does express what a modern suicidologist might interpret as a threat of suicide: "So that my soul chooseth strangling and death rather than these my bones. I loathe it; I shall not live always. Let me alone; for my days are vanity" (Job 7.15–16). Still, Job is really interested in a reaffirmation of his relationship with God.

Job maintains his innocence in his suffering (9.21), refusing to be silent (10.1), and again expressing weariness of life while calling on God for meaning, saying: "My soul is weary of my life" (10.1). Even so, he again refuses to be silent: "I will say unto God: Do not condemn me; make me know wherefore Thou contendest with me" (10.2). Job finds strength in his faith (position B): "Though He slay me, yet will I trust in Him" (13.15). Indeed, he will continue to trust God no matter what God does to him. He asks only that God maintain an open relationship with him: "Call then and I will answer, or let me speak and answer thou me" (13.22). Beginning in chapter 38, God does speak directly to Job, confirming the importance of their continuing relationship and God's care for His creation (38).

Jeremiah

A sense of grief and loss appears in certain passages of the book of Jeremiah and in the book of Lamentations, also ascribed to Jeremiah. In chapter 20, the prophet speaks of his disappointment with life in the most uncompromising terms:

> Cursed be the day wherein I was born!
> The day wherein my mother bore me,
> Let it not be blessed! . . .
> Wherefore came I forth out of the womb
> To see labor and sorrow,
> That my days should be consumed in shame.
> (Jeremiah 20.14,18)

These thoughts are the despairing words of a very sensitive man who is overwhelmed by the evil and suffering that he sees around him. Yet, protected by his faith (position B), there is no indication that he thinks of suicide, nor do the rabbinic commentators find any hint of suicide in his words. His belief that God will indeed punish evil comes across clearly in an earlier passage in chapter 20:

Sing unto the Lord;
Praise ye the Lord!
For he hath delivered the soul of the needy
From the hand of evil-doers.

(Jeremiah 20.13)

Rebecca

After participating in the deception by which Jacob obtains Isaac's blessing, Rebecca sends him away to his Uncle Laban, lest he be killed by an
angry Esau (Gen. 27.42–45). Immediately afterward, Rebecca tells Isaac
that her life has been made miserable (position A) by Esau's Hittite wives,
and she worries lest Jacob marry similarly:

And Rebecca said to Isaac: "I am weary of my life because of the daughters of
Heth. If Jacob take a wife of the daughters of Heth, such as these, of the daughters
of the land, what good shall my life do me?" (Gen. 27.46)

Although this has been read as a "suicidal ideation" narrative, such interpretation is far overdrawn and matches neither the wording of the text
nor the best of scholarly opinion. Rebecca's words seem more like a message to her husband—"please fix this situation because I can't stand it." In
any case, the tactic works, and Isaac involves God as a stopper in his command that Jacob not marry a daughter of Canaan so offensive to Rebecca.
Let him instead marry a daughter of Laban, a kinsman (position B). Rebecca is presumably satisfied, and there is no more mention of her "suicidal"
musings (Gen. 28.1–4).

SUMMARY

The Hebrew Bible contains many stories in which God intervenes in the
lives of characters who express some sort of death wish. He does not place
characters in a Hobson's choice situation in which they are compelled to
make a decision that will destroy them. Further, God plays the role of a
stopper, offering the characters a chance to overcome their problems. All
these narratives thus resemble the story of Jonah. Individuals are offered
special support (B) to prevent them from committing suicide. This is not a
suicidal return to an "inanimate state," as Freud described it, but rather a
protective intervention that allows the individual to understand that his
life is important to God and that God will help him to seek fulfillment in
his relationship with God and with the world.

NOTES

1. See Herman van Praag (1986) on the depression of King Saul.
2. Showing consideration for others by giving them food shows up several times

in the Biblical account of Elijah. God sends Elijah food, carried by ravens, from the table of King Asa of Judah. It is Elijah whom God sends to announce the end of the frightful famine in Ahab's kingdom. Elijah also saves the woman of Zarephath and her son from starvation. After the excitement and exhaustion of the confrontation on Mt. Carmel, it is Elijah who reassures King Ahab and gets him to eat and drink. Finally, when Elijah comes to Elisha to anoint him as his successor, Elisha slaughters his two oxen to provide a feast for his family and friends to celebrate his new elevation (Radak on 1 Kings 18.4, 19.14).

3. The rabbinic commentator Rashi has suggested that Moses could not bear to see the punishment that he thought was coming to his people.

III

FAMILY INFLUENCES

Chapter 7

Couples: Polarization versus Growth

When he had made the lovely curse, the price for the blessing of fire, he brought her to a place where gods and men were gathered, and the girl was thrilled by all her pretty trappings, given by mighty Zeus' daughter with grey eyes. Amazement seized the mortal men and gods, to see the hopeless trap, deadly to man.

Hesiod, Theogony, 11.587–593

And the Lord God said: "It is not good that man should be alone; I will make a helper fit for him." . . . And the man called his wife's name Eve, because she was the mother of all living. And the Lord God made for Adam and for his wife garments of skins, and clothed them.

Gen. 2.18, 3.20–21

Couples in the Greek world oscillate between enmeshment and disengagement. Mothers show a fear of individuation (position A), while fathers manifest a fear of attachment (position C). Couples in the Biblical world, in contrast, show greater balance or congruence between individuation and attachment (the BED axis). Although parents with problems in the areas of enmeshment and disengagement may not always be suicidal themselves, they are more likely to produce offspring who are. In his important book on family treatment of suicide, Joseph Richman (1986) has emphasized the suicidogenic implications of family symbiosis and separation issues. First, a child's efforts at individuation disrupt the family system and are seen by the family as a threat. Second, members of the family may see the formation of intimate attachments outside the family as threatening, as if there can be only one intimate attachment or one social group. The threat to the family is that of loss or separation. Finally, disturbances in the family communication system, an intolerance for crisis, and an accumulation of crisis situations all culminate in double-bind dilemmas in which suicide is perceived as the only possible solution.

Pathological and healthy couples are distinguished in Figures 7.1 and 7.2 (Kaplan 1990b). Figure 7.1 presents the pathological AC axis. Position AA represents an enmeshed couple type, position CC a disengaged couple type, and position AC, a rejection-intrusion couple type.[1]

Enmeshed couples (position AA) are afraid of autonomy but not of bonding. They are attached but not individuated. Conflict emerges when the parties in the couple become too remote from each other. Disengaged couples (position CC) are afraid of bonding but not of autonomy. They are individuated but not attached. Conflict emerges when the two people become too intimate (Kohut 1971; Minuchin 1974). In a rejection-intrusion couple (AC), one partner (C) is afraid of entrapment while the other (A) is afraid of responsibility and abandonment. The A partner wants togetherness while the C partner wants freedom (Napier 1978; Willi 1982).

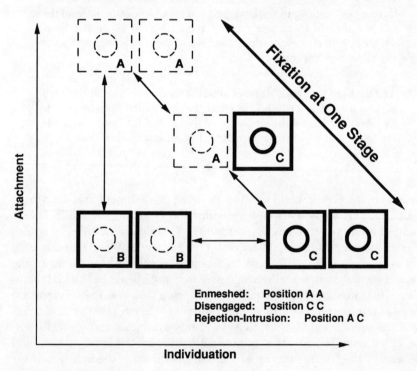

Figure 7.1
The Couple Clinical Axis

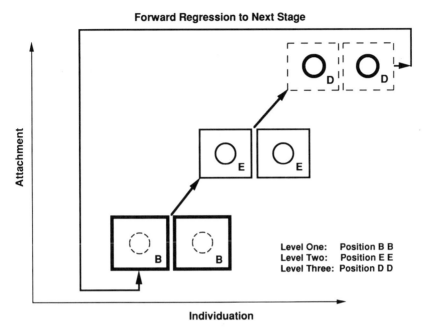

Figure 7.2
The Couple Developmental Axis

Figure 7.2 describes healthy couple development. Immature reciprocal couples (BB) are neither individuated nor attached, fearing both bonding and autonomy. Conflict emerges when the partners become too intimate with each other or too remote. Emerging reciprocal couples (EE) are semi-individuated and semi-attached. The partners do not fear either bonding or autonomy, nor do they need it. Their relationship is neither close nor distant. Mature couples (DD) are highly individuated and highly attached, needing both bonding and autonomy. They can enjoy both intimacy and separation.

Healthy couple growth involves the step-by-step replacement of inter-personal defenses or walls by healthy self-definition or boundaries. Weak-ening the walls before the boundaries are strong enough or leaving them up after the boundaries have formed leads to pathological outcomes. Let us use this model to study two early Greek and two early Biblical "couples."

GREEK MARITAL PATTERNS

Prometheus and Pandora are the closest thing to a Greek first couple. Deucalion and Pyrrha are the couple who experience a great flood.

Prometheus and Pandora

The choice of Prometheus and Pandora requires some explanation, since they are not actually a couple at all. It is Prometheus' brother, Epimetheus, who is married to Pandora. Nevertheless, the leading male and female roles in this story are played by Prometheus and Pandora, even though there is no indication in the myth that they ever meet each other. This lack of a true original couple may in itself indicate the underlying feeling among the Greeks that male-female relationships are somewhat of an aberration.

The following events can be highlighted for our purposes:

1. Prometheus attempts to make man autonomous by stealing fire and the mechanical arts from the gods. This enrages Zeus who obtains revenge by sending Pandora, a seductive but deceitful woman to Epimetheus, the brother of Prometheus, to be the "ruin of mankind" (Hesiod, *Works and Days*, 60–86).

2. Prometheus warns Epimetheus against becoming entrapped by Pandora and tells his brother not to accept any presents from Zeus. Epimetheus forgets the warning (87–90).

3. Pandora opens Epimetheus' jar, releasing every manner of pain and evil into the world, leaving hope alone still locked up (90–96).

4. Prometheus is bound to a cliff at the edge of the world to punish him for helping man (Hesiod, *Theogony*, 616–620).

5. Pandora becomes the progenitress of women and female kind. From her comes the deadly female race, who live with mortal men and bring them harm (591–594).

Because Epimetheus fails to carry out the job of achieving autonomy for mankind, Prometheus must intervene, but on the sly. He steals fire and the technical arts for man; these are the basis for human civilization (Plato, *Protagoras*, 320–322). A tragic figure, Prometheus must act in isolation (C) from the gods (see Figure 7.3).[2] At the same time, Prometheus unsuccessfully warns Epimetheus against becoming entrapped by Pandora (A), who releases evils, such as sickness and old age, into the world. This enmeshment is exacerbated by the suicidogenic hopelessness of the situation; hope alone is still trapped in the jar of Epimetheus and unavailable to man.

Epimetheus is thus a passive object between Prometheus and Pandora. Prometheus is wary and rejecting, warning Epimetheus against Pandora, while Pandora is controlling and entrapping, undoing Prometheus' hard-won autonomy with her jar of evils (AC).[3]

Zeus's acquiescence and even desire for this type of narcissistic male-female relationship is evidenced by his role in the entire affair. His cruelty and pathological need for control set up the antagonism between Prometheus and Pandora. It is, after all, Zeus who withholds fire from man,

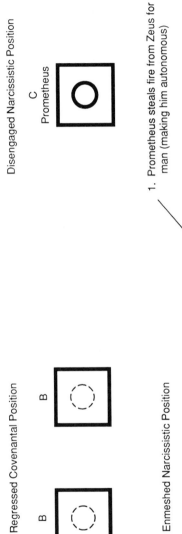

Regressed Covenantal Position

Disengaged Narcissistic Position

C
Prometheus

B   B

Enmeshed Narcissistic Position

A
Pandora

Narcissistic Collusion

1. Prometheus steals fire from Zeus for man (making him autonomous)

3. Prometheus warns Epimetheus not to be trapped by Pandora

5. Prometheus is now led to a cliff at the edge of the world for being champion of men

2. Deceitful Pandora created by Zeus to punish mankind

4. Pandora opens Epimetheus' jar (entrapping him)

6. Pandora creates race of women and female kind

Advanced Covenantal Position

D   D

Figure 7.3
Prometheus and Pandora

forcing Prometheus to steal it. It is Zeus who makes Pandora deceitful and sends her to entrap man. And finally, it is Zeus who attempts to maintain the respective narcissistic positions of man and woman by arranging their continuing enmity.

Deucalion and Pyrrha

This polarized pattern is further illustrated in the Greek story of the flood and of Deucalion and Pyrrha. As depicted in Apollodorus (1.7–2), the conflict is not between Deucalion and Pyrrha, who seem decent enough people, but between them and Zeus, who, out of personal pique, sends a great flood to destroy mankind. He fails in his aim; a few people escape the flood by climbing onto high mountain peaks. Deucalion and Pyrrha survive by building a boat on the sly with help from Prometheus. When the flood is over, Deucalion sacrifices to Zeus who allows him to rebuild the human race. Zeus has the last laugh, however, for mankind is created from stones cast separately by Deucalion and Pyrrha. He makes the men, and she the women.

Ovid focused on Deucalion and Pyrrha, good and decent people who are lonely for human company. They pray to Themis (not to Zeus, as in Apollodorus) and eventually puzzle out the instructions of the goddess to toss the bones of their "great mother" earth over their shoulders. Her "bones" are stones that repeople the wet and empty world (Ovid, *Metamorphosis*, 1.381–398).

The following events in the above narratives may be highlighted (Figure 7.4 represents this schematically):

1. Deucalion is the son of Prometheus; Pyrrha is the daughter of Pandora (and Epimetheus).
2. Zeus sends a flood to destroy the Bronze race of men without warning Deucalion and Pyrrha.
3. Prometheus, however, warns Deucalion and advises the couple how to build a boat.
4. Deucalion and Pyrrha are saved by the ark during the flood and are described as a happy couple. After the flood, Deucalion and Pyrrha emerge from the boat. Deucalion asks the gods (either Zeus or Themis, depending on the account) for a renewal of the human race.
5. Zeus responds and arranges to repopulate the world by having men spring from stones thrown by Deucalion and women from stones thrown by Pyrrha (rather than from their sexual union).

At first, Pyrrha and Deucalion seem to fall into the rejection-intrusion (AC) pattern of their respective parents, Pandora and Prometheus. Zeus sent a flood to destroy humanity. His narcissistic attempts to drown them

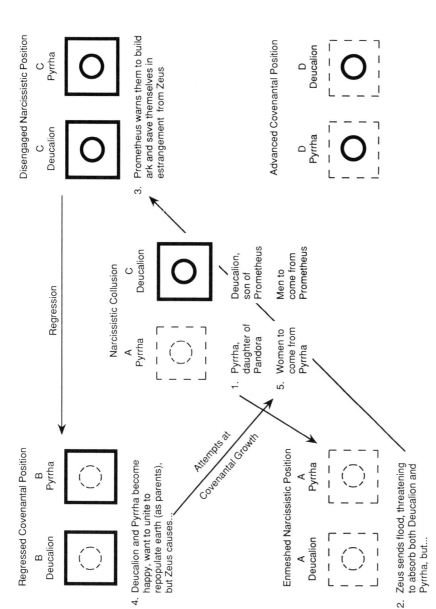

Figure 7.4
Deucalion and Pyrrha

drive the couple into an enmeshed (AA) collusion with him, while Prometheus' intervention pushes them to the opposite polarity, a disengaged (CC) collusion against Zeus. They escape the flood by building a boat of which Zeus is ignorant. Their time together on the boat seems to tilt them off their narcissistic collusion, establishing the beginning of a developmentally healthy relationship (position BB); Ovid described them as a happy couple. Rather than allow this relationship to mature, however, Zeus quickly repolarizes it, causing women to come from Pyrrha and men to come from Deucalion,[4] reestablishing the narcissistic (AC) collusion. Zeus seeks thereby to weaken the basis of family life and the continuity of generations so that people will never be able to develop secure, harmonious, and supportive family patterns.

BIBLICAL MARITAL PATTERNS

Adam and Eve are the original Biblical couple; Noah and his wife live through the great flood and the subsequent renewal of life.

Adam and Eve

Adam and Eve differ from Prometheus and Pandora in that they are clearly a married couple.

The following events can be summarized:

1. God commands Adam not to eat of the tree of knowledge lest he die (Gen. 2.16–17).
2. God creates Eve for Adam from his rib (2.18–22).
3. The serpent entraps Eve to eat of this tree; Eve entraps Adam (3.1–7).
4. Adam and Eve hide from God, attempting unsuccessfully to deny their act (3.8–10).
5. When they are caught, Adam blames Eve; Eve blames the serpent (3.11–12).
6. Instead of killing them, God makes clothes and exiles them from Eden (3.22–23).
7. In exile, they will come to know the pain and toil of earning a livelihood and raising children (3.17–20).

Adam and Eve are in a rejection-intrusion (AC) dilemma with each other. She is entrapped by the serpent to eat the fruit and in turn entraps Adam to eat. Adam retaliates by blaming Eve while she, in turn, blames the serpent. Beneath Eve's entrapment of Adam lies a fear of alone taking the responsibility and consequences for her act (position A). Thus Figure 7.5 portrays her as being initially in the A position. Adam's blaming reflects his effort to place the entire responsibility on Eve and avoid any share

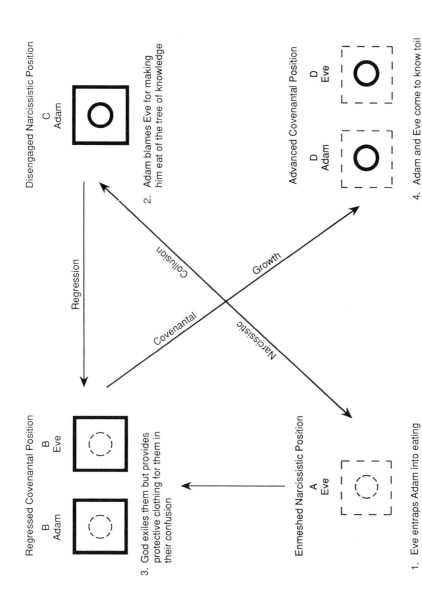

Disengaged Narcissistic Position

C
Adam

2. Adam blames Eve for making him eat of the tree of knowledge

Regression

Collusion

Growth

Covenantal

Narcissistic

Advanced Covenantal Position

D
Adam

D
Eve

4. Adam and Eve come to know toil and pain and parentage

Regressed Covenantal Position

B
Adam

B
Eve

3. God exiles them but provides protective clothing for them in their confusion

Enmeshed Narcissistic Position

A
Eve

1. Eve entraps Adam into eating of the tree of knowledge

Figure 7.5
Adam and Eve

of God's anger (position C). This pattern resembles the narcissistic collusion of Prometheus and Pandora, with Adam blaming and Eve entrapping. The Biblical God, unlike Zeus, however, will have none of it.

Indeed, some commentators have argued that the reason for God's exile of Adam and Eve is precisely his disapproval of this narcissistic pattern. For example, a midrash (*Gen. Rabbah*, 19.12) states that the main reason that man and woman are driven from the garden is that each attempt to blame someone else for their sins (also see Rashi, on Gen. 3.12). Similarly, Eve's entrapment of Adam can be seen as an attempt on her part to avoid solitary death: "She [Eve] came to him and said, 'Do you think that I will die and another Eve will be created for you? Do you think that if I die you will survive me?' " (*Gen. Rabbah*, 20.8).

Despite His disapproval of their narcissistic pattern, God continues to care for Adam and Eve. He does not kill them but provides them with clothing to protect them in their exile (an impermeable wall) and confusion (an inarticulated boundary). This allows them to regroup (position BB). They then begin to develop their marital relationship, learning to live with the labor and pain of life and parenthood (position EE). They later bear a third son, Seth, after the tragic events surrounding Cain's murder of Abel and his banishment (position DD).

In the Greek story, Pyrrha and Deucalion get along but Zeus is hostile to both. Zeus uses his power to try to destroy human development, whereas the God of Genesis opens an important dialogue with the couple, providing them with the protection of clothing in their exile. This enables Adam and Eve to renew their relationship with each other and with Him despite their sin and their expulsion from the garden. With God's help, they slowly mature and finally achieve the successful joint parenthood of their third son, from whom mankind is descended.[5]

Noah and His Wife

A similar suicide-preventive, covenantal pattern emerges in the narrative of Noah and his wife. First, the descent of Noah (and his wife) from Adam and Eve is asserted. God then warns Noah of the impending flood and makes arrangements for his safety.

The following events in the story of Noah may be highlighted:

1. Noah and his wife are descendants of Adam and Eve (Gen. 5.1–32).
2. God sends a flood to destroy mankind (6.17).
3. God warns Noah and instructs him how to build an ark and to save two or more of each creature, male and female.

> And God said unto Noah, "The end of all flesh is come before me. . . . But I will establish my covenant with thee; and thou shalt come into the ark, thou, and thy sons, and thy wife, and thy sons' wives with thee. And of every living

thing of all flesh, two of every sort shalt thou bring into the ark, to keep them alive with thee; they shall be male and female (6.13, 18–22).

4. After the flood, Noah and his wife and all the creatures, male and female, re-populate the earth according to God's design (8.15–19; 9.1).

5. God places a rainbow in the heavens as a sign of His covenant with man that there will not be another flood to destroy man (9.12–17).

Figure 7.6 visually illustrates this process. First, God sends the flood because of mankind's wickedness. God, unlike the narcissistic Zeus, however, does not try to destroy Noah and his wife but provides an ark to protect them from the flood (BB position). Moreover, God provides the plan for them to reemerge as grandparents (DD position). The continuing race of people (both men and women) come from the union of Noah's sons and daughters-in-law. The rainbow symbolizes the ongoing covenant, even in the face of human sinfulness.[6]

This signal of faith stands in marked contrast to the suicidogenic hopelessness that pervades the conclusion of the Prometheus-Pandora myth. Pandora releases evils from the jar of Epimetheus into the world. Hope alone remains locked up, and man is provoked into a quixotic quest to release it.

IMPLICATIONS FOR SUICIDE

These Greek couples seem pathologically fixated and tragic while those in the Biblical world have hope for development. The relationship between men and women in Greek narratives cycles endlessly between enmeshment and disengagement, with men exhibiting a fear of absorption and women a fear of abandonment. Men and women in the Biblical narratives, by contrast, turn expectantly to God to overcome these fears.

Recent research (Kaplan and Maldaver 1990a) has pointed to the suicidal implications of this difference. A review of eighty-five research studies over the past twenty years has yielded the following results. Marriages on the clinical AC axis are generally more suicidogenic for their offspring than those on the developmental BED axis. Adolescent suicidal behavior (completions, attempts, or plans) occurs more frequently in the disengaged (CC) parental style, followed respectively by the immature reciprocal (BB) parental pattern, the enmeshed (AA) pattern, and the rejection-intrusion (AC) pattern. Our literature review has revealed no suicidal attempts or completions for the offspring of more mature reciprocal (EE or DD) parents.

Particularly striking results are apparent in an empirical study. The parents of twenty-five adolescent suicides were compared to the parents of twenty-five comparable nonsuicidal adolescents. As can be seen in Figure 7.7, only 16.7 percent of the adolescent suicides came from families with

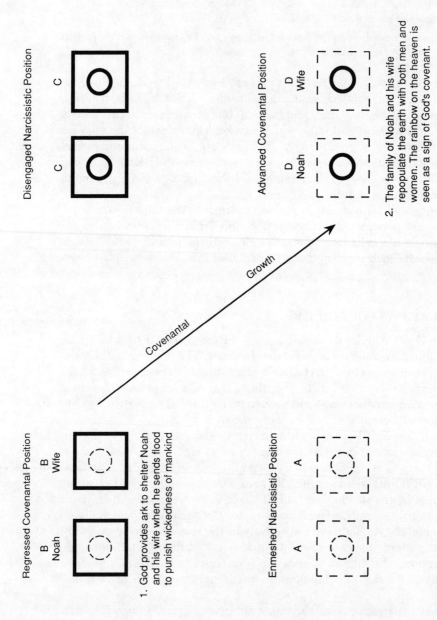

Disengaged Narcissistic Position

C   C

Advanced Covenantal Position

D   D
Noah   Wife

2. The family of Noah and his wife repopulate the earth with both men and women. The rainbow on the heaven is seen as a sign of God's covenant.

Covenantal   Growth

Regressed Covenantal Position

B   B
Noah   Wife

1. God provides ark to shelter Noah and his wife when he sends flood to punish wickedness of mankind

Enmeshed Narcissistic Position

A   A

Figure 7.6
Noah and His Wife

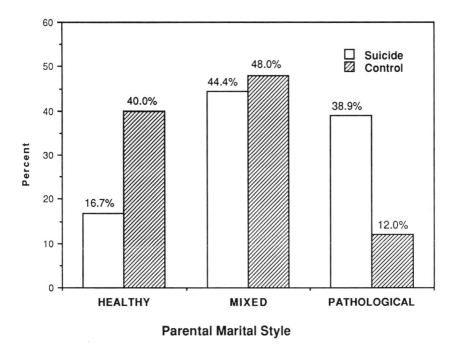

Figure 7.7
Marital Pathology and Completed Adolescent Suicide

two healthy (BED axis) parents, while 44.4 percent came from a mixed parental pattern (one healthy BED-axis parent and one clinical AC-axis parent), and 38.9 percent came from two pathological (AC axis) parents. The nonsuicidal families showed a dramatically different pattern. Forty percent of the control adolescents had two healthy (BED axis) parents, 48 percent had a mixed parental pattern (one BED and one AC parent), and only 12 percent had two pathological (AC axis) parents (Kaplan and Maldaver 1990b).[7] Approximately three times as many suicides came from pathological families while three times as many nonsuicides came from healthy families.[8]

NOTES

1. This summarizes the conceptual framework of a number of the most important marital and family theorists and therapists (e.g., Bowen 1960; Minuchin 1974; Stierlin 1974; and Wynne et al. 1958). D. M. Olson, D. M. Sprenkle, and C. S. Russell (1979) have worked with the same single dimension, although they have broken the scale into four points (disengaged, separated, connected, and enmeshed) rather than into three.

2. It is clear that Prometheus does not descend to Zeus's level of villainy and that, despite suffering, he holds fast to his standard of morality and of right and wrong. His reaction may be the best possible one in the face of a narcissistic Zeus, but moral autonomy, although heroic, is not sufficient. There is no safe space for Prometheus in Zeus's world, and he is therefore isolated on a cliff at the earth's farthest edge (position C). Prometheus is often used as a standard of heroism for Western man. Unfortunately, in the absence of covenant, such Promethean struggle often degenerates into pointless rebellion and even suicide.

3. Curiously, the modern stereotype of the devouring "Jewish mother" fits Pandora better than Eve, and it certainly applies to Hera as described by Philip Slater (1968). The issue of how the modern Jewish mother came to be seen in ancient Greek rather than Biblical terms is a complex one deserving of serious study.

4. To be sure, a subsequent account in Apollodorus does suggest a sexual union between Deucalion and Pyrrha. "Deucalion had children by Pyrrha, first Helen, . . . second Amphicyton, and third, a daughter, Protogenia" (Apollodorus, 1.7–3). Nevertheless, the account of separate parentage seems highly significant in a society as misogynistic as classical Greece. Women, in this story, continue to be seen as "a race apart," cloning women after themselves.

5. In one Midrashic version, Noah's wife is a descendant of Cain (*Gen. Rabbah*, 22).

6. See Rabbi A. I. Kook's *Musar Avicha* (34–39) for a comparable argument.

7. The Chi-square statistic describing this interaction equals 5.16 and is significant at the .075 level.

8. An alternative, "backward" explanation is that experiencing the suicide of a child will make the parents more pathological. However, the research of M.D.S. Ainsworth (1972) has provided support for the "forward" interpretation, specifically, importance of secure parenting, especially mothering, for a later resilient sense of self that is capable of withstanding life stressors (c.f. Bowlby 1977; Main, Kaplan, and Cassidy 1985; Kaplan and O'Connor, in press; Kaplan and Worth, in press).

An interesting recent study of suicide in Yiddish literature (Hadda 1988) has pointed to a pervasive theme in relationships. Women are passionate and men passive, at least in suicidal relationships. This is more reflective of a Greek rejection-intrusion (AC) pattern than a Biblical reciprocity (DD).

Chapter 8

The Suicide-Promoting Structure of the Greek Family: Oedipus and Electra

From what manner of parents did I take my miserable being! And to them I go thus, accursed, unwed, to share their home.

Sophocles, *Antigone,* 862–863

Ah! Hapless mother, what a love was thine! . . . Where will this history end? That "love" has been our curse from the time long past.

Euripides, *Hippolytus,* 337–343

Ah me! alas! and whither can I go? What share have I henceforth in dance or marriage rite?

Euripides, *Electra,* 1198–1199

Conflictual family structure is one of the greatest contributing factors to the urge toward suicide in Greek thinking. Mothers are intrusive, not allowing their children any space for growth or autonomy. Fathers are disengaged, with children feeling rejected and abandoned. The child's energies become completely involved in attempting to solve the insoluble problem of gaining the recognition and love of each parent (Orbach 1986; 1988). In this system, the child has no real right to live, and he is burdened with a deeply guilty feeling that he is not wanted. Suicide becomes a predictable result of this oppressive sense of worthlessness.

The child is caught in the destructive interplay between the two parents themselves. The wife feels abandoned and demeaned, while the husband often feels irrelevant and controlled. Each partner uses the child as an ally in the battle against the other. This pattern can be seen in the relationship of the first divine Greek family (Apollodorus, 1.1.1). Sky, the father, is unrooted and disengaged, while Earth, the mother, is fixed but intrusive.

Such a mix is deeply destructive, even homicidal or suicidal, to children. The father provides no support, and the mother gives no space. This is the experience of insecure parenting that leads to Oedipal problems:

Grieved at the loss of the children who were thrown [by Sky] into Tartarus, Earth persuaded the Titans to attack their father and gave Cronus a steel sickle . . . Cronus cut off his father's genitals and threw them into the sea. Having thus elimi- nated their father, the Titans brought back their brothers who had been hurled to Tartarus and gave the rule to Cronus. (Apollodorus, 1.1.4)

This vicious family pattern continues as Cronus swallows his own new- born children to avoid being supplanted by them, but Zeus, his youngest son, survives. He overpowers Cronus with the collusion of Rhea, his mother, and becomes king. Zeus, in turn, devours Metis with an embryo still in her womb (Apollodorus, 1.1).

The sociologist Phillip Slater (1968) has demonstrated the constant pres- ence of aggression between parents and children in Apollodorus: forty- seven cases between fathers and sons, twelve between mothers and sons, one between mother and daughter, and sixteen between fathers and daughters. These often lead to suicide or self-mutilation. Our selection of narratives in Table 8.1 first examines sons, and then daughters.

GREEK FATHERS AND SONS

In these stories, Greek fathers and sons are in a bitter rivalry, with sons seen as a threat and the fathers as a block. Sons must not threaten their fathers' position in any way, and it is perfectly legitimate for fathers to

Table 8.1
Greek Parent–Child Narratives

	Fathers	Mothers
Sons	Laius - Oedipus ---------------- Creon - Haemon	Medea - sons ----------------- Jocasta - Oedipus
Daughters	Agamemnon-Iphigenia ------------------- Oedipus - Antigone	Clytemnestra-Electra -------------------- Hecuba - Polyxena

practice infant exposure. Cronus eats his children, and Zeus begets and abandons bastards all over the earth. The son in this system has no real right to live. Two relationships exemplify this pattern: (1) Laius and his son Oedipus and (2) Creon and his son Haemon.

Laius and Oedipus

Consider first the story of Oedipus, who unknowingly slays his father Laius, replaces him as king of Thebes, and marries his own mother Jocasta. What is relevant for present purposes is, first, the nature of the relationship between Laius and Oedipus and, second, the fact that Oedipus winds up mutilating himself.

The story of Oedipus begins with a warning to King Laius that there is danger to his throne at Thebes if his new-born son should reach man's estate. This warning leads Laius to give his son to a herdsman to be destroyed. The herdsman, after piercing the infant's feet, gives him to a fellow shepherd, who carries him to King Polybus of Corinth and his queen, by whom he is adopted and called Oedipus (meaning swollen feet).

An oracle presents Oedipus with a riddle, rather than an intelligible prophecy, and it leads him to destruction. The oracle prophesies that Oedipus will kill his father, whom Oedipus apparently takes to be his adoptive father with whom he has a good relationship. Note the strange tone of the oracular pronouncement: Avoid the parent you love lest you hurt him, rather than to honor him as in the Biblical creed of "Honor thy father and mother." The oracle picks on the weakest link in the relationship between father and son — that point of primal suspicion and fear that must exist in some small amount in even the best of relationships. Further, the prophecy brings about what it purports to warn against, the murder of Oedipus' biological father and the destruction of any chance that Oedipus has for fulfillment.

The oracle thus places Oedipus in a no-win situation. It becomes impossible for Oedipus to maintain any type of relationship with his father and derive the sense of security essential to his normal development. When Oedipus rebels, he is doomed. Precisely because he is so well-intentioned, Oedipus is unable to face his parents in the next world, and he blinds himself with a brooch from his mother's clothing. The immediate precipitant to his self-blinding is his mother's suicide. Despite his fury toward her, he is enmeshed with her.

Creon and Haemon

The relationship between Creon and Haemon in Sophocles' *Antigone* shows some of the same characteristics, except that here it is not an outside oracle but the father, Creon himself, who places his son in an impossible situation, a Hobson's choice. Shall Haemon obey his father and consign his fiancée Antigone to her doom, or shall he oppose his father in an attempt to save her? Haemon's attempt to express his own point of view is seen by his father Creon as disloyalty to the family agenda. Creon's first words are to question whether Haemon will remain loyal to him (635). Haemon responds mildly at first, submitting to his father's authority (636), but then he attempts to defend Antigone to his father (699). Creon responds: "Men of my age, are we indeed to be schooled by men of his?" (727–728). The exchange between father and son becomes quite bitter. Haemon demands that his father judge him by his merits rather than his years (728–729). Creon responds by accusing Haemon of shamelessly feuding with his father (743). Creon emphasizes his control and power by introducing the notion of Haemon's death: "Thou canst never marry on this side of the grave" (750). Haemon's response contains a clear suicidal threat: "Then she must die, and in her deeds, destroy another" (751). Creon calls his son's bluff (759–760), and Haemon raises the ante to suicide (761–763). When Creon interrupts Haemon's mourning for the now-dead Antigone, Haemon reacts violently. He first attempts unsuccessfully to murder his father and then kills himself.

GREEK MOTHERS AND SONS

Slater's studies of Greek mythological families has led him to focus on mother-son relationships as potentially more destructive than those between father and son. The mother's low self-esteem intensifies her fear of being abandoned. She responds to her miseries by using her sons to hurt her husband, thus venting her rage on those who she feels keep her in her wretched state.

Typically, the Greek mother will hurt her children as well. She expresses her guilt, anger, and self-hatred by creating disharmony and conflict within the family. She does this by "triangulating," allying with the son against the father. Sometimes this leads to the mother's murder of her son, sometimes to the son's self-destructiveness. An example of the first is Medea and her sons; an example of the second is Jocasta and Oedipus.

Medea and Her Sons

The potential brutality of the mother is expressed in Euripides' magnificent drama *Medea*. The legend of Medea's aid to Jason and the Argonauts in their quest for the Golden Fleece is among the best known of ancient Hellenic tales, and it also forms the subject of the third-century epic poem *The Argonautica*, by Apollonius of Rhodes.

The action in Euripides' *Medea* begins some years later, when Jason rejects his wife Medea to marry a wealthy princess of Corinth. Medea is devastated: "And she [Medea] lies fasting, yielding her body to her grief, wasting away in tears" (24–26). She plots a terrible revenge, the murder of the new bride and of Medea's own two sons with Jason. As the plot develops, Medea expresses her misery at being a woman and her resentment toward both Jason and her sons: "Curse you and your father too, ye children, damned sons of a doomed woman! Ruin seize the whole family!" (112–114). She despises her role as a woman, since a man's role is so much pleasanter (213–266). Both she and Jason demean the woman's role: "And yet they say we live secure at home, while they are at the wars, with their sorry reasoning, for I would gladly take my stand in battle array three times o'er, than once give birth" (Euripides, *Medea*, 244–251).

She cannot bear the thought of being rejected and abandoned by Jason or of being mocked by her enemies. Jason criticizes her for being illogical and impractical. Jason's misogyny and disdain for women are clear. Men are truly superior, and women bring ruin: "Yea, men should have begotten children from some other source, no female race existing; thus would no evil ever have fallen on mankind" (573–575).

Medea hates Jason's disdain for her sex but is disgusted with the role of woman. She will not be a weak, feeble-spirited stay-at-home. What is horrible here is Medea's solution, which is so self-destructive as well as so frighteningly inhuman to others. It reveals much about the deep rage and hostility inherent in the typical Hellenic family. She feels she can respond most effectively by destroying everything.[1]

Medea sends Jason's bride a beautiful white dress and a golden crown as wedding gifts. They have been treated with poison, however, so that they burn the princess to an agonizing death when she puts them on. Medea then completes her revenge with the murder of the two boys. In the final scene, Medea appears above the house in a chariot drawn by flying dragons; the bodies of her sons are with her. Jason pleads to be allowed to bury them. Medea torments and rebukes him cruelly (1354–1360).

Medea is motivated largely by the feeling that Jason is abandoning her. If she cannot be with him any longer in marriage, she will still be united with him. She slays her sons to vex Jason and to gain his full attention. Jason may now hate her, but he can no longer scorn her as weak, powerless, and irrational. Medea proves herself cleverer, more macho, and more destructive than any warrior (1370–1406). She punishes Jason for abandoning her and, at the same time, repays her sons for making her a mother and contributing to her abasement. Medea does not acknowledge her sons as individuals with their own rights to live but sees them simply as enmeshed extensions of herself. She murders them to punish Jason.[2]

Jocasta and Oedipus

The mother in Greek mythological families is in constant conflict with her husband and uses her sons against her husband. Like Rhea, she can support them in overthrowing their father, or, like Medea, she can murder them to deprive her husband of an heir, fulfilling her own hatred of them at the same time. The royal couple of the gods, Zeus and Hera, presents a prime example of the second pattern. Hera, bitterly hostile to Zeus, constantly plots the destruction of his numerous bastards. She herself, according to some accounts, bears him no children.

The passive role of Jocasta in Sophocles' *Oedipus Rex* can be seen as representing a pale reflection of this deep and hostile pattern on the part of the Greek mother-wife. This time, it takes a self-destructive rather than a homicidal form. First, Jocasta hangs herself; immediately afterward, Oedipus puts out his eyes with the golden brooches that she wears.

Oedipus has been set up by the riddling oracle and placed in an insoluble dilemma. He has married his biological mother. When he discovers this, Oedipus feels betrayed and wishes to murder her. She has already killed herself, however, awakening Oedipus' sense of abandonment. He turns his anger inward and blinds himself, using an article of her clothing, saying that he does not wish to see his parents in the next world.

THE OEDIPUS COMPLEX AND SUICIDE

As described by Freud, the Oedipus complex represents an archetypal dilemma for the son within the family and is directly linked to suicidal pathology. The Oedipal son wishes to replace his father and have his mother for himself: "King Oedipus, who slew his father Laius and wedded his mother Jocasta, is nothing more or less than a wish-fulfillment, the fulfillment of the wish of our childhood" (Freud 1954, 296). Because of this, the son is rejected by his father from his very birth and fails to develop a sense of his own worth. He becomes bound to and dominated by his "earth" mother and at best will have a standoffish relationship with his "sky" father. Indeed, Greek father-son myths abound with instances of castration and incorporation (again, see Apollodorus, 1.1). In none of these stories does the son feel even the most minimal acceptance from his father. The son either revolts against his father or acquiesces in his own destruction.

Split between enmeshed and disengaged states, the child is simply torn apart and is likely to produce a persistent pattern of self-defeating and self-destructive behaviors. The son becomes a pawn in the battle between his parents, neither of whom sees the son as an individual with a right to independence and his own creativity. He lacks the approval, permission, and indeed the blessing of his parents to live his own life. Greek plays constantly return to the theme of the curse on the house of Labdacus and the curse of Oedipus on his own sons: "The glory of wealth and of pride, with iron, not gold, in your hands, ye shall come, at the last, to divide" (Aeschylus, *Seven Against Thebes*, 785–786), a curse so horribly fulfilled when his sons murder each other. What makes this especially tragic is that Oedipus in many ways is a good and well-meaning man who is trapped by an all-enveloping suicidal doom. This situation was keenly perceived by the Greek dramatists who understood the tragic drives underpinning their great society but felt helpless to provide any antidote or solution.

The link between the Oedipus complex and suicide is diagramed in Figure 8.1. The Greek husband-father is disengaged (C) and deprecating to his wife (MW), yet terrified of absorption by her.[3] He also fears displacement by his son (MS)[4] and threatens to demean and castrate him. The Greek wife-mother, in contrast, is enmeshed (A). She envies her husband (WM), yet fears that he will abandon her. She also attempts to control and seduce her son (WS). This, of course, evokes the classical Oedipal complex of the son wanting to displace his father (SM = C) and possess his mother (SW = A). The son thus is anomic (A/C),[5] driven to possess his mother and displace his father. Anomic suicide is a serious risk unless something drastic changes in the situation (see Figure 8.1, top).[6]

According to classic psychoanalytic thinking, the father counters the son's threat of displacement by activating his own threat of castration. This serves to neutralize rather than resolve the son's desire to displace the father, resulting in a mutual standoffishness (SM = C, MS = C) in the father-son relation (Figure 8.1, bottom). The husband-wife relationship, however, remains unchanged, with the husband still deprecating his wife (MW = C) and the wife still envying her husband (WM = A). The mother will still try to seduce her son (WS = A) but the son has given up his desire to possess his mother, now fearing incorporation by her (SW = C). He has displaced the fear of castration from his father to his mother. This ambivalent neutralization of the Oedipal dilemma leaves the son in the disengaged C position with both his father and his mother. The son, of course, remains at suicidal risk, now falling into Durkheim's egoistic suicidal type, which is so typical of the Sophoclean plays. He cannot genuinely attach to anyone.

Saddest indeed is the dependence on fear in achieving this neutralization. No fundamental resolution has occurred in the relationship of father and son. There is no sense that the father accepts his son's right to exist. The child is expendable! Still driven to displace his father, he is simply inhibited in this desire by fear of punishment. As the superego is internalized in this process (Freud 1923a; 1923b; 1924), the son's moral identification with his father must have a detached and isolated quality, leaving him susceptible to egoistic (position C) suicide. Furthermore, this pathology, without outside intervention, is likely to reproduce itself from generation to generation. Escaping self-destruction, the disengaged (C) son will himself grow up to be a disengaged father. If he marries an intrusive (A) woman, they will pass on the unresolved Oedipal conflict, with its suicidal implications, to their sons.[7]

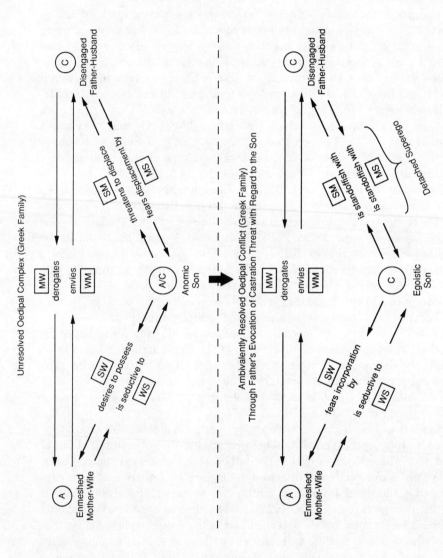

Figure 8.1
The Oedipus Complex and Suicide

GREEK MOTHERS AND DAUGHTERS

Although the basic relationship between mother and daughter is very close in the Greek literary tradition, it is tainted by a potentially suicidal lack of genuine self-esteem. Woman is seen as the mysterious "other," closely associated with the devouring earth. This "otherness" is implied in the creation of Pandora as a curse to man, rather than as a helpmeet and a source of life. Woman's "alien" nature is perhaps most clearly expressed in taboos regarding the uncleanliness of her menstrual blood. Taboos about menstruation lead to envy of the male (cf. Stephens 1962) and the daughter's willingness to abandon the mother and to look to her father. The Greek mother's only defense in this regard is to lower her daughter's self-esteem by eliciting even further shame about the latter's menstruating condition, to make it risky for the daughter fully to abandon the mother lest she herself wind up totally alone — without either mother or father. This is obviously a poor solution to the daughter's low self-esteem. Any attachment between Greek mother and daughter is permeated with a suicidal symbiotic quality, leaving the daughter unable to cope with life stresses. Psychoanalysis has understood this problem in terms of the Electra complex.

Clytemnestra and Electra

In his play *Electra*, Euripides depicted Electra, daughter of Agamemnon, as waiting for years, completely obsessed by plans for the return of her brother Orestes and their revenge on Clytemnestra for her murder of Agamemnon (188). Raised by both mother and father to see herself as debased in her womanhood, Electra is hostile both toward men and toward her mother, as well as toward her own lowly role. She is married to a farmer of good family, "one of a noble nature" (262). Yet Electra treats him badly and boasts to strangers that she is still a virgin (255). Plotting to murder Clytemnestra, Electra sends to tell her that she has just given birth. When Clytemnestra arrives, Electra lets out her long-cherished hostility in a lengthy speech, accusing her mother of betraying and cuckolding Agamemnon (1067–1083).

Clytemnestra's response to Electra is not without insight as to the preference of the daughter for her father over her mother: "Daughter, t'was ever thy nature to love thy father. This too one finds; some sons cling to their father, others have deeper affection for their mother" (1102). Although Electra (with the help of Orestes) murders her mother rather than herself, her reaction further displays her essential feeling of debasement as a woman: "Ah me! alas! and whither can I go? What share have I henceforth in dance or marriage rite? What husband will accept me as his bride" (1198–1200).

Electra's sister Iphigenia significantly carries these same feelings of worthlessness into suicide. Agamemnon tricks Iphigenia into coming to the camp of the Greek army to be sacrificed to Artemis by pretending that she is to marry the great warrior Achilles (Euripides, *Iphigenia at Aulis*, 104–106). Clytemnestra soon discovers the truth about the "marriage" (841–842, 873–883). Still, she feels powerless and does nothing but bemoan her lot: "O, we are lost, my child and I. Lost, lost!" (886). Even before she knows of the plot, Clytemnestra reveals her fear that her daughter will prefer her father to Clytemnestra. Rather than show support when Electra runs to embrace her father, she emphasizes the bitter triangular rivalry: "Go, go, my girl. You always loved your father more than the other children" (653–656). This line, of course, shares the same reproach as that previously cited from *Electra*. Clytemnestra is poignantly aware that both of her daughters prefer their lordly father to their ineffectual mother, and they share her low self-esteem.

Hecuba and Polyxena

A second mother-daughter narrative involves the relationship between Hecuba and Polyxena described in Euripides' *Hecuba*. Hecuba, the brave widow of King Priam of Troy, is a captive of the Greeks. Her first speech reveals the depths of her own despair and distaste for life:

Woe, woe is me! What champion have I? Sons, and city — where are they? Aged Creon is no more; no more my children now. Which way I am to go. . . . Ye have made an end, an utter end of me; life on earth has no more charm for me. (Euripides, *Hecuba*, 163–170)

When Odysseus informs them that Polyxena will be sacrificed to the ghost of Achilles, Hecuba's own emotional structure crumbles so badly that she cannot function as a mother. When Polyxena attempts to talk to her mother about her impending disaster, Hecuba seems unable to concentrate on anything but her own problems.[8] When Polyxena says, "Unwedded I depart, never having tasted the married joys that were my due!" (416), Hecuba replies, "Tell them of all women I am most miserable" (424). Hecuba is without hope. Further she expresses this fatalism to her daughter: "Alas, my daughter! . . . Woe for the life! Ah, my daughter, a luckless mother's child" (179–185).

Faber (1970, 117) has offered a radical interpretation that Hecuba's own paralyzing depression and inability to show a full empathy pushes Polyxena to suicide. For Faber, the Greeks actually offer Polyxena a means of escape (562–563) that she will not use, instead expressing a preference for death over life:

Alas, for thy cruel sufferings! My persecuted mother! Woe for thy life of grief! . . .
Not more shall I thy daughter share thy bondage, hapless youth on hapless age
attending! . . . For thee I weep with plaintive wail, mother doomed to a life of
sorrow! For my own life, its ruin and its outrage, never a tear I shed; nay, death is
becoming to me a happier lot than life. (200–216)

GREEK FATHERS AND DAUGHTERS

The father-daughter relationship in the Greek family presents the final
link in the chain of interlocking hostility and conflict within the nuclear
family. The father carries uncertain feelings about his own manhood into
the relationship and transmits ambivalent signals to his daughter. He demands that she idealize him as a male, but he simultaneously degrades her.
If she does not idealize him, she is threatened with rejection and abandonment. At the same time, she is so debased that she is worthy of nothing
other than rejection and abandonment. Both signals are apparent in Agamemnon's attitude toward his daughter, Iphigenia.

Agamemnon and Iphigenia

Iphigenia, like many young girls, desperately wants her father's attention. She is literally willing to be sacrificed for her father's interests and
seems to prefer him to her mother. Her self-esteem is so low that she leaps
at the chance to be martyred in her father's name. Iphigenia allies herself
with her father against her mother: "O mother, blame me not! Let me go
first. And put my arms about my father's neck. Father, how glad it makes
my heart to see you! It is so long since you have been away!" (Euripides,
Iphigenia in Aulis, 631–637).

Agamemnon has no interest in his daughter but only in himself. His response to her upcoming sacrifice is totally self-involved: "O *my* wretched
fate" (1135, emphasis added). Iphigenia pleads with her father for her life
and recognition, revealing her feeling of powerlessness: "I have only tears.
. . . They are all my power. I clasp your knees, I am your suppliant now. I
am your own child; my mother bore me to you. O kill me not ultimately!"
(1215–1218). When he rejects her, she is unable to express her anger to
him. She complains instead to Clytemnestra: "Mother, my father has gone,
left me, betrayed and alone!" (1313–1315). Finally, her basic behavioral
pattern reasserts itself. She accepts her martyrdom and glorifies it as heroic
altruism: "My death will save them, and my name will be blessed. She who
freed Hellas" (1383). She tells her mother not to mourn for her and not to
hate Agamemnon.

It is likely that Iphigenia gives herself over to the total idealization of her
father and, simultaneously, to uttermost self-debasement by dying to preserve *his* honor. Perhaps taking her fate "like a man" is also an effort to win

his approval. Agamemnon has made use of his daughter both to aggrandize himself and to debase his wife. His daughter is not real to him as a person, and he easily abandons, exposes, and even sacrifices her if he stands to achieve personal gain by such action, even if that gain is merely to buttress his own shaky ego in relationship to his wife.

Oedipus and Antigone

A second suicidogenic relationship between father and daughter is that of Oedipus and Antigone. Antigone is obsessed with the incestuous sin of her parents: "Alas for the wretched mother's slumber at the side of her own son, — and my sire! From what manner of parents did I take my miserable being!" (Sophocles, *Antigone*, 859–868). She sees this sin as a curse leading to her own death: "And to them I go thus, accursed, unwed, to share their home" (869). Antigone seems obsessed with dying to fulfill her relationship with Oedipus (1–3). She even sees death as a sort of marriage (808–814). Furthermore her suicide by hanging mimics that of her mother, Jocasta (1219–1221). Perhaps this is Antigone's way of replacing Jocasta as his wife or even his mother.

Even more curious is Antigone's obsession with burying her dead brother in defiance of Creon's order. Her defiance has been interpreted by many scholars as the height of individualism. Nevertheless, her more fundamental enmeshment with her family of origin is revealed in a bizarre speech in which she states that she would not have felt compelled to bury a husband or child as she would a brother: "The husband lost, another might have been found, and child from another to replace the first born: but father and mother hidden with Hades, no brother's life could bloom for me again" (913–918). This enmeshment is bad enough if we take Antigone's concern to be directed toward her slain brother Polyneices. We should remember, however, that her father Oedipus too is her brother! This desire to merge is clearly expressed in her desire to lie with her "brother" in death: "I shall rest, a loved one one with him whom I have loved"[9] (74). Deeply enmeshed with her father, as was Iphigenia, Antigone can nonetheless show great indifference toward her lover, Haemon, and severe independence toward King Creon. One doubts that Iphigenia has this capacity for independence.

THE ELECTRA COMPLEX AND SUICIDE

The Electra complex, based on the myth of Electra, describes the ambivalent desire of the daughter to abandon her mother and possess her father. It is neutralized through the daughter's giving up of her father as a sexual object and coming to identify with her mother. As the basis for this identification is not punitive, as in the Oedipus complex, it may be accomplished through the introjection of an ego ideal rather than a superego.[10] In Freud's view, however, the daughter does not rest easy because she has already been castrated and because of the remaining penis envy she feels toward her father. One dynamic in this process may be a shame about menstruation elicited in the daughter by the mother as a means of neutralizing the mother's own fear of abandonment. Penis envy may be a result rather than a cause of this process.[11]

More generally, the place of the daughter in the Greek family is tenuous at best. She idealizes her father because she needs him. At the same time, he typically ignores or rejects her because he is preoccupied with his own needs. Her mother may neglect her, as Clytemnestra does to Electra, or may find it difficult to see her as an independent being. The daughter is thus caught between rejection and smothering, and her shaky self-esteem is further diminished by her mother in the latter's attempt to bind her. She remains highly vulnerable to a variety of pathologies including suicide.

Figure 8.2 diagrams the link between the Electra complex and suicide. The Greek wife-mother is enmeshed (A), envying her husband (WM) yet terrified of abandonment by him. She also fears abandonment by her daughter (WD) and seeks to arouse menstrual shame in her. The Greek husband-father, in contrast, is disengaged (C), deprecating his wife (MW) and terrified of absorption by her. He is willing to abandon, expose, or sacrifice his daughter (MD). This, of course, evokes the classic Electra complex for the daughter who is eager to abandon her mother (DW = C) in her idealization of her father (DM = A). The daughter thus becomes a potential anomic (A/C) suicide (see Figure 8.2, top).

Classic psychoanalytic thinking gives an unsatisfactory account of how this conflict may be neutralized, arguing that the mother has no real deterrent since the daughter has already been castrated. We suggest an alternative explanation. The mother counters the daughter's threat of abandonment by activating her shame of menstruation.[12] This lowers the daughter's sense of self-esteem and merely transforms the daughter's desire to abandon her (both FD and DF = A). The wife-husband relationship, however, remains unchanged, the wife still envying her husband (WM = A) and the husband still deprecating his wife (MW = C). As such, the father will try to abandon his daughter (MD = C), but the daughter still idealizes her father (DM = A). In other words, the neutralization of the Electra dilemma between father and daughter leaves her enmeshed (A) with both her father and her mother, vulnerable to threat of abandonment and at risk of altruistic (A) suicide.

The Greek daughter too is thus at risk for suicide, albeit of the altruistic type. Her relationship with her mother remains basically unresolved. The drive to escape her mother remains, although inhibited by low self-esteem. As the ego ideal is thus internalized, a girl's sense of morality must have an enmeshed and undifferentiated aspect to it, as is apparent in many of Euri-

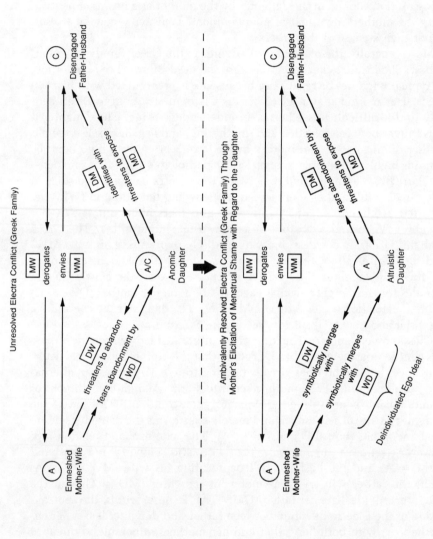

Figure 8.2
The Electra Complex and Suicide

pides' self-sacrificing female martyrs. Furthermore, this pathology, untreated, is likely to recur from generation to generation. The enmeshed (A) daughter will grow up to be an (A) enmeshing woman who is likely to find a disengaged (C) man to marry. Together, this couple will pass on the unresolved Electra conflict and suicidal vulnerability to yet another generation of daughters.

NOTES

1. Erich Wellisch (1954) has employed the term "Medea complex" in *Isaac and Oedipus*. It was coined by Edward Stern (1948).

2. A poignant example in English literature of this expendable condition occurs in Thomas Hardy's *Jude the Obscure*. The scribbled suicide note left by three unwanted children says it all: "Done because we are too menny" (1974, 356).

3. Bruno Bettelheim (1955) has argued that one illustration of this male fear of absorption by the female is the theme of *vagina dentata* (castrating vagina with teeth) in Greek art.

4. In this narration, the husband-father is designated by M (man) and the wife-mother by W (woman). The son is designated by S and the daughter by D.

5. Olympiodorus' emphasis on Plato's curious suggestion of suicide as a remedy for a man possessing uncontrollable erotic passions for his mother (Taylor 1834) becomes more comprehensible, given this analysis.

6. Certain passages in the New Testament can be read as placing the family of Jesus in this rejection-intrusion (AC) pattern. Jesus' last words on the cross emphasize the theme of abandonment by the Father: "My god, My God why has thou forsaken me?" (Matt. 27.46). In another passage, Jesus seems to want to distance himself from his mother. Jesus responds to his mother's request for wine during the wedding in Cana, "Woman, what do I have to do with you?" (John 2.4).

7. An example of this recurrence of narcissism across generations can be found in the family history of Otto Weininger, the suicide discussed in Chapter 4. In a letter to his biographer, the psychiatrist Dr. David Abrahamsen, Weininger's sister Rosa described their parents' marriage:

The married life of my parents was not peaceful. That was due to my father's strong personality, his sharp criticism, and his great demands upon his family. We children let Mother spoil us, we confided in her, but to us Father was the supreme judge. (Abrahamsen 1946, 213)

Abrahamsen went on to speculate:

Undoubtedly, the disharmony between his parents impressed young Otto deeply. Having a highly gifted but severe father and a mother of quite ordinary talents affected his sensitive mind. . . . Apparently Otto tried to identify himself with his father and developed hostility, unconscious though it may have been, toward his mother. (Abrahamsen 1946, 13)

8. Hecuba lacks the religious perspective and the hope shown in the parable of Rabbi Wasserman (chapter 3).

9. The pattern of a daughter committing suicide to rejoin a dead father has been vividly illustrated in the late Sylvia Plath's poem "Daddy." Here she describes weeping at her father's grave immediately before swallowing fifty sleeping pills in her mother's cellar:

> At twenty I tried to die
> And get back, back, back to you.
> I thought even the bones would do.
> (Alvarez 1982, 20; Plath 1986, 134–137)

10. Ego ideals emerge out of the earlier anaclitic identifications of a child, primarily with the mother. In current psychoanalytic thinking, it has become the convention to reserve the term "superego" for the punitive basis for conscience achieved in the boy child through the resolution of the Oedipus complex and the term "ego ideal" for the seemingly more benign basis for conscience that is available to the girl child in the resolution of the Electra complex (cf. H. B. Lewis 1976).

11. In a cross-cultural study, William Stephens (1962) has found a relationship between indices of "castration anxiety" and the severity of menstrual taboos, and one may argue not only that severe menstrual taboos presuppose a high castration anxiety among males but also strong penis envy and resentment of males by females (cf. Slater 1968). The disorders of anorexia nervosa and amenorrhea may represent reactions to strong menstrual shame. Note the wasted states of Medea and of Echo, the ultimate idealizing narcissist.

12. This may involve invoking a prepubescent girl's anticipation of menarche.

Chapter 9

The Suicide-Preventing Structure of the Hebrew Family: Isaac and Ruth

Behold, I will send you Elijah the prophet before the coming of the great and terrible day of the Lord. And he shall turn the hearts of the fathers to the children, and the hearts of the children to their fathers; lest I come and smite the land with utter destruction.

Mal. 3.23–24

A woman of valour who can find? For her price is far above rubies. The heart of her husband doth safely trust in her. . . . She looketh well to the ways of her household, And eateth not the bread of idleness. Her children rise up and call her blessed; Her husband also, and he praiseth her.

Prov. 31.10–11, 27–28

Therefore shall a man leave his father and mother and shall cleave unto his wife, and they shall be one flesh.

Gen. 2.24

The Biblical and Greek literatures present very different ideas on married life. The Greek theogony portrays a primal and fatal antagonism between husband and wife. Husband is sky, wife is earth, and their descendants are destructively pulled between a disengaged, freedom-seeking father and an intrusive, devouring earth-mother. The Biblical world has no such view: "In the beginning, God created the heaven and the earth" (Gen. 1.1). The two elements are harmonious rather than conflictual; they are not divided in a male-female conflict. Adam himself is made of the ground and is given a soul: "Then the Lord God formed man of the dust of the ground, and breathed into his nostrils the breath of life; and man became a living soul" (Gen. 2.7).

The Biblical relationship between husband and wife has an essential compatibility. Normal strains and conflicts occur, but there is no sense of a primal antagonism between man and woman that is so endemic to the Greek literature nor are children suicidally torn between the two. The success of the Biblical family structure in meeting challenges is only partly a result of the character of the people who constitute that family. The Biblical family is based on the premise that every human—woman or man—is created in the divine image, is therefore worthy of respect and consideration, and likewise has certain well-defined but not rigid obligations toward others. The divine love for a person is unconditional, and it is the person's role to fulfill that trust.[1]

Biblical accounts of families often portray supportive relationships in what could be very trying circumstances. Abraham, Isaac, and Elkanah show the highest respect and affection toward wives who are barren. When Hannah becomes depressed over her infertility and does not eat, Elkanah responds tenderly that he loves her as much as if she had ten sons (Malbim on Sam. 1.8). Men in the Bible are not always so exemplary. The patriarch Jacob is not sufficiently supportive when Rachel complains to him about her barrenness (Gen. 30.1–2), and the Midrash criticizes him for this. The importance of harmony between husband and wife is a ubiquitous theme in the rabbinic understanding of the Bible. Sarah refers to her husband Abraham as "old," and God Himself modifies the statement before repeating it to Abraham. Again, the Midrash states that the Hebrews mourned more at the death of Aaron than at the passing of Moses because Aaron had done much to help improve relations between couples with marital problems (Rashi on Deut. 34.8).

The Bible rejects the suicidal, incestuous sexual and emotional patterns so destructive to the Greek world. Leviticus provides a list of the blood relatives whom a man may not marry. These include his father, his mother, his father's wife, his sister, his half-sister, his granddaughter, his daughter-in-law, or his aunt, whether natural or by marriage (Lev. 18.26). This passage is nowadays read in the synagogue on the afternoon of Yom Kippur.[2]

The Greek child, according to the pattern discussed above, is put in the position of an unwanted burden, a threat to his parents, and is raised to feel expendable, indeed guilty for existing. No wonder suicide is such a high-risk outcome. By contrast, the Hebrew child is much wanted and desired, and this knowledge helps him to withstand the normal stresses of life. The resiliency given to the child by the parents helps him to give the same to his own offspring. Instead of a drive to destroy one's family and oneself, as with the children of the house of Labdacus, there is every incentive to continue the family tradition. Although the deeds of the parents clearly affect the children, there is no sense of predetermination or fate.

The present chapter will examine narratives illustrating the ways in which Biblical families protect their offspring from self-destruction and encourage them toward development and creativity. Table 9.1 first examines the position of sons, and then of daughters.

HEBREW FATHERS AND SONS

Parental aggression toward children, which so dominates Classical thought and Freudian psychology, has no place in Biblical or rabbinic thought. Indeed, it is taken as natural that a father will be happy if his child surpasses him. God expresses His pleasure when the rabbis base a legal decision on their own scholarship despite heavenly signals to reverse the decision (*Baba Metzia*, 58).

Abraham and Isaac

The covenant of circumcision signals an important victory over the terrible conflict between fathers and sons. In the Bible, God makes a covenant with Abraham and his descendants. God will bless Abraham and give him the land of Canaan as his own; in return, Abraham and his progeny will follow God's law (Gen. 17.9–11).

The father is not the owner of his son as with the Roman *patria potestas*, nor does he hold the power of infant exposure. The relationship between father and son is seen in terms of the fulfillment of the covenant. The child honors his father and mother as an aspect of obedience to God, not of personal obligation to the parent. The urge of father and son to destroy each other is superseded by the obligation of both to the fulfillment and continuity of the covenant. One of the most significant themes in the rabbinic literature is the command to the father to teach his children thoroughly

Table 9.1
Biblical Parent–Child Narratives

	Fathers	Mothers
Sons	Abraham - Isaac ---------------- Jacob - sons	Rebecca - sons ---------------- Hannah - Samuel
Daughters	Amram - Miriam ------------------- Jephthah - Daughter	Naomi - Ruth

(Deut. 6.7; *Kiddushin*, 30a). The father's identity is not threatened by the son. He wants to see his son develop and surpass him.

The son learns that he is not an unwanted burden and that his well-being is beneficial both to God and to his father. He does not need to feel guilty for existing, nor does he entertain thoughts of self-destruction, even in his darkest hour. Isaac, for example, goes up on the altar on Mount Moriah not to fulfill a wish for suicide but in obedience to God. Neither Abraham nor Isaac wants Isaac's death, yet they wish to fulfill the will of God (*Genesis Rabbah*, 56.8).

It is particularly significant psychologically that the covenant is partly symbolized by physical circumcision (*berith hamilah*).[3] The Hebrew Bible seems to offer an unambivalent resolution for both the father's fear of displacement and the son's fear of castration and murder. The father willingly passes down the covenant, making displacement by the son unnecessary.[4] The son becomes aware that the father could have castrated him and destroyed his power of procreation and creativity but chose not to, instead offering a sanctified noninjurious circumcision as the very symbol of the father's love and assent to the son's right to succession.[5] This pattern results in increased security, making attacks on each other unnecessary.

Abraham goes through a series of tests, culminating in the binding of Isaac, that demonstrates that his devotion to God is of a different order than that of the idolater who actually does sacrifice his children to his deity. The final test begins with God's command to Abraham to sacrifice his son Isaac on Mount Moriah (Gen. 22). Abraham binds Isaac on the altar, but God will not allow the sacrifice:

And the angel of the Lord called unto him out of heaven, and said, "Abraham, Abraham!" and he said, "Here am I." And he said, Lay not thine hand upon the lad, neither do thou anything unto him; for now I know that thou art a God-fearing man, seeing thou hast not withheld thy son, thine only son, from me. (22.11–12)

God leads Abraham through an experience in which Abraham comes to realize something very significant. Unlike the Greek earth mother, the God of Genesis will never demand ritual murder, heroic self-sacrifice, or human suicide. Full obedience to this God instead demands a rejection of these destructive tendencies. This understanding has to be lived through and understood so that Abraham, Isaac, and all their descendants are released from the terrible forces that bludgeon a thinking Greek like Antigone into self-destruction.[6]

Jacob and His Sons

The story of Jacob and his sons offers another situation of great potential destructiveness. Joseph's special talents and Jacob's recognition of them arouse fear and jealousy among his brothers, to the point of their contemplating Joseph's murder and their actually selling him into slavery, while convincing Jacob that Joseph has been destroyed by a wild beast (Gen. 37). But Joseph thrives and develops morally in Egypt, even as a slave. In one particularly challenging moment, the love that he still feels from his father gives him the moral strength to reject the adulterous advances of Potiphar's wife. In this moment of trial, the image of his father comes to his mind (*Sotah*, 37). Years later, Joseph, as viceroy of Egypt, orchestrates a reunion with his brothers so that they are able to demonstrate, both to their satisfaction and to his, their sincere regret over their treatment of Joseph and their acceptance of the obligation to support all their brothers and their father (Gen. 42–45).

Jacob, now a very old man, provides the successful dénouement to the drama. He comes to Egypt, renews his relationship with Joseph, and makes certain that Joseph's sons, Ephraim and Manasseh, even though born in Egypt, are included within the family and are full recipients of its teachings and traditions. Finally, Jacob blesses his sons in terms of each one's unique strengths and weaknesses, affirming each as an individual personality, and recognizing his unique role and creativity in the covenant (Gen. 49): "All these are the twelve tribes of Israel, and this is what their father spoke unto them and blessed them, every one according to his blessing he blessed them" (Gen. 49.28).

This individual recognition of both the strengths and weaknesses of each son provides a high degree of approving acceptance for the son to develop and carry on the covenant according to his special emotions and abilities. Such a paternal blessing is the very essence of a nonsuicidal society and the strongest possible antidote to the destructive curse of Oedipus on his own sons who fight and kill each other. The destructive pathology and determinism of the Greek family undermines the basically well-meaning Oedipus. Jacob's blessing, in contrast, softens the rivalry between his sons, encouraging each to develop his own talents.

HEBREW MOTHERS AND SONS

The role of the mother in both Biblical and later Jewish families also is fundamentally different from that in the Greek family. She too is part of the covenant and plays a major role in its continuance. She has no need to defend or avenge herself by pitting her husband and sons against each other (Gen. 28.5; Hirsch 1876 on Gen. 27.42).

The Greek pattern of a mother seducing her son to displace her husband or murdering her son to deprive her husband of an heir is totally foreign to the Hebrew family. Biblical sons do not simply represent extensions of the mother, as do Medea's sons. They are human beings in their own right. Perhaps because the woman's status in the Biblical family is highly respected, she feels less need to compete with her husband and sons. Rather than encourage and exploit the primitive impulse toward rivalry between fathers and sons (the Oedipal conflict), she helps to promote a sense of harmony between them. Rather than evoke fears of incorporation and suicide in the son through the threat of either seduction or murder, she helps to guide the son to manhood as a potential heir of the covenant. Her role is different from that of her husband but no less integral. An ideal of womanhood is the *eishet chayil* (a woman of valor in Prov. 31).

Rabbinic literature stresses the significance of woman's support for the Torah study of her husband and sons (*Berakhot*, 17a; *Ketubot*, 62b). Numerous stories are related, such as that of the mother of Rabbi Joshua (ca. 50–125 CE) who brought him while still in the cradle to the house of study of the Torah. The rabbis of the Talmud also showed a great respect to their mothers. When Rabbi Joseph heard the footsteps of his mother approaching his house, he would hasten to meet her saying, "Let me rise to meet the Divine Presence" (*Kiddushin*, 31b).

Rebecca and Her Sons

A classic example of the Jewish mother is Rebecca. Abraham's servant is sent to Haran to find a suitable wife for Isaac. He plans to test the women of Haran by asking them for a drink of water from the well. Rebecca is the first to respond to his request and also volunteers to draw water for his ten camels, which are thirsty from their long journey. By this act of kindness and lively intelligence, she proves herself to be a fit wife for Isaac (Gen. 24.12–20; see also Abravanel 1964, on Gen. 24.12).

During her marriage to Isaac and particularly in the incident of the passing down of the blessing, Rebecca proves her compassion, ability, and courage as a wife and mother. Isaac, now an elderly man and dim of sight, lives a retiring life. He is drawn toward the vigorous Esau, perhaps because he possesses a type of earthy physical strength, a wildness, that Isaac himself lacks (Hirsch 1976, on Gen. 25.28). Apparently realizing that Jacob is the more fit of his two sons in spiritual matters, he decides to bestow his blessing of material wealth and power on Esau, who will likely need it more than Jacob. Rebecca learns of Isaac's intention and feels that he is mistaken. Jacob will be the follower of Abraham's covenant and will need the support of material well-being too. Rather than confront Isaac directly, she plans a deception that will obtain the material blessing for Jacob without bruising Isaac's feelings. When Jacob hesitates, Rebecca assures him that she is the mother and is assuming full responsibility for the plan (Gen. 27.13). The plan succeeds, and Jacob receives the blessing of material well-being, "dew of the heavens and the fat of the land and much corn and wine" (Gen. 27.28–29).

Rebecca bears no hatred toward Esau, even through the hard times that follow. She does not desire his destruction, but she sees more realistically than Isaac the threat to the continuity of the covenant should Esau, not Jacob, receive the blessing. When Rebecca hears of Esau's fury and his threats to murder Jacob, she again acts in a manner that saves Jacob's life and sets up the basis for the ultimate restoration of harmony to the family. She protects both her sons, each of whom she still loves (Gen. 27.43; 28.5; she is still "mother of Jacob and Esau"), and again avoids hurting Isaac. Without informing Isaac of Esau's threats and without filling his ears with "I told you so's," she suggests that it would be suitable for Jacob to go to Haran to find a wife, as indeed Eliezer had done for Isaac himself. Rebecca does not try to hold on to Jacob but instead arranges for him to be sent away to save his own life. Isaac agrees, without even realizing the full danger in the situation, and gives Jacob the spiritual blessing that he had planned for him all along (Gen. 28.3): "And give thee the blessing of Abraham and to thy seed with thee" (Gen. 28.4). Jacob now has both the spiritual blessing and the material assurance of carrying on the covenant. Family harmony is not shattered, and, when Jacob returns to Canaan years later, he and Esau are reconciled. Rebecca does her best to preserve the self-esteem of her two sons, each in his own way. Neither is driven to fratricide or to suicide!

Rebecca's role as a mediator in the Hebrew family ensures the successful passing down of the covenant and the restoration of family harmony. Throughout, she avoids creating a father-son rivalry. She is not interested in destroying either her son or her husband.

Hannah and Samuel

The relationship of Hannah and her son exemplifies the importance of the interplay of a supportive mother and, indeed, a supportive family. Hannah is deeply saddened over her failure to bear children (1 Sam. 1.5–10). Elkanah, her husband, is very supportive to her. Hannah goes to the Tabernacle to pray, and when the priest Eli hears of her problems, he too is supportive (1.17). Basically a positive thinker, Hannah accepts this reassurance (1.17). Within a year, Hannah gives birth to a son whom she names Samuel, indicating her gratitude to God: "because I have asked him of the Lord" (1.20).

When Samuel is old enough, Hannah brings him to serve at the Tabernacle. She reminds Eli that God had answered her prayers for a child; she feels that the child was lent to her by God and now she is lending him back. Hannah then recites a poem of praise and thanks to God in which she expresses her strong sense of closeness and hope in Him "who guards the steps of His holy ones" (2.9). Although still young in years, Samuel is clearly a child of exceptional sensitivity and intelligence, and he takes a serious part in the divine service in the Tabernacle. He is not merely a servant to Eli, who loves him deeply although Samuel seems to be far brighter and of better character than his own sons (2.12–20).

Hannah makes Samuel a special robe (*me'il*) and brings new ones to him as he grows. This is a garment typically worn by the leading priests and is a means for Hannah to express her love and confidence in her son (2.19; see Radak). Hannah continues to love Samuel; she does not wish to control him, however, feeling that what they both owe to God and to Samuel's own development far exceeds in importance the pleasure she would derive from keeping him at home. It is noteworthy that all through his life Samuel wears a *me'il* and even wears it in the other world (28.14; see Rashi and Radak). Hannah goes on to bear five other children.

In strong contrast is Hagar's treatment of Ishmael in the desert. After the bread and water given to them by Abraham are gone, she casts the child under a shrub and goes some distance off, saying, "Let me not look upon the death of the child" (Gen. 21.16). This pattern should remind the reader of Artemis' withdrawal from the dying Hippolytus (Euripides, *Hippolytus*, 1432–1433) rather than the Hebrew mothers. Hirsch (1976) has argued that Hagar's behavior is not characteristic of a Jewish mother who would not forsake her child and would help him in any way she can. Hagar, on the other hand, casts her child behind some bushes, quite indifferent to where he may fall and possibly even adding unnecessary pain to his thirst (356–357).

THE AKEDAH MOTIF AND SUICIDE PREVENTION

The Biblical stories provide a model for transforming the pathological position of the child in the Greek family into the life-affirming orientation of the Biblical family. The child feels that he is valued in his own independence and creativity. He is not presented with the intolerable choice of deep enmeshment versus estranged isolation. Instead, he can remain part of the tradition while becoming a worthy individual.

In *Isaac and Oedipus* (1954), Erich Wellisch has pointed to the Akedah narrative as the foundation story of this process. A good father-son relationship, unavailable in the story of Oedipus, establishes an effective encouragement to life, which prevents suicide in Biblical families. Wellisch has postulated that the Akedah experience encourages "instinct modification" in the attitudes of fathers toward sons and vice versa. His view has been severely criticized in psychoanalytic circles as mixing religion with psychology. Even someone as sympathetic to Wellisch as Theodore Reik has viewed Wellisch's claim for a modification of instincts in the Akedah experience as a psychological impossibility (Reik 1961, 225).[7]

Wellisch's claim for instinct modification is supported by a closer examination of Freud's analysis of the Oedipus complex.[8] The son threatens to displace his father, taking over his power as symbolized by possession of the mother.[9] The father threatens castration in response. The ambivalent neutralization of the Oedipus complex available to Greek society may be seen as a cold war between these two forces — the threat of displacement balanced by a threat of castration. Covenantal circumcision provides for a modification of the entire familial situation. The father knows that the son will inherit the covenant and thus will not try to displace him (the father); the son knows that the father could have castrated him but did not. Instead, circumcision becomes the very symbol of the son's right of inheritance and to his own life (Kaplan 1990a).

The suicide-preventive aspects of the Akedah story are diagrammed in Figure 9.1, bottom. The covenantal matrix within which the son develops, as expressed in circumcision, changes all of the familial relationships. The Hebrew husband (position D) honors and respects his wife (MW). She in turn loves him and helps him to pass on the covenant (WM = D). Her role as a mother is to nurture her son to his covenantal responsibilities, not to dominate his individuality (WS = D). The son in turn overcomes the Oedipal dilemma with his father. Not fearing displacement by the son, the father instructs him in the covenant (MS = D). The son does not need to desire to possess his mother or displace his father (thus resolving the Oedipal dilemma); instead he accepts protection and nurturance from his parents and learns from them. It is this assurance of outside protection that allows the son to develop in a healthy way (SM = B, SW = B) for his own role as a husband and father and his own place in the tradition (position D).

In summary, the Akedah experience provides an unambivalent resolution to the potentially suicidal Oedipal conflict.[10] The son's existence is not conditional on his staying infantile or becoming disengaged. He receives full support to develop into healthy manhood (BED axis). The Biblical family pattern blocks the transmission of narcissism and the Oedipal conflict from one generation to the next. The son does not grow into the male participant (position C) in a suicidogenic parental collusion in the next generation. Rather, he carries the potential of emerging as a developed male participant (BED axis) in a healthy, suicide-preventive (DD) parental relationship.

HEBREW MOTHERS AND DAUGHTERS

Although the Hebrew Bible is filled with stories of women of great character and significant accomplishment, there is almost no information in the Biblical text specific to mother-daughter relations. We can only assume that highly developed and revered women such as the matriarchs, Miriam, Huldah, Abigail, Esther, and Ruth came out of a healthy familial and societal background. Nevertheless, the story of Ruth and her mother-in-law Naomi provides a Biblical example of an intergenerational relationship between women.

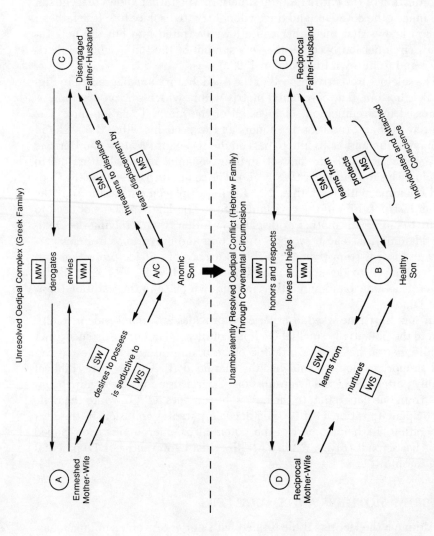

Figure 9.1
The Akedah Motif and Suicide Prevention

Naomi and Ruth

Naomi and Ruth support each other in very sensitive areas. Naomi offers Ruth a sense of belonging, even after her son, Ruth's husband, has died; she also helps her to find a fine husband and position in her new nation. Ruth refuses to abandon Naomi, even when they seem to have lost everything. This relationship is far removed from the enmeshment and abandonment conflicts of the classical Greek families. Ruth shows no desire to abandon Naomi in order to marry. Indeed, her loyalty to Naomi is exemplary. In turn, Naomi does her best to enhance Ruth's self-esteem and instructs her how to approach her kinsman Boaz. After Boaz and Ruth do marry, Naomi is included in their happiness, becoming nurse to their son Obed, who becomes the father of Jesse, the father of David.

The story begins when Naomi, her husband, and their two sons leave Judah to reside in Moab. After the death of her husband, Naomi's two sons marry women of Moab, Orpah and Ruth. Then Naomi's sons die, and she sets out to return to Judah accompanied by her two daughters-in-law. At this point, Naomi blesses her daughters-in-law and tells them to go back to Moab, to their own people. They both cry and insist that they will return with their mother-in-law to Judah. Naomi again urges them to go, stating that she is too old to have more sons for them to marry (Ruth 1.11–12). Unlike Clytemnestra, Naomi does not try to bind her daughters-in-law to her but unselfishly urges them to go on their way to find husbands. She recognizes their right to their own lives. They are not simply objects to serve her.

Orpah kisses her mother-in-law and departs, but Ruth will have none of it. In a moving speech, Ruth expresses her devotion to Naomi as a person, rather than as only a producer of a son. Unlike Electra, Ruth refuses to abandon Naomi:

And Ruth said, "Entreat me not to leave thee, or to return from following after thee: for whither thou goest, I will go; and where thou lodgest, I will lodge: thy people shall be my people, and thy God my God. Where thou diest, will I die, and there will I be buried: the Lord do so to me, and more also, if ought but death part thee and me." (Ruth 1.16–17)[11]

This beautiful reciprocity continues throughout the story, Naomi continuously encouraging and helping Ruth to fulfill her own needs and Ruth being certain to include Naomi in any good fortune she may experience. Ruth meets Boaz, a kinsman of Naomi's late husband, who is greatly moved by Ruth's treatment of Naomi: "It hath fully been told me, all that thou hadst done unto thy mother-in-law since the death of thy husband" (2.11). Naomi continues to look out for Ruth's welfare unselfishly. Rather than diminish Ruth's self-esteem (as Clytemnestra does to Electra), Naomi instructs Ruth about how to win Boaz (3.1–4).

Ruth follows Naomi's advice, and ultimately marries Boaz. She does not fail to include Naomi in her happiness. Naomi becomes the nurse to their son and is even described by the neighbors as the child's mother:

And he shall be unto thee a restorer of life and a nourisher of thine old age; for thy daughter-in-law, who loveth thee, who is better to thee than seven sons, hath borne him. And Naomi took the child, and laid it in her bosom, and became nurse unto it. And the women her neighbors gave it a name, saying, "There is a son born to Naomi." And they called his name Obed; he is the father of Jesse, the father of David. (4.5–17)

The Moabite woman Ruth is a fit ancestress of the Davidic dynasty.

HEBREW FATHERS AND DAUGHTERS

The attitude of the father in the Greek family — seducing his daughter in order to abandon her mother and then sacrificing her — is unthinkable within a Hebrew covenantal family, nor does the daughter idealize her father in the same desperate way. The father sees the daughter as a real person and does not employ her against her mother. We consider here two father-daughter stories; first, Amram and Miriam; second, Jephthah and his daughter.

Amram and Miriam

The Hebrew father sees his daughter as a full person in her own right, as one whose advice and opinions are worthy of respect and attention. This attitude finds full expression in the relationship of Amram and Miriam. Miriam is the daughter of Amram and Jochebed and the elder sister of Moses and Aaron. The Talmud (*Sotah*, 12b), filling out the rather cryptic account in Exodus 1–2, tells that when Pharaoh decreed that all Israelite infant boys would be murdered, Amram and Jochebed separated in despair over the doom impending on any male children they would bear. Miriam, still a very little girl, went to her father, and argued that, "Pharaoh's decree affected only the sons; your act affects daughters as well."

Amram accepts his daughter's advice and her sense of faith, and he and Jochebed remarry, with Miriam dancing at their wedding. In due course, this reunion produces Moses. Exodus 2 narrates the story of Moses' birth and the efforts of his family to hide him. When it is no longer safe to hide him in the house, his mother puts him in a little ark in the rushes. It is Miriam who is sent to watch over and protect him. She does not hesitate to approach the Egyptian princess who finds the ark, suggesting that the boy be nursed by his own natural mother. The critical issue here is that Amram trusts and respects his daughter. This trust should enhance Miriam's self-esteem and resiliency and give her the confidence to grow in a healthy and an integrated way.

The incident (Num. 27) of the five daughters of Zelophahad supports this picture of father-daughter relationships. Zelophahad dies, leaving five daughters but no sons. The five girls are as yet unmarried and therefore presumably rather young. They approach Moses with the claim that, since there are no sons, they themselves should inherit the father's portion of the land, so that his name should not be removed from his family. The Talmud (*Baba Batra*, 119b) says that the daughters argue their case wisely and to the point. Moses is impressed by them, and he brings their case straight to God Himself. God agrees with the girls' argument and praises them (*Sifre* on Num. 27.7). Rashi records the comment, "Happy is a person to whose words the Holy One gives agreement." Although there is no description of Zelophahad, his daughters are clearly independent and capable. They are also realistic about their father, neither idealizing him nor showing hostility to him (Num. 27.8).

Jephthah and His Daughter

Consider the single example of father-daughter sacrifice in the Hebrew Bible—that of Jephthah and his daughter. A child sacrifice story is of course repugnant. Nevertheless, a number of striking differences emerge between this sacrifice story and that of Agamemnon and Iphigenia. First, although both Agamemnon and Jephthah are offering a sacrifice in return for military success, Jephthah does not realize that he will be sacrificing his daughter. Rather, he offers to sacrifice "the first living creature that cometh forth of my house to meet me when I return" (Judg. 11.30–31). He apparently expects it to be an animal. Second, upon seeing his daughter emerge (11.34) and realizing the full import of his earlier vow, Jephthah shows genuine remorse: "He rent his clothes and said, 'Alas my daughter thou hast brought me very low. . . . I have opened my mouth to the Lord and I cannot go back' " (11.35). Thus, although his vow is ill-considered and foolish, it is not premeditated and callous like Agamemnon's. Furthermore, Jephthah does not employ deceit to carry out the vow the way that Agamemnon creates the ruse of a marriage. Finally Jephthah's response to his daughter is not self-centered in the same sense that Agamemnon's is. This is especially dramatic in light of the greater insecurity in Jephthah's social and political position. Nevertheless, the rabbis have been quite harsh in their evaluation of Jephthah. He is used in the Talmud as an example of one unfit to rule. They have also criticized Jephthah's obstinacy for not having gone to a priest or a sage to have his vow annulled (*Genesis Rabbah*, 60.3; *Midrash Tanhuma Buber Behukotai*, 112–114).[12]

The Biblical narrative does not idealize the death of Jephthah's daughter nor is there any sense of self-sacrificing altruism. In fact, it is not clear that she actually is sacrificed. Some say she is (*Midrash Tanhuma Buber Behu-kotai*, 112–114), but others maintain that she is not put to death but instead becomes a recluse (see *Tanach Mikraot Gedolot*, glossators on Judg. 11). There is no sense of self-sacrificing or altruistic suicide in the death of Jephthah's daughter. She is willing to go along with her father's vow, but only after she goes away for two months of mourning (Judg. 11.39–40).[13]

THE RUTH MOTIF AND SUICIDE PREVENTION

The typical Biblical mother-daughter relationship thus is very unlike the Greek. The emphasis shifts from competition between mother and daughter to a united effort toward fulfilling the covenant. The father also teaches children as a fulfillment of the covenant (Bakan 1979). The child honors his father and mother as an aspect of obedience to God, not simply out of a personal obligation to the parent.

The daughter's role in the Hebrew family is quite different from the son's but no less important. Menstruation does not cause the same shame and diminution in self-esteem as in the Greek society. Rather, it is transformed in Judaism into part of the woman's unique role. It is her task to observe carefully the laws that govern and sanctify the physical aspects of her role as a woman. In practice, the essential law of *nidah* is that a woman ceases sexual contact with her husband at the onset of her menstrual period. Seven days after the termination of her menstrual flow, she may immerse herself in the ritual water, after which full sexual contact between husband and wife may be resumed (Blumenkrantz 1969; Tendler 1982). A woman's sexuality is accepted as part of civilized society, and she need not be ashamed of it.[14] A young girl thus does not need to attempt to abandon her mother and possess her father to achieve security. Likewise, a mother need not evoke her daughter's shame of menstruation. A girl is not an expendable object but a person with her own unconditional right to exist.[15]

This covenantal structure also overcomes the daughter's fear that her father will abandon her. Leaving her father's house to become a wife and mother on her own is a joyous and sacred fulfillment of her duty as an *eishat chayil* (a woman of valor). The Midrash recounts that when Rabban Gamaliel's daughter was getting married, he blessed her thus: "May you never return to my house, and may the word 'woe' never depart from your mouth." He then explained to her, "May you be so happy with your husband that you have no need to return to your parent's home; and may you have children and be devoted to raising them well" (*Genesis Rabbah*, 26.4).

The relationship between the Ruth narrative and suicide prevention is presented in Figure 9.2. The covenantal matrix within which the daughter develops is symbolized by the ritual purification in relation to menstruation (*nidah* and *mikva*). This matrix fundamentally changes all of the fa-

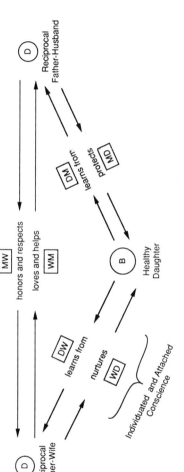

Unresolved Electra Conflict (Greek Family)

Unambivalently Resolved Electra Conflict (Hebrew Family)
Through Covenantal Purification

Figure 9.2
The Ruth Motif and Suicide Prevention

milial relationships. The Hebrew husband honors and respects his wife
(MW = D). She, in turn, helps him to pass on the covenant (WM = D).
Her role as a mother is to guide her daughter on the path to finding spiritual, emotional, and material fulfillment with God and her family. Essential to this is their femininity without shame (WD = D). The daughter
gives up any attempt to abandon her mother and ally with her father (thus
resolving the Electra dilemma), instead coming to accept nurturance and
learning from her mother without being symbiotically connected to her. It
is this assurance of nurturance that allows the daughter to be a daughter
(DW = B). The daughter does not fall into the oral-narcissistic dilemma
with the father, neither fearing abandonment by him nor desiring to fuse
with him. She comes to trust him not to use her for his own interests and
allows him to protect her.

The mother knows that her daughter is a partner in the tradition and
that she need not try to abandon the mother; the daughter knows that the
mother need not evoke shame in her. The father's transformation in the
family is pivotal. He is transformed from child exposer to protector, resolving the daughter's Electra complex and strengthening her hold on life. Parents can relate in a truly nurturant (D) manner to their daughters and to
each other, and they provide the genuine protection and support the
daughter needs for healthy development (BED axis).

The daughter's avoidance of the enmeshment-abandonment pathology
endemic to the AC axis has profound implications for blocking the transmission of narcissism and suicidogenics from one generation to the next.
The daughter avoids becoming the enmeshing partner in her own pathological (AC) marriage. Rather, her development (BED axis) facilitates life-
affirming, healthy (DD) parental and marital relationships.

No family pattern is totally foolproof against suicide for either daughters
or sons. As we shall see in Chapter 10, however, all is not lost in the Biblical
scheme of things, for God himself provides a safety-net for the family. He
will provide the stopper to prevent the pattern of suicidal destruction.

NOTES

1. These characteristics seem to have insulated the Jewish family to some degree, even in modern times. In a national survey conducted in a six-month period
in 1965, the National Opinion Research Center (NORC) studied the family background of child abuse victims; 164 fatalities resulting from child abuse were reported. Although Jews represent approximately 3 percent of the population, not
one of the above fatalities involved a Jewish mother.

2. The Hebrew Bible allows polygyny but definitely not incest. Nevertheless,
several seemingly incestuous relationships are described; for example, Lot and his
two daughters (Gen. 19) and Judah and Tamar (Gen. 38). Lot's daughters, for example, mistakenly believe their father to be the last man on earth. The widowed
Tamar feels rejected by her father-in-law with regard to his promise to marry her to

his youngest son. In neither case is the man aware of the incestuous nature of the sexual act. Lot is made drunk by his daughters, while Tamar disguises herself as a harlot. Significantly, the rabbis have not seen Tamar's act as incestuous under the religious law of that time.

3. A sense of participation in the covenant is experienced even among those sons for whom the law forbids circumcision for medical reasons.

4. It is noteworthy too that although a double portion of the material inheritance generally goes to the first-born son, there is no comparable notion of primogeniture in carrying on religious leadership. In this, all sons are equally responsible, and the leaders attain their status through ability and merit. Isaac, Jacob, and Joseph are not the first-born to their fathers, nor are Levi and Judah, upon whom priesthood and kingship later devolve.

5. Covenantal circumcision must be distinguished from circumcision that is simply used as a rite of passage into manhood. Despite these social-benefit arguments, Judaism stresses that only God knows the deepest reasons for the laws of Torah.

6. The British psychotherapist Erich Wellisch has argued that the entire experience produces a fundamental modification of instinct in Abraham:

A fundamental effect of Abraham's change of outlook was the realization that God demanded life and not death. Abraham realized that the meaning of the commanded sacrifice was not to kill his son but to dedicate his son's lifelong service to God. He completely rejected the former dominance of his death instinct and entirely abandoned his aggressive tendencies against Isaac. His life instinct was tremendously prompted and with it a new love emerged in him for Isaac, which became the crowning experience of his religion. (89)

7. Wellisch has suggested that the moral relationship of parents to their children can be considered in three main stages. The first and most primitive stage is characterized by intense aggression and possessiveness of the parents. The aggression is particularly severe in the father and directed mainly at his sons, in the first place at his first born son. In early societies, it not infrequently culminated in infanticide. The second stage is caused by a reaction of guilt about aggressive and possessive tendencies, especially about committed infanticide. It results in a compromise solution between the opposing tendencies of the wish to possess the child completely or even kill him and the desire not to do so (i.e., Freud's Oedipus complex). These mental sufferings can be overcome only when the third stage of moral development of the parent-child relationships is reached. It consists in the almost entire abandonment of possession and in a covenant of love and affection between parent and child.

8. Significantly, the possibility of the modification of instincts is accepted in rabbinic thought and particularly emphasized in the Musar teaching of Rabbi Israel Salanter and his school.

9. The mother, though seemingly the center in a sexual triangle, is again not valued in her own right. She represents the "keys to the kingdom" rather than an end in herself.

10. Christianity, of course, has its own primal relationship between father and son — that of God the Father and his son Jesus Christ. The Akedah experience works to eliminate tendencies toward child sacrifice in the human being. God cannot and does not allow the sacrifice of a human being, nor does God allow the sacrifice of the child of the promise. The Golgotha narrative reintroduces the child-sacrifice

theme so apparent in Oedipus and other Greek myths but with a twist. It is connected to God's love for the world. Indeed, this is the central Christian proclamation: "For God so loved the world, that he gave his only begotten son, that whoever believes in him should not perish, but have eternal life" (John 3.16). The question of why God does not intervene to save his own son, as he did to save Isaac, is the theme of Kazantzakis' *The Last Temptation of Christ* (1960). This connection between love and sacrifice fits the altruistic suicide theme so typical in the plays of Sophocles and Euripides. The proclamation in John reads like a suicide note: "I have died to save you." Christianity opposes suicide, yet its central figure is an altruistic martyr whose aim is to save the world rather than just Thebes. The question can be raised as to whether believing Christians may experience "survivor guilt."

11. The Midrash amplifies the religious intent behind Naomi's words. When Naomi tells Ruth to remain behind because Jewish women do not frequent theaters and circuses, Ruth replies, "Whither thou goest, I will go." When informed that Jewish women dwell only in houses sanctified by mezuzot, Ruth responds "where thou lodgest, I will lodge." The phrase "Thy people will be my people" reveals her intent to give up idolatry, and "thy God shall be my God" indicates Ruth's acceptance of the Torah (*Midrash Ruth Rabbah* and Rashi on Ruth 1.16).

12. It is instructive to compare Jephthah's vow with Abraham's binding of Isaac. Jephthah's vow is a thoughtless unilateral act. Abraham, by contrast, is commanded directly by God to offer up Isaac. This is not a vow but divine command.

13. It should be pointed out that there is some disagreement about the ultimate fate of Iphigenia as well. While most accounts of the myth claim that Iphigenia was indeed sacrificed at Aulis by Agamemnon, one version maintains that she was miraculously snatched away to safety by Artemis at the last moment and subsequently became the priestess of a human sacrifice cult (see Graves 1955, 2.73–80 and Euripides, *Iphigenia at Taurus*).

14. The Midrash says on Numbers 23.9 that a man cannot number the *mitzvot* that he fulfills with the seed of sexual intercourse. Semen and menstrual blood are both sacred parts of God's creation.

15. The mother may be seen as the person who prepares the daughter to accept her role as a wife and mother in marriage. Rather than eliciting menstrual shame in her daughter, a mother may set the stage for the daughter's subsequent attention to the laws of purity. The daughter must purify herself with regard to sexual relations with her husband but in a manner that enhances her self-esteem as a woman rather than diminishes it.

IV

THE PREVENTION OF SUICIDE

Chapter 10

From Tragedy to Therapy:
A Psychology of Hope

But now, I am forsaken of the gods, son of a defiled mother, successor
to his bed who gave me my own wretched being.
                                    Sophocles, *Oedipus the King*, 1359–1361

Pray thou no more; for mortals have no escape from destined woe.
                                    Sophocles, *Antigone*, 1336

Cast me not off, neither forsake me, O God of my salvation. For
though my father and mother have forsaken me, the Lord will take me
up.
                                    Psalms 27.9–10

Even if a sword's edge lies on the neck of a man he should not hold
himself back from prayer.
                                    Berachot, 10a

In the Greek world, man feels trapped and desperate, with all hope still
locked up in Pandora's box and unavailable (Hesiod, *Works and Days*,
90–98). His gods show little interest in him. Suicide offers itself as a way to
gain freedom and security, whether through egoistic Promethean rebellion, altruistic self-sacrifice, or anomic confusion between the two. Far
from providing a stopper, Greek thought seems actually to push the individual in his rush to self-destruction. Biblical man has a sense of being created and watched over by a concerned and caring God and of having a
purpose and hope.[1] The rainbow in the sky after the flood reaffirms this
relation and gives the individual hope (Gen. 9.12–14). Man is an important creature with significant responsibilities and does not have to destroy
himself to please God. It is sufficient and expected that he show gratitude

and make good use of the gift of life. He has no need to justify his existence beyond this and is not pushed into deeds of impossible heroism or altruism.

The story of Jonah offers a prime example of this process. Jonah runs away in confusion, because he is not able to answer God's command to go to Nineveh. God, however, provides a great fish to shelter him in his state of regressed confusion. Narcissus, by contrast, lacks protection in his confusion and falls to self-destruction.

Often Biblical intervention is very simple. Elijah is given food and water, and Moses is offered help for his burden. The Greek Ajax, in contrast, is left alone in his depression, with neither food nor emotional support. The Biblical story of Naaman and Elisha (2 Kings 5.1–14) illustrates the importance of simple interventions. Naaman, a Syrian general stricken with leprosy, approaches the prophet Elisha for help. Elisha proposes a simple cure: "Go and wash in the Jordan seven times, and thy flesh shall come back to thee, and thou shalt be clean." Naaman becomes angry that Elisha does not propose something grander, and his own servants criticize him for his disparaging attitude toward a simple intervention: "My father, if the prophet had bid thee do some great thing, wouldst thou not have done it? How much rather then, when he saith to thee, 'Wash and be clean'?" Naaman dips in the Jordan and is cured.

BIBLICAL FAMILY THERAPY

Effective psychotherapy must be two-pronged. It must provide for the restoration of the entire family when this is possible, and it must remove the individual from the family when the family cannot be restored. The unsalvageable family can actually promote self-destruction in the individual, and here the therapy must protect the individual from the family.

An effective modern psychotherapy must avail itself of the Biblical world-view. First, the individual is not abandoned nor need he feel enmeshed. This is true even if his own family is deficient in these ways. Second, the individual's life improves when he realizes that he can recover from mistakes. He must learn to hope. Finally, therapy must involve nurturance at both the symbolic and material levels.

The suicidogenic Greek family feels abandoned by the gods and is often hopelessly enmeshed. Generational boundaries are blurred, family members take sides against each other, and relations between the genders are often fatally antagonistic. This impossible condition is agonizingly expressed in the Oedipus stories: "But now, I am forsaken of the gods, son of a defiled mother, successor to his bed who gave me my own wretched being" (Sophocles, Oedipus the King, 1359–1361). Biblical families, however, are neither abandoned by God nor hopelessly enmeshed. Generations are clearly differentiated from each other, and triangulation between the genders is discouraged. Further, the relationship between the genders is complementary rather than antagonistic: "Therefore shall a man leave his father and his mother, and shall cleave unto his wife, and they shall be one flesh" (Gen. 2.24).

The basic goal of covenantal family therapy is to transform suicido-genic families into hopeful families. This requires the redirecting of entire families off the enmeshed-disengaged axis onto a healthy axis that allows a genuine integration of individuation and attachment.

Both Greek and Biblical couples may face problems. The difference is in the response of the divine therapist. Zeus creates the entire context in which Prometheus must steal fire for mankind and Pandora is sent to en-trap man. Further, Zeus actively intervenes to block a happy couple, Deucalion and Pyrrha, from achieving joint harmonious parenthood. He calls for male-female antagonism, with Deucalion throwing stones over his shoulder to create men and Pyrrha doing the same to create women.[2] The Biblical God, on the other hand, provides protection for Noah and his wife, presenting them with the instructions to build the ark. He does not force them into a Promethean rebellion to save themselves. Earlier, the Biblical God interrupts the emerging narcissistic collusion between Adam and Eve, providing protection to enable them to regroup and to rebuild their lives.[3]

A family approach to suicide prevention involves the transformation of a Greek family into a Biblical family. Practically, this transformation must be divided into three phases: separation, protection, and integrated devel-opment.

Separation. The suicidal youth is trapped by his pathological family be-tween enmeshment and disengagement. His attempts at individuation are interpreted by his parents as abandonment. Family attempts at unity are perceived as enmeshment. Each generation has its own symbols, and even potentially resolvable issues can lead to shattering crises. A graphic clinical experience serves as an illustration here. A rigidly homophobic Vietnam veteran was brought to treatment by his wife because he threatened to pull the earring out of the left ear of his adolescent son. The father stormed, "No son of mine is going to be a fruitcake." The son, equally homophobic, responded, "Left is right, right is wrong." This statement turned out to be an attempt by the son to express, in the idiom of his generation, his self-assertion of being straight as opposed to gay. Though neither party realized it at the time, the boy was very much his father's son. He dropped out of school (against therapeutic advice), enlisted in the army, and went with the American forces to Saudi Arabia. In such a case, the therapist must provide a temporary protective shield between the child and his parents. The child must be protected from pathological family dynamics.

Protection. At this phase, the therapist must encourage both the child and the family to give up their shared polarity between individuation and attachment. The family must come to understand that the child must stake out his own identity. The child, in his turn, must come to understand the meaning and supportive functions of family. Old behaviors and response patterns must be unlearned, and new ways of transmitting and receiving symbols must be incorporated. This can be very confusing. The child is helped to give up the illusory and dangerous temptations of premature autonomy or intimacy. The therapist must provide a protective shield to allow the child time to grow. The parents too must be weaned away from the rigid choices between enmeshed loyalty and expulsion that they place on the family. They too will be confused and must be protected by the therapist.

Integrated Development. Until this phase, the therapist is dealing with the child separately from the parents. Now he brings them together, helping to create a shared agenda in which the child's needs for integrated development are not seen by his parents as abandoning nor are parental responses designed to keep the child enmeshed. The child must perceive unconditional supports for his right to exist, to achieve, and even to surpass his parents. The therapist must now begin to withdraw from his role as a buffer between the youth and the parents and to solidify a new family environment based on harmony. The critical issues here are to elicit parental and family support for the youth to develop and for the youth to learn to differentiate himself in ways that maintain harmony. A sense of freedom must be instilled that is not in opposition to the family but congruent with it. It is critical that the family learn to recognize this individuation-attachment conflict and to resolve it in a constructive way.

BIBLICAL INDIVIDUAL THERAPY

Sometimes, a family is unsalvageable and indeed may contribute to the suicidal crisis. Findings from one recent study suggest that disturbed parents tend to be potentially suicidogenic for their children unless the children insulate themselves from the family dynamics (Kaplan and Maldaver 1990b).[4]

Greek literature sees such a situation as hopeless. The child is enmeshed in the pathology of his family of origin with no concept of how to escape. The attempts by Oedipus to avoid his fate only sink him deeper into it. He flees from his step-parents in Corinth, hoping to spare them from the curse of the oracle but then encounters his biological parents in Thebes and plays out the curse. There is no hope: "Pray thou no more, for mortals have no escape from predestined woe" (Sophocles, *Antigone*, 1336). For people so obsessed with tragedy, therapy is useless!

In the Biblical world, all is not lost, even when a family is unredeemable. "Cast me not off, neither forsake me, O God of my salvation. For though my mother and father have forsaken me, the Lord will take me up" (Psalms 27.9–10). Parents have been sent by God to do the job of rearing children. God Himself as the third partner in parenting offers the children the security and respect they need. The parents too must recognize their reliance on God. One must not lose hope, no matter how desperate the situation. The prophet Isaiah foretells King Hezekiah's death because he has produced no offspring. Hezekiah responds: "The idea has been passed down from the house of my fathers: Even if a sword's edge lies on the neck of a man, he should not hold himself back from prayer" (*Berachot*, 10a).

A classic illustration of this theme is the story of Abraham. God commands him to leave the house and the country of his father and to go to a new land where God will make of him a great nation (Gen. 12.1–3). Rashi has explained Abraham's need to separate himself from the corrupting influence of his family of origin: "In the land of idol worship, Abraham is not worthy to rear sons to the service of God" (Rashi on Gen. 12.1).[5] Several accounts in the Talmud illustrate the possibility of individuals overcoming the deleterious influences of their parents to become righteous people. The descendants of the wicked Haman teach the Torah in Bnei Brak, while those of the cruel Assyrian King Sennacherib (Shemaiah and Abtalyon) become the teachers of Hillel (*Gittin*, 57b).

Greek stories are filled with accounts of the destructive effects of family, from which individuals seem never to escape. In the Biblical narratives, God intervenes, lifting the person above the limitations of his familial background. Abraham leaves the house and land of his father Terah and is protected by God. In Biblical thought, people can find in their faith the ability to overcome deep problems. When characters in Greek literature return to their roots, they are overwhelmed by primordial forces.

Therapeutic support can help to provide extraparental protection. As such, the therapist is acting in a Biblical framework, whether or not he realizes it. He is placing his bet on the belief that he can help a patient to overcome the tragic effects of a dysfunctional family that the individual, with secure support, is free to change. The therapist is opting for a therapeutic as opposed to a tragic vision of life.

Individual therapy resembles the family approach, with one important difference. There is no reintegration between parents and child. The therapist must substitute for the parents, ultimately helping the patient to find a parental substitute either within himself or in the extrafamilial environment. The three phases of this kind of individual psychotherapy are as follows:

Permanent Separation. The suicidal youth must be *permanently separated* from his pathological family. He must be taught to think in an untrapped manner and to free himself from the stark alternatives of enmeshment and estrangement that provoke his self-destructive tendencies.

Protection. The therapist must provide protection for the patient while he is vulnerable, so that the patient can strengthen himself without feeling threatened. This is a period of unlearning pathological ways of coping, and the individual needs to be protected.

Integrated Development. The therapist must guide and protect the individual in his integrated development. Such protection allows him to escape the destructive quick fixes of misdirected attachments and achievements. He must learn a repertoire of behaviors that provide both individuation and attachment.

SUMMARY

A covenantal psychotherapy can free children and parents from narcissistic polarities and self-destructive tendencies. A healthy family assures protection and nurturance and allows and encourages a person to develop his own unique creativity.

The therapist may provide substitute parenting to facilitate this process. Biblical concepts can be employed so that parents protect their children and set limits for them, rather than simply permitting certain behaviors. They do this not to block the children, as in the typical Greek family, but to enable them to grow in ways that are not self-destructive. Freedom is instilled not in the Graeco-Roman sense of escape but in the Hebrew sense of opportunity for commitment. Suicide is prevented rather than promoted. Living rather than dying is assisted.

Hope can free the individual from the threat of a tragic, deterministic, and suicidal view of life. Further, it offers a therapeutic alternative to a fixation on impossible choices. The quest for the heroic "noble death" of the Graeco-Roman tradition[6] becomes irrelevant as human life becomes more hopeful and possible. This has been the great insight of the Hebrew tradition.

NOTES

1. The work of Aaron Beck and his colleagues (1985) has pointed to the relationship between hopelessness and suicide.

2. In Greek mythology, aggression in cross-sex parent-child dyads occurs more than twice as often as aggression in same-sex parent-child dyads (Slater 1968, 403). Slater has pointed out that this finding runs counter to the cornerstone of orthodox psychoanalytic thinking. The pattern becomes understandable in light of our analysis. The ambivalent resolution of the Oedipal and Electra dilemmas available from the Greek perspective (Wellisch 1954) transfers parent-child conflicts from the same-sex arena to the cross-sex domain.

3. The Biblical perspective provides unambivalent and full resolution of the Oedipal and Electra conflicts. This should drastically reduce cross-sex parent-child conflicts. Indeed, the work of David Bakan (1971; 1979) has pointed to the involvement of fathers in Biblical families; these fathers overcome their tendency to abandon their children, especially their daughters, which was a widespread practice in

the Hellenistic world (Rostovtzeff 1964, 623–625, 1329, 1547). Even Tacitus, the anti-Semitic Roman historian, noted that Jews do not kill their new-born infants and thus provide for an increase in their numbers (Tacitus, *History*, 5.5).

4. The Kaplan and Maldaver results suggest that the marital pathology score differentiates adolescent psychopathology independent of suicide and adolescent suicide independent of psychopathology. Further, reported adolescent psycho-pathology and suicide are largely independent of one another. In other words, pathological adolescents in dysfunctional families are not the ones who commit suicide; rather, it is the adjusted adolescents in these same dysfunctional families. The results in this sample suggest that some seemingly pathological defensive be-haviors (e.g., communicative withdrawal) on the part of adolescents growing up in disturbed families actually serve a suicide-preventive function by protecting the adolescent from the pathological dynamics of the family. In other words, some de-fensive pathologies actually represent self-therapy on the part of adolescents in dis-turbed families. These results have strong implications for our family therapy approach to adolescent suicidal behavior and are consistent with the work of Laing and Esterson (1970).

5. Abraham does not let Isaac go back to his ancestral homeland but brings a wife from there to him. Jacob does go, under duress, but brings his wives back to Canaan with him.

6. The therapeutic answer to the question posed by Hamlet, with which we opened the book, is to "B"; that is to temporarily withdraw to a protected position (B) which avoids the suicidal dialectics of enmeshment and abandonment (the AC axis) so likely to provoke the futile heroic gestures so common in the Graeco-Roman world.

Bibliography

Abrahamsen, D. 1946. *The Mind and Death of a Genius.* New York: Columbia University Press.

Abravanel, I. [15th cent.] 1964. *Perush al Hatorah*, 3 vols. Jerusalem: Bnai Arbael.

Adams, J. 1700. *An Essay Concerning Self-murder.* London: Privately printed for T. Bennett.

Aeschines. 1919. *The Speeches of Aeschines* [including Against Ctesiphon]. Trans. C. B. Adams. London: W. Heinemann.

Ainsworth, M. D. S. 1972. Attachment and Dependency: A comparison. In *Attachment and Dependency*, ed. J. Gerwitz. Washington, DC: V. H. Winston and Sons.

Alighieri, D. 1977. *The Divine Comedy.* Trans. J. Ciardi. New York: W. W. Norton.

Alvarez, A. 1970. *The Savage God.* New York: Random House.

Apocrypha of the Old Testament. 1965. New York: Oxford University Press.

Apollodorus. 1976. *The Library.* Trans. M. Simpson. Amherst: University of Massachusetts Press.

Apollonius. 1912. *Argonautica.* Trans. R. C. Seaton. Cambridge, MA: Harvard University Press (Loeb Classical Library).

Appianus of Alexandria. 1912–1913. *Appian's Roman History.* Trans. Horace White. New York: Macmillan.

Aquinas, Thomas. 1981. *Summa Theologica.* 5 vols. Trans. Fathers of the English Dominican Province. Westminster, MD: Christian Classics.

Aristotle. 1936. *The Poetics.* Ed. and trans. S. H. Butcher. London: Macmillan.

Aristotle. 1976. *The Ethics of Aristotle: The Nichomachean Ethics.* Trans. J. A. K. Thomson. New York: Penguin.

Athenaeus of Naucratis. 1924. *The Deipnosophists.* London: Heinemann.

Augustinus, Aurelius. 1955. *The Problem of Free Choice.* Trans. Dom Mark Pontifex. London: Longmans, Green.

Augustinus, Aurelius. 1957–1972. *The City of God Against the Pagans*, 7 vols. Trans. Willima M. Green. Cambridge, MA: Harvard University Press.

Augustinus, Aurelius. [1631] 1960. *St. Augustine's Confessions*. 2 vols. Cambridge, MA: Harvard University Press, Loeb Classical Library.

Augustinus, Aurelius. 1963. *The Trinity*. Trans. S. McKenna. Washington, DC: The Catholic University of America Press.

Avot D' R. Nathan. 1887. Ed. S. Schechter. Vienna: n.p.

Babylonian Talmud. Vilna edition. 1975. Jerusalem.

Bachya Ibn Pakuda. 1965. *Duties of the Heart*. Trans. M. Hyamson. Jerusalem: Boystown Publishers.

Baechler, J. [1975] 1979. *Suicides*. New York: Basic Books.

Bakan, D. 1971. *Slaughter of the Innocents*. San Francisco: Jossey-Bass.

Bakan, D. 1979. *And They Took Themselves Wives: The Emergence of Patriarchy in Western Civilization*. New York: Harper & Row.

Battin, M. P., and D. J. Mayo. 1981. *Suicide: The Philosophical Issues*. London: Peter-Owen.

Bayet, A. 1922. *Le Suicide et la Morale*. Paris: F. Alcan.

Beavers, W. R. and M. Voeller. 1983. Family models comparing and contrasting the Olson circumplex model with the Beavers system model. *Family Process* 22: 88–95.

Beck, A. T., R. A. Steer, M. Kovacs, and B. Garrison. 1985. Hopelessness and eventual suicide: A ten year prospective study of patients hospitalized with suicidal ideation. *American Journal of Psychiatry* 142: 559–563.

Ben Gurion, Joseph. 1956. *Sefer Yosippon*. Jerusalem: Hotstaat Hominer.

Berlin, M. 1943. *Rabban Shel Yisrael*. New York: Histadrut Ha Mizrachi.

Bettelheim, B. 1955. *Symbolic Wounds*. London: Thames and Hudson.

Blumenkrantz, A. 1969. *The Laws of Nidah: A Digest*. Far Rockaway, NY: n.p.

Bohannan, P. 1960. *African Homicide and Suicide*. Princeton, NJ: Princeton University Press.

Bowen, M. 1960. The family as the unit of study and treatment. *American Journal of Orthopsychiatry* 31: 40–60.

Bowlby, J. 1969. *Attachment*. New York: Basic Books.

Bowlby, J. 1973. *Separation: Anxiety and Anger*. New York: Basic Books.

Bowlby, J. 1977. The making and breaking of affectional bonds: Etiology and psychopathology in the light of attachment theory. *British Journal of Psychiatry* 130: 201–210.

Brandt, R. B. 1975. "The Rationality of Suicide" from "The Morality and Rationality of Suicide." In *A Handbook for the Study of Suicide*, ed. S. Perlin. Oxford: Oxford University Press.

Breiner, S. J. 1990. *Slaughter of the Innocents: Child Abuse through the Ages and Today*. New York: Plenum Press.

Buchler, A. 1922. *Types of Jewish-Palestinian Piety from 70 B.C.E. to 70 C.E.* London: Jews' College, Publication #8.

Camus, A. 1948. *The Plague*. New York: Modern Library.

Camus, A. 1955. *The Myth of Sisyphus and Other Essays*. New York: Alfred A. Knopf.

Caro, J. 1977. *Shulchan Aruch*. Tel Aviv: n.p.

Cavan, R. 1928. *Suicide*. Chicago: University of Chicago Press.

Cicero. 1914. *De Finibus Bonorum et Malorum.* Trans. H. Rackham. New York: Macmillan.

Cicero. 1945. *Tusculan Disputations.* Trans. J. E. King. Cambridge, MA: Harvard University Press, Loeb Classical Library.

Cohen, S. J. D. 1982. Masada, literature, tradition, archaeological remains, and the credibility of Josephus. *Journal of Jewish Studies* 33: 385–405.

Cohn, H. 1976. Suicide in Jewish legal and religious tradition. *Mental Health and Society* 3: 129–136.

Conon. 1798. *Narrationes Quinquaginta et Parthenii Narrationes Amatoriae.* Gottingae: J. C. Dietrich.

Cyprian. 1951. In *The Ante-Nicene Fathers,* 5. Ed. A. Roberts and J. Donaldson. Grand Rapids, MI: Wm. B. Eerdmans.

d'Holbach, P. H. T. [1770] 1821. *Système de la Nature.* Paris: Etienne Ledoux.

Dio Chrysostom. 1932. *Diochrysostrom.* Trans. J. W. Cohoon. London: W. Heinemann.

Diogenes Laertius. 1972. *Lives of Eminent Philosophers.* 2 vols. Trans. R. D. Hicks. Cambridge, MA: Harvard University Press, Loeb Classical Library.

Donne, J. [1608] 1984. *Biathanatos.* Ed. Ernest W. Sullivan II. Cranbury, NJ: Associated University Press.

Douglas, J. D. 1967. *The Social Meanings of Suicide.* Princeton, NJ: Princeton University Press.

Droge, A. J., and J. D. Tabor. 1992. *A Noble Death: Suicide and Martyrdom among Christians and Jews in Antiquity.* New York: Harper Collins.

Durkheim, E. [1897] 1951. *Suicide.* Trans. J. A. Spaulding and G. Simpson. Glencoe, IL: Free Press.

Elwin, V. 1943. *Muria Murder and Suicide.* London: Oxford University Press.

Epictetus. 1890. *The Discourses of Epictetus: With the Enchiridion and Fragments.* Trans. G. Long. London: G. Bell and Sons.

Epstein, Y. M. (n.d.) *Aruch Hashulchan.* Jerusalem: n.p.

Erikson, E. 1968. *Identity, Youth, and Crisis.* New York: W. W. Norton.

Faber, M. 1967. Shakespeare's Suicides: Some Historic, Dramatic, and Psychological Reflections. In *Essays in Self-Destruction,* ed. Eishneldman. New York: Science Houses.

Faber, M. D. 1970. *Suicide and Greek Tragedy.* New York: Sphinx.

Fedden, H. R. 1938. *Suicide: A Social and Historical Study.* London: Peter Davies.

Finley, M. I. 1959. *The World of Odysseus.* New York: Meridian.

Frend, W. H. C. 1952. *The Donatist Church: A Movement of Protest in Roman North Africa.* Oxford: Clarendon Press.

Frend, W. H. C. 1965. *Martyrdom and Persecution in the Early Church: A Study of a Conflict from the Maccabees to Donatus.* Oxford: Blackwell.

Freud, A. 1936. *The Ego and the Mechanisms of Defense.* New York: International Universities Press.

Freud, S. 1913. *Totem and taboo.* In *Standard Edition of the Complete Works of Sigmund Freud, 13,* 1–161, ed. and trans. J. Strachey. London: Hogarth Press.

Freud, S. 1914. *On Narcissism: An Introduction.* In *Standard Edition of the Complete Works of Sigmund Freud, 14,* 73–102, ed. and trans. J. Strachey. London: Hogarth Press.

Freud, S. 1917. *Mourning and Melancholia*. In *Standard Edition of the Complete Works of Sigmund Freud*, *14*, 243–258, ed. and trans. J. Strachey. London: Hogarth Press.

Freud, S. 1923a. *The Ego and the Id*. In *Standard Edition of the Complete Works of Sigmund Freud*, *19*, 12–59, ed. and trans. J. Rivere. London: Hogarth Press.

Freud, S. 1923b. *The Infantile Genital Organizations: An Interpolation into the Theory of Sexuality*. In *Standard Edition of the Complete Works of Sigmund Freud*, *19*, 141–148, ed. and trans. J. Strachey. London: Hogarth Press.

Freud, S. 1924. *The Dissolution of the Oedipus Complex*. In *Standard Edition of the Complete Works of Sigmund Freud*, *19*, 173–179, ed. and trans. J. Strachey. London: Hogarth Press.

Freud, S. 1954. *The Interpretation of Dreams*. In *Standard Edition of the Complete Works of Sigmund Freud*, *4* and *5*, ed. and trans. J. Strachey. London: Hogarth Press.

Genesis Rabbah. (Vilna edition.) 1961. Jerusalem.

Goethe, J. W. von [1774] 1957. *The Suffering of Young Werther*. Trans. B. C. Morgan. New York: F. Ungar.

Gordis, R. 1955. *Koheleth: The Man and His World*. New York: Bloch.

Gottschalk, H. B. 1980. *Heraclides of Pontus*. Oxford: Clarendon Press.

Graves, R. 1955. *The Greek Myths*. 2 vols. Baltimore: Penguin.

Greek Commentaries on Plato's Phaedo. 1976. Ed. and trans. L. G. Weserink. New York: North-Holland.

Greek Tragedies. 1960. Ed. D. Grene and R. Lattimore. Chicago: University of Chicago Press.

Haberman, A. 1946. *Sefer Gezerot Ashkenaz Ve Tsarfat*. Jerusalem: Mosad Ha Rav Kook.

Hadda, J. 1988. *Passionate Women, Passive Men: Suicide in Yiddish Literature*. Albany: State University of New York Press.

Haim, A. 1970. *Adolescent Suicide*. New York: International Universities Press.

Halliday, W. R. 1970. *The Pagan Background of Early Christianity*. New York: Cooper Square.

Hankoff, L. D. 1979a. Judaic origins of the suicide prohibition. In *Suicide: Theory and Clinical Aspects*, ed. L. D. Hankoff. Littleton, MA: PSG.

Hankoff, L. D. 1979b. Suicide and the after life in ancient Egypt. In *Suicide: Theory and Clinical Aspects*, ed. L. D. Hankoff. Littleton, MA: PSG.

Hardy, T. [1896] 1974. *Jude the Obscure*. London: Macmillan.

Hartmann, H. 1964. *Essays in Ego Psychology: Selected Problems in Psychoanalytic Theory*. New York: International Universities Press.

Heillig, R. J. 1980. Adolescent suicidal behavior: A family systems model. In *Research in Clinical Psychology*, *1*, ed. P. E. Nathan. Ann Arbor, MI: UMI Research Press.

Herodotus. 1924. *The Famous History of Herodotus*. Trans. B. Rich. London: Constable.

Hesiod and Theognis. 1973. *Theogony and Works and Days* [Hesiod] *and Elegies* [Theognis]. Trans. D. Wender. Middlesex, England: Penguin Classics.

Hill, T. E., Jr. 1983. Self-regarding suicide: A modified Kantanian view. *Suicide and Life-threatening Behavior* 13: 254–275.

Hirsch, S. R. [19th Cent.] 1976. *The Pentateuch.* 6 vols. Trans. I. Levy. Gateshead, England: Judaica Press.

Hirzel, R. 1908. Der selbstmord. *Archiv. fur Religionwissenschaft* 11: 75–104.

Holy Scriptures, The. 1955. Philadelphia: The Jewish Publication Society of America.

Homer. 1951. *The Iliad.* Trans. R. Lattimore. Chicago: University of Chicago Press.

Homer. 1967. *The Odyssey.* Trans. R. Lattimore. New York: Harper & Row.

Hooper, F. 1967. *Greek Realities.* New York: Charles Scribner's Sons.

Huizinga, J. 1955. *Homo Ludens.* Boston: Beacon Press.

Hume, D. 1984. *An Essay on Suicide.* With a historical and critical introduction by G. W. Foote. London: R. Forder.

Ignatius. 1968. *Epistles. Early Christian Writings,* ed. B. Radice. Baltimore: Penguin Books.

Ionesco, E. 1963. *Exit the King.* In *Plays,* vol. 5. Trans. D. Watson. London: John Calder.

Josephus, Flavius. 1985. *Complete Works.* Trans. W. Whiston. Grand Rapids, MI: Kregel.

Justinian. 1985. *The Digest of Justinian.* Trans. A. Watson. Philadelphia: University of Pennsylvania Press.

Kant, I. 1788. *Grundlegung zur Metaphysik der Sitten.* Riga: J. F. Hartknoch.

Kaplan, K. J. 1987. Jonah and Narcissus: Self-integration versus self-destruction in human development. *Studies in Formative Spirituality* 8: 33–54.

Kaplan, K. J. 1988. TILT: Teaching individuals to live together. *Transactional Analysis Journal* 18: 220–230.

Kaplan, K. J. 1990a. Isaac and Oedipus: A reexamination of the father-son relationship. *Judaism* 39: 73–81.

Kaplan, K. J. 1990b. TILT for couples: Helping couples grow together. *Transactional Analysis Journal* 20: 229–241.

Kaplan, K. J. 1991–92. Suicide and suicide prevention: Greek versus Biblical perspectives. *Omega* 24: 227–239.

Kaplan, K. J., and M. Maldaver. 1990a. Parental marital patterns and adolescent suicide: A theoretical taxonomy and literature review. Presented at the 22nd Annual Meetings of the American Association of Suicidology. New Orleans, LA, April.

Kaplan, K. J., and M. Maldaver. 1990b. Parental marital style and completed adolescent suicide: An empirical study. Presented at the 22nd Annual Meetings of the American Association of Suicidology. New Orleans, LA, April.

Kaplan, K. J., and N. O'Connor. In press. From mistrust to trust: Through a stage vertically. In *The Course of Life,* vol. 6, ed. S. I. Greenspan and G. H. Pollock. New York: International Universities Press.

Kaplan, K. J., and M. W. Schwartz. 1990. Walls and boundaries in Rabbinic-Biblical foreign policy: A psychological analysis. Presented at the 13th Annual Meetings of the International Society for Political Psychology. Washington, DC.

Kaplan, K. J., M. W. Schwartz, and M. Markus-Kaplan. 1984. *The Family: Biblical and Psychological Foundations.* New York: Human Sciences Press.

Kaplan, K. J., and S. Worth. In press. A developmental-clinical view of suicide: Through a stage darkly. In *The Course of Life,* vol. 7, ed. S. I. Greenspan and G. H. Pollock. New York: International Universities Press.

Kaufman, R. V. 1982. Oedipal object relations and morality. *The Annual of Psychoanalysis* 11: 245–256.

Kaufmann, Y. 1972. *The Religion of Israel.* Trans. M. Greenberg. New York: Schocken.

Kazantzakis, N. M. 1960. *The Last Temptation of Christ.* Trans. P. A. Bien. New York: Simon and Schuster.

Kegan, R. 1982. *The Evolving Self: Problem and Process in Human Development.* Cambridge: Harvard University Press.

Kohut, H. 1971. *The Analysis of the Self: The Psychoanalytic Study of the Child.* Monograph No. 4. New York: International Universities Press.

Lachs, S. 1974. The Pandora-Eve motif in Rabbinic literature. *Harvard Theological Review* 67: 341–345.

Lactantius. 1964. *The Divine Institutes (Books I–VII).* Trans. Sister M. F. McDonald. Washington, DC: Catholic University of America Press.

Ladouceur, D. J. 1987. Josephus and Masada. In *Josephus, Judaism and Christianity,* ed. L. Feldman and G. Hata. Detroit: Wayne State University Press.

Laing, R. D., and D. Esterson. 1970. *Sanity, Madness, and the Family.* New York: Penguin Books.

Lebacqz, K., and H. T. Englehardt, Jr. 1977. Suicide and Covenant. In *Death and Dying & Euthenasia,* ed. D. J. Horam and D. Mall. Washington, DC: University Publications of America.

Lewis, C. 1972. Jonah — A parable for our time. *Judaism* 21: 159–163.

Lewis, H. B. 1976. *Psychic War in Men and Women.* New York: New York University Press.

Libanius. 1969. *Selected Works of Libanius.* Trans. A. F. Norman. Cambridge: Harvard University Press.

Lindell, K. 1973. Stories of suicide in ancient China. *Acta Orientalia* 35: 167–239.

Livy. 1909–1919. *The History of Rome.* Trans. D. Spillan, C. Edmons, and W. A. M'Devitte. London: G. Bell.

Lucian of Samosata. 1959, 1967. *Lucian.* 8 vols. Trans. A. M. Harmon. London: W. Heinemann.

Mahler, M. S. 1968. *On Human Symbiosis and the Vicissitudes of Individuation.* New York: International Universities Press.

Main, M., N. Kaplan, and J. Cassidy. 1985. Security in infancy, childhood, and adulthood: A move to the level of representation. In *Growing Points of Attachment Theory and Research,* ed. I. Bretherton and E. Everett. Chicago: University of Chicago Press.

Malbim, M. L. 1957. *Ha Torah ve Ha Mitzva.* Jerusalem.

Marcus Aurelius. 1964. *Meditations.* Trans. and ed. M. Stramforth. Baltimore: Penguin Books.

Markus-Kaplan, M., and K. J. Kaplan. 1984. A bidimensional view of distancing: Reciprocity versus compensation, intimacy versus control. *Journal of Nonverbal Behavior* 8: 315–326.

Melville, H. [1851] 1926. *Moby Dick.* New York: Modern Library.

Midrash Rabbah. 1961. Jerusalem: n.p.

Midrash Tanhuma. Vilna edition. 1885. Ed. S. Buber.

Minuchin, S. 1974. *Families and Family Therapy.* Cambridge: Harvard University Press.

Napier, A. 1978. The rejection-intrusion pattern: A central family dynamics. *Journal of Marital and Family Counseling* 4: 5–12.

NASB Interlinear Greek-English New Testament. 1984. Grand Rapids, MI: Zondervan.

Neuringer, C., and D. J. Lettieri. 1982. *Suicidal Women: Their Thinking and Feeling Patterns.* New York: Gardner Press.

Nussbaum, C. 1992. *Semblance and Reality.* New York: KTAV.

Oates, W. J., and E. O'Neill, Jr., eds. 1938. *The Complete Greek Drama*, 2 vols. New York: Random House.

Ohara, K. 1961. A study of main causes of suicide. *Psychiatric Neurology of Japan* 63: 107–166.

Olson, D. M., D. M. Sprenkle, and C. S. Russell. 1979. Circumplex model of marital and family systems. I. Cohesion and adaptability dimensions, family types, and clinical implications. *Family Process* 18: 3–28.

Optatus. 1917. *The Work of St. Optatus, Bishop of Miletis Against the Donatists, with Appendix.* Trans. O. R. Vassall-Phillips. London: Longmans, Green.

Orbach, I. 1986. The "unsolvable problem" as a determinant in the dynamics of suicidal behaviors in children. *American Journal of Psychotherapy* 40(4): 511–520.

Orbach, I. 1988. *Children Who Don't Want to Live.* San Francisco: Jossey-Bass.

Orbach, I., S. Feschbach, G. Carlson, L. Glaubman, and Y. Gross. 1983. Attraction and repulsion by life and death in suicidal and normal children. *Journal of Consulting and Clinical Psychology* 51: 661–670.

Orbach, I., I. Milstein, D. Har-Even, A. Apter, S. Tiano, and A. Elizur. In press. A multi-attitude suicide tendency scale for adolescents. *Psychological Assessment: A Journal of Consulting & Clinical Psychology.*

Origen. 1954. *Prayer. Exhortation to Martyrdom.* Trans. John J. O'Meara. Ancient Christian Writers, No. 19. London: Longmans, Green.

Orosius, P. 1964. *The Seven Books of History Against the Pagans.* Trans. J. Deferrart. Washington, DC: Catholic University of America Press.

Ovid. 1955. *The Metamorphosis.* Trans. M. Innes. London: Penguin Classics.

Pascal, B. [1558] 1958. *Pensées.* New York: E. P. Dutton.

Pauly, A. F. 1916. *Real Encyclopaediae der Classichen Alterrumswissenschaft.* Stuttgart: J. B. Metzler.

Pausanias. 1907. *The Attica of Pausanias.* New York: Ginn.

Pesikta Rabbati. 1885. Ed. M. Friedmann. Vienna: n.p.

Pfeffer, C. R. 1981. The family system of suicidal children. *American Journal of Psychotherapy* 35: 330–334.

Plath, S. [1963] 1986. *The Bell Jar.* New York: Bantam Books.

Plato. 1954. *The Last Days of Socrates* [including *Euthyphro, The Apology, Crito, Phaedo*]. Trans. M. Tredennick. Middlesex, England: Penguin Classics.

Plato. 1955. *The Republic.* Trans. D. Lee. Middlesex, England: Penguin Classics.

Plato. 1970. *The Laws.* Trans. T. J. Saunders. Middlesex, England: Penguin Classics.

Plato. 1976. *Protagoras.* Trans. G. Taylor. Oxford: Penguin Classics.

Pliny the elder. 1857. *The Natural History of Plinius Secundus.* Vol. 6. Trans. J. Bostock and H. T. Riley. London: Henry G. Bohn.

Pliny the younger. 1963. *The Letters of the Younger Pliny.* Trans. B. Radice. Baltimore: Penguin.

Plotinus. 1918. *Complete Works.* Trans. K. S. Guthrie. London: George Bell and Son.

Plutarch. 1932. *The Lives of the Noble Grecians and Romans.* New York: Modern Library.

Polybius. 1922–1927. *The Histories.* Trans. W. P. Paton. London: W. Heinemann.

Pope, W. 1976. *Durkheim's Suicide: A Classic Analyzed.* Chicago: University of Chicago Press.

Quintilian. 1921–1922. *Institutiones Oratoriae.* Trans. H. E. Butler. London: W. Heinemann.

Rank, O. 1936. *Will Therapy.* Trans. J. Taft. New York: Alfred A. Knopf.

Rank, O. 1971. *The Double.* Ed. and trans. H. Tucter. New York: New American Library.

Rashi. 1978. *Commentary on the Bible.* Mikraot Gedolot edition. New York: n.p.

Reik, T. 1961. *The Temptation.* New York: George Braziller.

Richman, J. 1986. *Family Therapy for Suicidal Behavior.* New York: Springer.

Rin, H. 1975. Suicide in Taiwan. In *Suicide in Different Cultures,* ed. N. Farberow. Baltimore: University Park Press.

Ringel, E. 1981. Suicide prevention and the value of human life. In *Suicide: The Philosophical Issues,* ed. M. P. Battin and D. J. Mayo. London: Peter Owen.

Robert, C. 1915. *Oidipus Geschichte Eines Poetischen Stoffs im Griechischen Altertum.* Berlin: Weidmannsohe Buchhandlung.

Rosenstock-Huessy, E. 1969. *Judaism despite Christianity: The Letters on Christianity and Judaism between Eugene Rosenstock-Huessy and Franz Rosenzwig.* New York: Schocken Books.

Rosner, F. 1970. Suicide in Biblical, Talmudic, and Rabbinic writings. *Tradition* 11: 25–40.

Ross, L. T., and Kaplan, K. J. 1993. Life-ownership orientation and attitudes toward abortion, suicide, doctor-assisted suicide and capital punishment. To be presented at the 101st Annual Meeting of the American Psychological Association, Toronto, Canada, August.

Rostovtzeff, M. 1964. *Social and Economic History of the Hellenistic World.* Oxford: Clarendon Press.

Rousseau, J. J. [1761] 1925. *La Nouvelle Héloise.* Paris: Hachette.

Samuel. 1976. Ed. A. J. Rosenburg. New York: Judaica Press.

Schneid, H. 1973. *Family.* New York: Leon Amiel.

Schwartz, M. 1985. Koheleth and Camus: Two views of achievement. *Judaism* 35: 29–34.

Schwartz, M., and K. J. Kaplan. 1992. Judaism, Masada, and suicide: A critical analysis. *Omega* 25: 127–132.

Seneca, L. A., the younger. 1918–1925. *Ad Lucilium Epistulae Morales.* 3 vols. Trans. R. M. Gummere. London: W. Heinemann.

Seneca, L. A., the elder. 1974. *Oratorum et Rhetorum Sententiae Divisiones, Col-*

ores. [The elder Seneca declamations] Trans. M. Winterbottom. Cambridge: Harvard University Press.

Seneca, L. A., the younger. 1979. *Seneca.* Cambridge: Harvard University Press.

Servius. [4th century] 1946. *Servianorum in Vergilii Carmina Commentariorum Editionis Harvardianae Volumen Edwardas Kennard Rand Confecerunt.* Lancaster, PA: American Philological Association.

Shakespeare, W. 1959. *Hamlet.* Cambridge, MA: Houghton Mifflin.

Shneidman, E. S. 1968. Classifications of suicidal phenomena. *Bulletin of Suicidology* 1–9.

Shneidman, E. 1981. *Suicide Thoughts and Reflections, 1960–1980.* New York: Behavioral Science Press.

Shneidman, E. 1982a. On "Therefore I must kill myself." *Suicide and Life-threatening Behavior* 12: 52–55.

Shneidman, E. 1982b. The suicidal logic of Cesare Pavese. *Journal of the American Academy of Psychoanalysis* 10: 547–563.

Shneidman, E. 1985. *Definition of Suicide.* New York: John Wilcy and Sons.

Shneidman, E. S., and N. L. Farberow. 1957. The logic of suicide. In *Clues to Suicide*, ed. E. S. Shneidman & N. L. Farberow. New York: McGraw-Hill.

Sifre. 1957. Jerusalem: n.p.

Slater, P. 1968. *The Glory of Hera: Greek Mythology and the Greek Family.* Boston: Beacon Press.

Soloveitchik, J. 1973. *Bet Halevi.* New York: n.p.

Soloveitchik, J. 1983. *Halakhic Man.* Trans. L. Kaplan. Philadelphia: Jewish Publication Society.

Sorasky, A. 1982. *Reb Elchonon.* Trans. L. Oshry. New York: Art Scroll History Series.

Stael, A. L. de. 1796. *Sur L'influence des Passions.* Paris: Charpentier.

Stael, A. L. de. 1814. *Réflexions sur le Suicide.* Paris: Charpentier.

Stark, R., D. P. Doyle, and J. L. Rushing. 1983. Beyond Durkheim: Religion and suicide. *Journal for the Scientific Study of Religion* 22: 120–131.

Stephens, W. N. 1962. *The Oedipus Complex.* New York: Free Press.

Stern, E. S. 1948. The Medea complex: The mother's homicidal wishes to her child. *Journal of Mental Science* 94: 321–331.

Stierlin, H. 1974. *Separating Parents and Adolescents: A Perspective on Running Away, Schizophrenia, and Waywardness.* New York: Quadrangle.

Stone, I. F. 1988. *The Trial of Socrates.* New York: Anchor Books.

Szasz, T. 1971. The ethics of suicide. *Antioch Review* 31(1).

Tacitus. 1942. *The Complete Works.* Trans. A. J. Church and W. J. Brodribb. New York: Modern Library.

Tatai, K., and M. Kato, eds. 1974. *Thinking of Suicide in Japan.* Tokyo: Igaka-Shoiu.

Taylor, T. 1834. *Translations from the Greek of the Treaties of Plotinus on Suicide and the Scholia of Olympiodorus on the Phaedo of Plato.* London: Privately printed for T. Taylor.

Tendler, M. D. 1982. *Pardes Rimonim: A Marriage Manual for the Jewish Family.* New York: Judaica Press.

Tertullian. 1959. "To the Martyrs" [Ad Martyres]. In *Disciplinary, Moral and As-*

cetical Works, Vol. 40, trans. R. Arbeshann, E. J. Daly, and E. A. Quain, ed. R. J. Deferrari. New York: Fathers of the Church.

Thakur, Y. 1963. *The History of Suicide in India*. Delhi: Musnshiram: Manoharlal.

Tuke, Reverend. 1613. *A Discourse on Death*. London: n.p.

Urbach, E. E. 1979. *The Sages: Their Concepts and Beliefs*, 2d ed., trans. I. Abrahms. Jerusalem: The Magnes Press, The Hebrew University of Jerusalem.

Valerius Maximus. 1823. *Valeri Maximi Factorum Dictorumque Memorabilium Liborinovem*. London: A. J. Valpy.

van Hooff, A. J. L. 1990. *From Autothanasia to Suicide: Self-killing in Classical Antiquity*. London: Routledge.

van Praag, H. M. 1986. The downfall of King Saul: The neurobiological consequences of losing hope. *Judaism* 35: 414–426.

Voltaire, F. M. A. 1973. *The Selected Letters of Voltaire*. Ed. and trans. R. A. Brookes. New York: New York University Press.

Weininger, O. 1975. *Sex and Character*. London: W. Heinemann.

Wellisch, E. 1954. *Isaac and Oedipus: Study in Biblical Psychology of the Sacrifice of Isaac. The Akedah*. London: Routledge and Kegan Paul.

Westcott, W. W. 1885. *Suicide: Its History, Literature, Jurisprudence, Causation, and Prevention*. London: Lewis.

Willi, J. 1982. *Couples in Collusion*. New York: Jason Aronson.

Willis, G. C. 1950. *Saint Augustine and the Donatist Controversy*. London: S.P.C.K.

Wynne, L. C., I. M. Ryckoff, J. Day, and S. I. Hirsch. 1958. Pseudo-mutuality in the family relations of schizophrenics. *Psychiatry* 21: 205–222.

Xenophon. 1854. *The Anabasis, or Expedition of Cyrus, and the Memorabilia of Socrates*. Trans. J. S. Watson. London: Henry G. Bohn.

Xenophon. 1857. *Minor Works [including the Apology of Socrates]*. Trans. Rev. J. S. Watson. London: Henry G. Bohn.

Yalkut Shimoni. 1876. Warsaw: n.p.

Yap, P. M. 1958. *Suicide in Hong Kong*. Hong Kong: Hong Kong University Press.

Zeller, E. 1962. *The Stoics, Epicureans, and Sceptics*. Trans. O. J. Reichel. New York: Russell and Russell.

Index

About the Authors

KALMAN J. KAPLAN is Professor of Psychology at Wayne State University, Adjunct Professor of Psychology at the University of Illinois at Chicago and at Spertus College of Judaica, and a Research Associate in Psychiatry at Michael Reese Hospital and Medical Center. He is also a licensed clinical psychologist. He is co-author of *The Family: Biblical and Psychological Foundations* (1984) and a contributor to *Metapsychology: Missing Links in Mind, Body, and Behavior* (1991). He has written numerous journal articles about Biblical psychology, interpersonal relations, human development, and suicide.

MATTHEW B. SCHWARTZ is Professor of History at Wayne State University and co-author, with Kalman Kaplan, of *The Family: Biblical and Psychological Foundations* (1984). He is also co-author of *Roman Letters* (1991) and a contributor to *History of the Jews of Detroit: Volume II* (1992).